SO MUCH LOVE

After my first summer season, I tried for pantomime. I saw that Jack Gillam, who was registered in Manchester, was going to do a pantomime, so I decided to go to this audition, or interview. My mother said to me before I went, 'Now don't forget, Beryl – there's *nothing* you can't do.' I set off with much more confidence than I've got now, because I was so ignorant. 'What do you do?' Mr Gillam asked me. 'Oh – *everything*,' I replied. 'How much money would you want?' I said, '£3 a week.' 'All my life,' said Mr Gillam, 'I've been looking for someone who could do everything for £3 a week!' I was hired!

D0351225

Beryl Reid
SO MUCH LOVE

with the assistance of
Eric Braun

ARROW BOOKS

Arrow Books Limited
17–21 Conway Street, London W1P 6JD

An imprint of the Hutchinson Publishing Group

London   Melbourne   Sydney   Auckland
Johannesburg and agencies throughout
the world

First published by Hutchinson 1984
Arrow edition 1985

© Strithon Ltd 1984

This book is sold subject to the condition that it shall
not, by way of trade or otherwise, be lent, resold,
hired out, or otherwise circulated without the publisher's prior consent in any form of binding or cover
other than that in which it is published and without a
similar condition including this condition being im-
posed on the subsequent purchaser.

Printed and bound in Great Britain by
Anchor Brendon Limited, Tiptree, Essex

ISBN 0 09 942420 7

For Anne Reid
Born Anne Burton McDonald, my mother, who gave me
security, strength, common sense and honesty. Without
her this lovely life of mine, which I enjoy so much, would
not have been possible

Contents

Illustrations

At Honeypot Cottage: Beryl and the swan (*Fox Photos*), and Beryl and Footy (*Royston Summers*)

Childhood photos: at a picnic, and with brother Roy (*sister-in-law Pat's collection*)

Beryl and Roy several years on (London News Agency)

Beryl as Gretchen (*sister-in-law Pat's collection*)

Beryl as Soubrette (*by kind permission of Brian Seymour*)

Wedding photos at marriage to Bill Worsley (*Kensington Press Agency*)

Beryl as Estelle in *Betty* (*Beryl's photograph*)

Beryl in *The Good Old Days* (*Beryl's photograph*)

Monica takes aim (*John Vickers*)

Marlene (*Willoughby Gullachsen*)

Beryl with Archie Andrews (*BBC copyright photograph*)

Aladdin, the Coventry Theatre panto (*Beryl's photograph*)

'I changed my sex a week ago today' (*John Vickers*)

'A middle-aged, middle-class barfly' (*John Vickers*)

'Black and White', with Sheila Hancock (*Angus McBean*)

'Spanish Maid' with Tony Selby and others (*Angus McBean*)

Rehearsing *The Merry Wives of Windsor* with Jimmy Edwards and Cedric Messina (*BBC copyright photograph*)

'Red Peppers' with Graham Payn (*David Barry*)

'Rockin' the Town' with Harry Secombe at the Palladium (*Beryl's photograph*)

Beryl with spastic children (*Beryl's photograph*)

South African rhythms (*Dosthuysen*)

Marriage to Derek Franklin (*Beryl's photograph*)

The Belles of St Trinian's (*Thorn EMI Screen Entertainment*)

The Dock Brief with Richard Attenborough (*MGM-British*)

The Beast in the Cellar with Flora Robson (*Tigon British/Leander*)

The Killing of Sister George: outside St Martin's Theatre, with Eileen Atkins and Lally Bowers (*George Palomar International and Associates*)

A birthday surprise from Robert Aldrich on the film set

With Susannah York in a scene from the film (*Rex Features*)

Entertaining Mr Sloane with Peter McEnery (*Thorn EMI Screen Entertainment*)

With Reginald Vincent at the première of *Entertaining Mr Sloane* (*PIC Photos*)

With Noel Coward at Simpson's (*Terry Moore*)

Il Campiello with Peggy Mount (*National Theatre*)

Psychomania with George Sanders (*Benmar-Scotia-Barber*)

'Beryl Reid, This is Your Life' (*Thames Television*)

'Blankety Blank', Christmas 1981, with Terry Wogan and other performers (*BBC copyright photograph*)

'Get Up and Go', with Mooncat (David Claridge) and Stephen Boxer (*Yorkshire TV*)

The Irish RM, as Mrs Knox, with Lettuce as Balthazar (*Channel 4 TV*)

The Godchildren: Verity Stauffer, Susan Reid and Brian Holland (*Beryl's photograph*)

'The right shoes for the character' (*Rex Features*)

Tinker, Tailor, Soldier, Spy, as Connie Sachs, with Alec Guinness (*Radio Times*)

Acknowledgments

There are so many people I want to thank for having helped in various ways with the preparation of this book, some of them reminding me of things long since forgotten. I never kept press cuttings in the early days; when a job was over, that was it, and it was on to the next. When Eric Braun started to look after my publicity he collected cuttings and pasted them into books – thirty volumes by now! – which have proved exceedingly helpful for reference, and for the more recent careful and research work on these I am grateful to Joan Giles. Audrey Smith spent several days in the Westminster Central Reference Libraries going through years of newspaper references and old *Radio Times*, while Brian Rust came up with invaluable information of early recording sessions: my thanks to both of them, and to all who wrote such helpful letters.

To a number of personal friends go my love and gratitude for most rewarding interviews. They include Bill Bryden of the National Theatre; William Chappell, director and loving adviser of so much of my work on the musical theatre and television; Anthony Cornish of Capital Radio; Andrew Gardner of the 'Pinnacle Storyteller' series; Ronnie Hill, so happily associated with early days in revue; John and Terry Hacking, my friends since the Midlands days; Robert Luff, my agent and friend for many years and his personal assistant Gillian Lindo; Roy Pike, loyal supporter and theatre buff; Betty Milne, my 'Minder' in the theatre since *Mr Sloane*, Norman Newell, who has directed and been responsible for most of my record sessions;

Pat Reid, my sister-in-law, who has provided so many happy memories and photographs of my dear brother Roy; Sue Stauffer, good friend and mother of my goddaughter Verity, the 'Boring Rotter'; my very special script-writer, Ronnie Wolfe; and last, but by no means least in this section, my great friend and stage accomplice, Jack Tripp.

Special mention for further help in research etc. must go to Ian Bevan of the Harold Fielding Organisation for details of my work with 'Music For The Millions'; Paul Ciani, BBC Producer of 'Smike!' the TV play and LP; Linda Cleeve of the BBC TV's 'The Time Of Your Life'; Hilary Sampson, PRO to John Counsell at the Theatre Royal, Windsor, for access to his book *Counsell's Opinion* and to their director Hugh Goldie; Commander Innes Hamilton, for many years my business manager and adviser; James Hill, director of *The Dock Brief*, who laid on a special showing for me of that film after the filming of a 'Wurzel Gummidge' episode recently; Terri Howard for information on *Mother Goose* in Brighton, where she was my understudy and Second Girl; David Quinlan, Film Editor of *TV Times*, for invaluable photographs and information; Wally Ridley, MD, record producer and originally assistant to Peter Brough.

My thanks to three very special friends; Brian Seymour and Terence and Olivia Ward, and to James (Jimmy) Sharkey who worked with me on the stage and now represents me for films and the legitimate theatre.

Further helpful information was received from Richard Armitage of Noel Gay Music, June Burgess of the Music For Pleasure Library, Colin Clark of the *Worthing Gazette*, Mrs Eden of the Coventry Theatre box office and Dave Duncan for a most informative 1950 Edition of *Who's Who in Variety* published by the now defunct Performer. Thanks also to Spike Milligan for his kind agreement to my reproducing the poem from his book published by Michael Joseph, *Small Dreams of a Scorpion*. To everybody, my sincerest thanks and love.

BERYL REID

1

Home Truths

After the BAFTA Award for *Smiley's People*, the postman was riveted by the sack of mail that he brought to my door every day. Later, after a few weeks, he walked in with only a couple of bills. 'Is that all?' I asked. 'Oh, yes,' he said, 'I'm afraid so; you see, fame doesn't really last, Beryl!'

They always let you know about things in Wraysbury. It's like the story of my window cleaner: I'd had a lot of friends to lunch, always a great pleasure to me because I love cooking. It was a very, very hot day, and we'd all enjoyed ourselves something rotten. Eventually, after they'd gone, I thought, Oh, how marvellous that was, took all my clothes off, threw myself on the bed and went straight to sleep. When I woke up, nothing had changed, but there was a note through my letter-box which simply said, 'All your windows have been cleaned!'

I think this started the rumour going about Wraysbury that I was a little eccentric. It isn't the only thing that might have earned me that reputation. My present count of cats is ten. One of them is called Dimly. He's actually anything but 'dimly' – in fact, he's rather 'brightly' – but two friends of mine, Olivia and her husband Terry, were staying with me, and Terry said, 'Oh, I haven't seen Beryl for quite a while.' Olivia looked across to my little car-port and said, 'I can just see her moving dimly.' So of course I had to have something called Dimly to move.

I got up one morning to go to the loo, in my nightdress, and under the bureau I found an enormous rabbit, with Dimly sitting proudly behind it: he'd brought it in through the cat-flap. I thought how best I could deal with this without any trouble, then said quickly, 'Oh, Dimly – what a clever boy: goodness, gracious me, a lovely rabbit!' and I picked the rabbit up, took it in my arms and walked through the door, as I was, in my nightdress. If I had stopped to dress, the rabbit would have been done away with, so it was a case of just bare feet, and down the lane, saying 'Oh – what a lovely boy!' with all ten cats following. And that looked fairly silly, you know. I had to walk quite a way until I reached a flat piece, so the rabbit could run away. I just hope that nobody saw me: I've had no reports yet, but it was quite recent.

Anyway, here I am, attempting to write a book, dictating into a tiny machine that seems to have a will of its own: it can stop recording, or change speed to make you sound like Minnie Mouse or a very weary Sydney Greenstreet, and it loves to play everything backwards just when you think you've got the hang of it.

When this book was first spoken about, a press report appeared: 'Beryl To Reveal All?' They'd better just apply to the window cleaner! So much has been 're-vealed' by so many people that I'm amazed there's anything left. I've got great respect for 'Proper People' of the press, but none at all for those Third-Class Citizens who scrabble for gossip about anybody at all in the limelight, and if there's none, just make it up. I will have nothing to do with scandal. Sheridan felt so strongly after he had been hurt by it that he sent it up brilliantly in his play *The School for Scandal* – and afterwards wrote no more.

Noel Coward's 'talent to amuse' represents everything that going on the stage means to me. I met him during the fifties through his great friend Graham Payn, with whom I was working at the time at the Theatre Royal, Windsor. We were doing *Tonight at 8.30*, including *Brief Encounter*, *Red Peppers* and *Family Album* for which Noel

Coward wrote some extraordinary music, really not fitted at times for the human voice because the range of notes was so enormous. But he could sort of skip over it himself, because he was much cleverer than any of us, while I tried to *sing* all the songs. During rehearsals I got a wonderful note from the director, Hugh Goldie, who said, 'Darling, don't forget to breathe when you're singing!' – which was, of course, very sound advice, or I might not be breathing now. Anyway, it all went so well that I got carried away and said to Noel Coward, 'We're the *best*!' Noel replied, 'Now – steady!'

Much later, I was to play Madame Arcati in *Blithe Spirit*. I'd kicked the idea about for a couple of years, because really *nobody* could follow Margaret Rutherford, who was so funny without really ever looking as if she knew it. I could have imitated her, but that wouldn't have been good enough. I needed a coat-hanger for myself. After two years I had thought of an idea, so I told Noel Coward, who invited me to see him at the Savoy Hotel. 'I want to play it like a refugee from Edinburgh,' I said. 'There are such wonderful things to say, like "ectoplasmic manifestations", in that genteel Morningside accent.' He laughed a lot at the thought, and so eventually in the summer of 1970 I did play the part at the Globe Theatre. At the Savoy Hotel we spoke of all sorts of things, we even got on to the subject of death – goodness know how. Noel said, 'When you die, you know, your hair keeps growing, and your fingernails keep growing, and the hair on your chest.' I said, 'Well, not on *my* chest.' He replied in that wonderful clipped voice of his, 'Oh – you give up hope so easily!'

So we were in production! I set off with a good heart to the rehearsals, and, with his approval, did it in my Edinburgh voice. The director said, 'You're not really going to do it like that, are you?', which is the most depressing sentence any actor can hear. I said, 'Well, yes I am.' I was determined that, as Noel Coward had approved it, I was going to press on, and I did. But I had a lot of unhappiness during the rehearsals, because I felt destroyed; in fact, I stayed without any confidence of any kind for a year.

During the rehearsals I'd just got back home to Honeypot Cottage one Friday night with tears streaming down my face when my telephone rang. It was the people further along the river from me. 'There's somebody trying to land at your house in a boat,' they said, 'and they're breaking your willow tree.' I'd gone to bed and put a couple of terrible Kirbigrips in my hair – I don't know what I thought that was going to do for me, because I looked an awful mess and nobody would have had me with a pound of tea – but thought, I'd better make some effort if there is somebody arriving by river, so I put on a Marks and Spencer's puce catsuit (which really didn't suit me at all), my face was all covered with mascara and I'd got no make-up on, but I set off down towards the water. I had nothing in my head at that time, but the extraordinary thing is that I get inspirations sometimes, and suddenly I saw my lovely friend Barbara Evans and her chap walking up the path. I said, 'Oh, I'm terribly sorry – I can't ask you in because, you see, I'm in bed with someone I don't know very well!' She was totally confused by this, and they just retreated. I couldn't *believe* the words that were coming out of my mouth, because I had nobody in the house!

Anyway, when *Blithe Spirit* finally opened, I had the most amazing First Night. The play was a tremendous success, and the director who'd given me all this hell during the rehearsals came to the dressing room and said, 'There you are – I told you so!' It took great self-control for me not to throw everything I could find at him!

At the end of the run in London we were invited to the O'Keefe Center in Canada, a 4000-seater. The set of Mr Condomine's house had to be sawn in half to fit into the aeroplane when we travelled. It was November when we went, and fourteen below zero. I was only one block from the theatre, but the tears which ran down my face in the bitter cold were frozen by the time I got to the stage door.

4

But my dressing room had eighty degrees of heat in it. I was like a Giles cartoon person, I couldn't find my eyes, even to make them up. I said to Patrick Cargill, 'I'm taking the Ugly Pills – and they're working.'

As the set couldn't be got up in time after being sawn in half for the journey, we did have a free day when we got to Canada, during which I did seven television and, I think, five radio shows. I continued to do these during the two weeks we were there, because you have to get people in from the Sioux country. We filled that 4000-seater every night, which amazed me. The snow was terrible, everything about the weather was terrible, and when I went to see Niagara Falls, which was frozen, the icicles were about six feet across. I said to Patrick, 'I hope I don't meet a thick lumberjack,' and he replied, 'This is no time to be choosy!'

I've been very lucky, though: my wonderful times go back to childhood, when I had total security. If I'm any good at all as a person, I owe that entirely to the way that I was brought up. If I shouted 'Mummy!' Mummy was there. She seemed to understand the needs of my brother Roy and myself. We had a very carefree time; we were real, proper children. We lived in Manchester, where we both went to school, but we had a cottage at a fishing village called Dunure, which is eight miles out of Ayr. My parents were both Scottish – my mother from Edinburgh, my father from Aberdeen – and every summer and school holiday we used to go to the cottage. My packing used to be a vest, two pairs of knickers, two pairs of socks, my sandals, two dresses, a cardigan, a bathing-costume and bathing-hat. That was it. At four o'clock in the morning we used to walk down to the harbour, which was two miles from the cottage, and meet the herring boats as they came in. The fishermen used to chuck the herrings at us and say, 'As many as you can carry for a ha'penny.' That was just grand – a great life.

My mother selected schools very carefully for us. I say mother because, though my father was brilliant at his own job, he didn't really understand very much about us. So she sent me to one of the first Progressive Kindergartens in the country, which was called Lady Barne House, in Withington. That was a school of self-discipline, where I was never told not to do anything. I was six when I went there, and I learnt Latin and English and French all at the same time, and all from phonetic sounds, which really means I can't spell, but I'm very good at listening to sounds and learning language from them. One day I fell out of the window and was sent to Miss Jenkin-Jones, the headmistress. She had a long talk to me and said, 'I can't imagine how a big girl like you' – 'big girl' mind you; I was six – 'could fall out of the window.' After about three-quarters of an hour when she's gone round all the questions she gets to the bit where she says, 'It isn't possible, *is it*, that you were hanging out too far?' With bleeding knees, which no-body's taken any notice of, and elbows scuffed and cut, I say, 'Yes, it *is*,' and she replies, 'Well, I don't expect you'll be doing it again.' Then she said something which I never understood until I was much older, 'It is easier to break bottles than to mend them.'

Another time I was summoned, and she said, 'I want you to come in, Beryl, because Brenda Johnson wants to kick you.' (Brenda Johnson's uncle, I remember, was called the Red Dean of Canterbury.) I asked indignantly, 'Why does she want to kick me?' Miss Jenkin-Jones answered, 'Well, I believe that you've just kicked her during your little break.' I said, 'Yes, I did.' I've always been so honest that it's frightening. 'Well,' she said, 'just stand there, because now she's going to kick *you*.' And of course I had to stand there. It was a wonderful way to learn – not perhaps for all children, but absolutely firsters for me.

My mother was always very far-sighted: she'd always be thinking of new experiences for me. For instance, I can never remember not being able to swim. I learned when I was three, taught by a beautiful huge fat lady called Mrs Bark; she was like a sort of floating island,

6

and she would say, 'Just swim to me, darling, just swim to me.' She had me diving when I was four so it's just something I've grown up with. Also I learned dancing when I was four and was in several dancing displays, and I always say now that every performer should learn to dance, and sing if possible, because if you've been taught how to dance, you're never at a loss as to what to do with your hands or body. When I went to talk to the London School of Acting, they said, 'Why sing?' Well, if you can sing it could mean you'd get an extra job, and it's a great asset and it teaches you how to breathe. Of course, both those things I'd learnt at a very early age. When I was four I said, 'I'm going on the stage, you know,' when I could hardly have known what a stage was. It was always in my blood. Apart from the dancing, I used to put on my father's hat and do impressions of Uriah Heep, and that sort of thing. My aunts thought that it was all wrong that I was being brought up like this.

I had a friend in those days – a made-up friend – who was called 'Envigamees, who was Born'. When my mother said, 'Why have you been out by yourself, Beryl?' I would say, 'Oh, I wasn't out by myself, Mummy; you see, Envigamees, who was Born, said it was perfectly all right for me to go out, because he was going to be with me.' He protected me when I met a lion on the streets and in all those kinds of adventures that my aunts all thought was telling lies. But my mother said, 'No,' in her gentle Morningside way, which would make the name Beryl sound so soft, 'no – it's just that she's got a very vivid imagination.' My mother was always concerned for me. We had one photograph, which I can't find anywhere now, where she is looking beautiful in a big hat and with an ermine tie around her neck. The lid of the pram – the hood, in fact – is up, and there I am, pushed right to the back. When I saw it, I said, 'Where was I, Mummy?' 'Well,' she said, 'I couldn't let anybody see you, Beryl. You were bald!'

Something I've suffered from all my life is dyslexia. In the words of Winnie the Pooh, my spelling is good

7

spelling, but a bit wobbly, and the letters get in the wrong places. It's particularly difficult for an actress, and it wasn't much fun at school. Even though it was a very advanced school, nobody there knew what dyslexia was then. When I was six years old I knew real terror, because I just couldn't read straight from the page. I tried to count the girls before me, when we were reading round the class, look for inspiration, put my fingers in my ears, and wildly read the paragraph that I thought was going to be mine. The other girls thought I was being silly, or showing off, but I was really terrified. I had beads of perspiration on my face. Apart from opening-night nerves, which I still suffer from, and generally being nervous about going onto the stage, this was the only time that I've ever known such real fright.

Though my mother encouraged me about going onto the stage, my father always said, 'I would rather see you dead at my feet.' But my mother realized it was the only thing I was going to be any good at. She had a proper sense of values and a wonderful unconscious humour: when I was eventually set to go on the stage I expected great sympathy from her, because I'd always been a very poor eater, and fragile, so that she would make me two puddings every time in the hope that I would eat one of them. I'd had pneumonia twice as a child, and was very thin, though since then I've always been very tough. I asked her, 'Mummy, what are the things I mustn't eat?' She knew about the theatre. She looked me straight in the eye and said, 'Soap and rusty nails.'

2

Stage Struck

At Withington Girls' School, Marghanita Laski, an 'older girl', was very good at lacrosse; you were jolly lucky if you were in her team, because you could count on winning. A great friend of mine there was Nancy Wrigley, who was Isobel Baillie's daughter. Nancy used to come to my house to play, and I used to go to hers. I thought that her father, Isobel Baillie's husband, Henry, was the most handsome man I had ever seen in my life. He used to sit on a sort of packing case in the garden and swing his legs – and he was totally beautiful. Once, when I went to Nancy's house, 'Moona', as we used to call her mother, had just come back from Hawaii, and she was telling wonderful stories about how six princes had serenaded her below her balcony. Of course, we were open-mouthed and goggle-eyed. But at the end of this romantic story, she asked, 'Would you like some chips now?' We both said yes, and so she put on her pinnie and made them.

Later she came back into my life when I was doubling the Watergate Theatre and the Albert Hall. I was called 'Interlude' at the Albert Hall: Phyllis Sellick and Cyril Smith opened the programme, then I came on, and Isobel Baillie finished it. I said, 'Oh, Moona, I never thought I'd see you again. You know, I've been on the stage for quite a long time.' She replied, 'I know, lovey, and we've seen everything you've done.' 'Why haven't you been round to see me?' I asked. She said, 'I didn't think you'd remember me.' Now, that was the true humility of that beautiful person, who had the purest voice I've heard in all my life. She said, 'I'd better see you on here: it's rather like the Christians being thrown to the lions. You have to walk up a ramp, you know.' I performed that night with great confidence. Later I asked her, 'What do you do if you have trouble with your voice, Moona?' 'I'll tell you what I do,' she said, 'I just go to bed and I write a few letters to my friends and I rest completely.' She had great composure, and I learned a lot from her. When she knew I really did want to see her, she came either to first nights or early performances of every show I did in London. That was a great joy to me.

But, to quote my Birmingham character Marlene, who was already in my life that night at the Albert Hall, though nameless in those days at the Watergate, 'I digress.' At Withington I was good at cricket, but that was neither here nor there as far as learning was concerned, and so I was sent to Levenshulme Girls' School, which was much stricter than anything I'd ever had in my life. There I became friendly with a girl called Pat Kirkwood. We were both to start our careers in the same way, 'on the wireless'. We were cycling home and Pat said, 'I'm going on the stage, you know.' 'Oh, you lucky thing!' I replied. My father had quite different ideas for *me*.

Daddy was set on my having a job 'with a pension'. He got me an apprenticeship at Kendal Milne's, the store in Manchester where he was an estate agent – auctioneer, valuer, etc – and very clever at his job. I on the other hand was determined *not* to be good at mine. I was in six different departments in six weeks. In the fur department I was furious; they kept the furs in glass cases then, and I had to polish the mahogany bottom of the case, and, of course, it used to mess my hair up, because it brushed against the fur coats. Then I broke a lot of things in the china department. I was eventually transferred to toys, where I did a demonstration with bakelite bricks. This was all because I was going to have a Pension. I was quite good at the demonstration, because it was a bit like being on the stage. But afterwards I used to look round in a very crafty way, and if Mr Kilby, the buyer, wasn't there, I'd whisper to the crowd I'd gathered, 'Don't have them – they're awful: they *all* fall to pieces!' One more nail in my coffin as a pensioner!

My compulsive, terrible honesty has done me damage in my career on occasion, but once, in childhood, it let me down as well. Grandfather McDonald, my mother's father, used to stay with us for about six weeks in the summer, wherever we were. He was mad about cats, and took home every cat that he could possibly find. Well, I certainly inherited *that* from him! My brother Roy and I as young children – he was four years older – were told that we must look after Grandad, entertain him, take him for walks, and all that sort of thing, and we dreaded it. But we knew that at the end of the holiday we'd each get half-a-crown and that's what we were working for all along, which was really rather terrible of us. When Grandad eventually left, and we were heaving a sigh of relief, we would say, 'Oh, Grandad – you're far too decent!' It was an awful hypocritical children's thing – but that's what children are like. They're usually honest, but when they have to put on an act, they do it really well.

At Dunure I'd go for wonderful walks with my brother, my two boy cousins, and Auntie Belle and my mother. The fathers came when they could get away from work. If the tide was in, we'd walk along the railway lines – I think there was one train a week – and if the tide was out we would walk along the beach and look at the sea anemones in all those beautiful rock pools, making our way to Culzean Castle near Croy Beach, where Eisenhower was later to live during the Second World War. There was a famous optical illusion at Dunure known as the Electric Brae. At a particular point you could cycle uphill without pedalling – in fact it was downhill, but any observer would swear the path went upwards.

On the beach we would bat around a lot of golf balls. My Uncle Jack once went missing for three days without a word, then came back and laid a pile of lost balls on the table. They must have been all the ones we'd been losing for months.

Once, during the war, when he and Auntie Belle lived in Glasgow, he came home from his allotment, took off his boots, sat down and said to Auntie Belle, 'I think I'd better drop a line to the police, Belle.' Auntie Belle was excitable. 'Why?' she cried, 'What have you done? What have you done?' 'Well,' said Jack, 'when I was digging on my plot I found an unexploded bomb: I've just put it to one side ...' Before he'd finished speaking Auntie Belle was at the police station, and the whole place was cordoned off. The demolition squad were there before you could say Will Fyffe.

When we met the fishing boats in the morning, we'd pass the house where Mr McCrindle lived. His relatives are on the stage: I met his nephew Alex when I was doing *Spring Awakening* for the National. Mr McCrindle was Dunure's postmaster and although he had never learnt to read or write at school, he'd taught himself. At four o'clock in the morning he'd be stripped to the waist in what we thought was freezing cold weather (although it was summer in that climate) and he'd shout rather fiercely, 'Good morning, children!' as we scurried past. In fact he was tending the rock plants that he'd brought from all over the world. He had the most fabulous collection, which was the pride of Dunure. The pride of Ayrshire, really, was his rock garden, although we children never realized it.

When Pat Kirkwood was being allowed to follow her heart by going on the stage, I was still on the road that led to a pension. But I was trying to do my own thing, and I got a lot of encouragement from Alice Dodds, who was employed by Sally Lobel of the Lobel School of Dancing, and who taught me elocution. I learned monologues from her, and she saw that I had acting potential. She also taught me a most valuable lesson. 'I don't care *where* you perform,' she said, 'you can act on a dustbin lid if you like, but it must be before *people*.' I've never forgotten that. Soon after that Bernard Habgood asked my parents if I could join an amateur dramatic group. I was given my chance – to play the maid, Pauline, in *No, No, Nanette*.

Sally Lobel, by the way, was a very dedicated ballet dancer, and she tried to extend people's knowledge and appreciation of ballet, sometimes with unfortunate results. Once she performed in a factory, dressed as a butterfly – and I'm afraid all the factory-women hooted with laughter.

The one good thing about being the junior at Kendal Milne's was that I could escape to lunch at 11.30 in the morning. One day there was an audition at Leslie's Pavilion in Manchester. Now, in those days people like Ronald Frankau used to go to what were called 'concert party dates'. All the famous concert parties went to this place, where a man called Fred Rayne was doing auditions. I had worked out a little turn; I was Ethel, a maid in a hotel, where I cleaned all the people's shoes, which I collected from outside the doors, put them on, and did an impersonation of the people whose shoes I was wearing. I did this for Fred Rayne and, miraculously, I got a job at £2 a week for a summer season at Bridlington – that was in 1936. My mother came with me to Bridlington to see that I had proper accommodation, for which Full Board was twenty-five shillings a week, but when she had seen me settled she went home. There I was, alone, and Going To Be An Actress – Going On The Stage.

The first big professional people I met were Jewel and Warriss: I was at the Floral Hall, and they were a little further along at a Proper Theatre. I used to tear along with whatever make-up I'd put on for my sketch, and throw a pebble up at their window. They would look out and say, 'That's OK' or 'That's terrible', and I'd rush back and get on with it.

When I started, I knew nothing about how to remove make-up, and I used Trex. I would wet a towel, rub all

13

this goo off my face and then send the towel home to my mother for laundering. By the time it arrived the grease was oozing through the parcel, and the postman said to her, 'I expect your daughter has sent you some kippers, Mrs Reid.' 'I expect she has,' she would agree.

I had extraordinary ideas in those days which I now realize must have been an awful pain to everybody else. You see, I didn't try to make up to look pretty; I made up badly, on purpose. I dressed with four other girls. We were all called 'principals', but really in concert party there are only eight or nine people and everybody plays all the parts, and you do concerted numbers and sing – all the things I say everybody should learn. When the other principals said, 'Why don't you try to look a bit better on the stage?' I answered, 'Ah, I can explain why. When the curtain goes up, they're not going to say, "Oh – what a lovely lot of girls," they're going to say, "Who's that awful one there" and pick me out!' I also remember I had one red thumbnail to help get me noticed. It's all very gauche and naïve, but it was my idea, because I had very little skill or talent at this time. It sounds terrible now, and very precocious and nothing like I am today, but I just thought I couldn't achieve anything by real talent. Those were my learning days. They're not over, but I do know a little bit more now.

After my first summer season, I tried for pantomime. I saw that Jack Gillam, who was registered in Manchester, was going to do a pantomime, so I decided to go to this audition, or interview. My mother said to me before I went, 'Now don't forget, Beryl – there's *nothing* you can't do.' I set off with much more confidence than I've got now, because I was so ignorant. 'What do you do?' Mr Gillam asked me. 'Oh – *everything*,' I replied. 'How much money would you want?' I said, '£3 a week.' 'All my life,' said Mr Gillam, 'I've been looking for someone who could do everything for £3 a week!' I was hired!

In *Aladdin*, I played the Genie of the Ring, and there I met Reginald Vincent, who has always been my greatest friend. He's the sort of friend who, if I knocked at the door and said, 'I've just murdered somebody,' would say, 'Well, come in, you must be very hungry.' I was the youngest member of the cast, and that's always a tricky position. Reggie took me aside for a serious talk. 'Do you realize you'll have to bring sandwiches for the entire cast during the whole run?' he asked. 'Well, no, I didn't actually, Reggie,' I said – thinking, oh, God, how could I possibly pay for that on £3 a week? Anyway, I did manage it, I took sandwiches every day and everybody ate them. Nobody told me that it was one of those terrible jokes that people played on apprentices. Reggie, who was playing Abanazar, was sorry at the end, especially when I gave him a Tootal tie, as brother Roy then had worked on the anti-crease process for the firm and we always had a Tootal's bundle, with ties a shilling each. Reggie got one as a sort of end-of-term present. He then told me about this terrible lie and that it was only his joke. When he appeared with me on 'This Is Your Life', he did say, 'I think she forgave me,' and, of course, I did. I absolutely adored him. He died just a year ago, when he was eighty and had gone blind. He really no longer wanted to live and he upset me very much by saying, 'I'm in God's Waiting Room.' But he was terribly funny and had great spirit right to the end; he put on a Hawaiian shirt when he was quite elderly and I went to see him, to be rather 'goey' when he took me out to lunch.

Aladdin went on an amazing tour, opening at the Hippodrome, Salford, the birthplace of Walter Greenwood, who wrote *Love on the Dole*, which was extremely successful just at that time and made the reputation of Wendy Hiller on the stage and Deborah Kerr in the cinema. He then wrote another play, called *Give Us This Day*, which he asked me to appear in, but unfortunately it never got off the ground. Another remarkable man who came from Salford was L. S. Lowry, who painted matchstick men and matchstick cats and dogs. He really is one of my favourite artists, and though he wasn't painting at the time I was at the Hippodrome he did a great deal of his painting in Salford, with all those terrible grief- and poverty-stricken faces and crowds of people all rushing to any work they could get. He touches my heart very much.

But that's taking me away from the story of being in the pantomime, which happily wasn't a disaster of that kind. I didn't know that everybody didn't tour, or that you could ever stay in one place doing anything. We went on to the Metropole, Openshaw – of course none of these places are still standing – and I remember that we had the Massa Hirakawa Troupe from Japan, a Speciality Act who used to go on before the finale, while we were changing for the Walk Down the Palace Steps. The leader, who was always frightfully drunk, used to slide blindfold, wearing those funny little sandals with a split for the big toe, down a rope attached to the gallery rail and onto the stage. It was an absolute sensation. Next we went to the King's Palace, Preston, which always made me think of a gents loo, because it was all white tiles – really, I thought, an awful place. But I was delighted to be doing it, regardless.

On the Sunday we went by train to Preston, Reggie made the bold suggestion that he should escort me to Blackpool, take me into a pub in the evening and buy me a drink. I'd never been in a pub, and when he asked, 'What do you want?' I didn't know. So I said, 'Oh, I'll have a Guinness.' I really hated it, because it was so bitter, but I downed it with a look of great glee on my face. This is it, I thought, I'm on the stage, and this is Living! No wonder! At different times during the pantomime I played, when the originals fell out through illness or old age or whatever, a Fairy, a Second Boy and a Principal Girl. On this last occasion, knowing Jack Gillam was in the gents, I sat outside the door and cried, asking for a raise to £3 10s a week. What is more, he gave it to me!

After that I invented a variety act for myself. It wasn't a lot of good, I admit: I came on in the best evening dress I had, sang a song, told some jokes and did some impressions, then sang another song and got off. One of the first weeks I ever did in variety was at the Argyll, Birkenhead. As I approached the theatre I saw the word REID written in great big letters and thought, really, for £5 a week they're overdoing the billing a bit, then when I got nearer I saw that it was Billy Reid and his Accordion Band, with Dorothy Squires as the singer, and I was tiny, tiny – down in the wines and spirits bit. There were the most wonderful rows with broken chairs and flying records from Billy Reid and Dorothy Squires, something I'd never witnessed before in my life. I was still quite sheltered and my brother drove me back home every night. During the performance I wore a cap and gown over a rather pretty evening dress, which I was going to reveal later, and did something about school. I suppose it was the beginning of the thought about a schoolgirl, only in this instance, a schoolmistress. I'd never been First Turn before on the bill, and I got The Bird and was booed off, though I did finish my act. There was no applause, just slow handclapping and booing. Roy said, 'It didn't go very well, did it?' I replied, 'No, I don't think it did, Roy, but I don't think it's in the right place!' I stuck the week out and got my £5. When he came for me on Saturday night he had to break the news to me that one of our cats, Jumbo, had been killed on the railway line. That was the end of the saddest week of my life till then. But I enjoyed the fighting in the dressing-room!

The schoolroom figured again during my next summer season, at the Arcadia, Scarborough. Arnold Crowther's show was my first experience with a ventriloquist's dummy, although Horace in his sailor suit certainly didn't turn me on as Archie did all those years later with Peter Brough. Arnold Crowther wrote two acts for me, 'The Schoolgirl Impressionist' and 'My Radio'. One paper said, 'Another very popular artiste in this show is Beryl Reid. Without the aid of anything but her own face she impersonates all the well-known movie, stage and radio stars, not only obtaining their vocal characteristics, but also their facial expressions ... something new in impressionist acts, well deserving the applause she receives.' Patrick Page kindly sent that cheering cutting from *The World's Fair*, which undoubtedly gave me a lift after Birkenhead.

But one good review wasn't enough. I had to do something drastic to get my act together. A man called Hyman Zahl seemed to think I was quite a snip at £8 a week, and he gave me a tour of theatres which now seem ghastly to contemplate. I went first to Blackburn. My mother came to see me when I was dressing in a place like a stable: 'Well, Beryl,' she said, 'if this is what it's going to be like, I'd just give it up!' 'Oh, no, Mummy,' I said, 'it's going to get better and better.' I never thought it was hard or difficult, and I never believed that I was going to be anything but what I then called 'famous'. I was such an ignoramus, and so filled with enthusiasm I thought that I couldn't look back.

Next I went to Burnley, not an easy place in those days. On the way in, I asked a lady who was cleaning the floor with a bucket and mop, 'What time is the band call?' She dried her hands on her canvas apron and said, 'Well, the piano's over there and I'm ready when you are.'

When you did a variety act you had your own lighting plot, which means that you had to know all about the lighting of the stage and the colour that the limes upon you should be. Whoever arrived earliest got their lighting plots and their band books on the floor; whatever order you arrived in you had to do your band call and lighting plots in that sequence. In those days I made very sure I was near the beginning so I could have a jolly good look round and find out what it was all about. Once I disagreed with the note the trumpet player was blowing – you also had to know about the music – and said, 'You're playing a B natural and it should be a B flat.' 'It's meant to be a B natural,' he insisted. 'No,' I said, 'I'm sorry, it isn't. You're playing the wrong note. You should be playing a B flat.' So he said, 'I don't have to do this, you know – I'm a first-class joiner!'

Another date for Hyman Zahl was at the Palace, Attercliff, near Sheffield, where the rats ate my knickers. You had to leave them in the dressing-room at night, and the rats always seemed to find them very tasty. Another choice date was Wednesbury, on the outskirts of Birmingham, where one of the acts I worked with was the Four Aces, who sang in close harmony. I thought they were the most glamorous men I'd ever met. They lived at a pub called the Pipe Hall, where they paid £5 *a week*, and they asked me over there to have a drink. Such sophistication! I just couldn't believe my luck! Stan, one of the Four Aces, even took me to the pictures twice. It was absolutely great that they took any notice of me. Stan and I later wrote to each other for years, well into the war, when three of them were killed. I'm afraid I lost touch with Stan, and I don't know what happened to him.

Then there was the Grand, Benwell, outside New-castle, where the orchestra pit was wired in – I mean, there was wire over the top of the orchestra because of all the things that the audience threw at the artists. Whenever a comic came on, there was a lady who walked about in the gallery saying, 'Razor blades, buy me razor blades – she does nowt but talk.' Quite a baptism! And that was about the end of *that* tour!

It was also the beginning of the mental notes I kept storing up on some of the great characters I met in those touring digs – usually warm and comfortable places where you were really made to feel at home and well looked after. There were exceptions, of course, as Jack Tripp reminded me recently. The lady in question asked me, 'Do you like fish and chips?' I said, 'Yes.' 'That's good,' she said, tightening her lips, 'because you'll be getting them all week!'

For contrast, back in Sheffield I had a wonderful landlady who dressed in black bombazine, tightly stretched over this enormous bust. They were superlative digs: I never saw her sit in an easy chair. She always sat in a Bentwood wooden chair, with her back as straight as a die as she waited for you to come in. She gave me some beautiful silver grapefruit spoons; she had a number of very beautiful possessions and we did get very fond of each other. She had a rather plain daughter called Jessie who, as Noel Coward (or was it Oscar Wilde?) once put it, was even plainer and possibly older than she. One day I asked her where Jessie was.

'Where d'you think? Out with a married man: red 'ot, our Jessie!' In fact, anything less red hot you'd never set eyes on in your life. They don't make them like that any more – the landladies, or the theatrical digs, I mean. And more's the pity.

My next piece of good luck – because everything to me then was good luck – was to meet Al Burnett, a gentleman who ran a nightclub. He owned clubs in London, and, though I thought of him as slightly sinister, I loved this because it seemed so sophisticated. He paid me only £7 a week, which was a bit of a come-down, but I could manage perfectly well on it, and I was thrilled to have a list of dates from him. We used to have a train call on a Sunday, which meant you all got on the same train at, I think, a reduced rate, in a reserved compartment. I used to watch Al Burnett play cards during these journeys with all the men in the show – and he always won their salaries back from them! I was a dead loss to him, because I couldn't play cards at all, I couldn't even tell a spade from a club or a knave from a queen. I kept my £7 a week, which really quite upset him. So, when we got to a theatre in Bedford, he set up a lot of electric light bulbs in a tree outside the County (where we were appearing) and produced a gun. He said to me, 'I bet you £5 you can't shoot all those lights out' – but what he didn't know was that I could shoot. So he lost his £5.

I was doing, in my own small way, well. When I had been on bills for Hyman Zahl I had worked with very good people – stars who are now legends. There was Max Miller, Nellie Wallace and Harry Champion – I was amazed at how many choruses they played while he changed his jacket on the side of the stage, but that didn't seem to matter in those days. Then, a short time after I'd started to work with George Formby (Junior, of course), George asked me if I would like to do a little bit in a film called *Spare a Copper* which he was making at Shepperton. Even his wife Beryl, who used to guard him like a tigress, let me in. When I was rash enough to inquire what they were doing next week – in variety you really lived from date to date – she said '*We're* learning a song!' I must say she wasn't really my favourite lady, but George was very sweet when he had the chance. In the film I sang a sort of soprano song – I was terribly thin, with pince-nez glasses on, and I really thought I was a film star and that everybody was going to be longing for me to work for them. Of course I didn't get a single offer, but that's just the way of the world.

Nellie Wallace had a cabin trunk, which people used to travel with then, which she paid a porter threepence to carry from the station at Bedford to the stage door. I remember thinking that was what happened when you got rich! I also worked with G. H. Elliott, who was a very charming but, I thought, lonely man. Also on the bill was a head-to-head balancing act. They were circus people and the lady's name was June. G. H. Elliott fell in love with her, but because circus people are so close, so terrified of losing a partner, her brother used to lock her in the dressing-room, so that they were unable to meet. The brother regularly smashed the bottles of perfume that G.H. used to send her, but at last his persistent devotion won, and he married June. They had a very happy marriage and she was with him to the very end of his life. A niece took her place balancing on her brother's head so it all ended very well indeed, but at the start it was touch-and-go. Circus people are very strict with each other. It's a discipline entirely of its own, a family thing, and they're jealous of anyone who intrudes.

I worked with Randolph Sutton, who sang the original version of 'On Mother Kelly's Doorstep'. He was a superlative light entertainer and we all had a great time with him – a very witty man. There was a second comic on the bill and I remember him coming into Randolph Sutton's dressing-room and saying, 'I've had such a lovely week with you – I would love to keep in touch.' He said, 'Well, you can find me any Sunday at number four platform at Crewe!'

Billy Russell, the fine character comedian, was the only person before me to push the Birmingham accent. Of course he came from there, like lots of others, including Tony Hancock and Sid Field, but none of them let the Birmingham accent come into their work. Billy Russell did a memorable sketch as a lady flowerseller, and that was the first time I'd ever heard the accent. Many years afterwards I myself was going to become fairly well known as 'Marlene – from the Midlands'.

Also extremely funny was Billy Bennett, whose billing was 'Almost a Gentleman'. He used to do that terrible shouting thing – monologues telling the workhouse master where to stick the Christmas pudding, and so on. It was very, very vulgar, but vulgarity doesn't seem bad to me at all. Good vulgarity is absolutely marvellous – it's just when it's a bit mucky I don't like it. Going from the ridiculous to the sublime, although I never worked with Dorothy Ward, the most enduring and famous Principal Boy of all, she was in pantomime when I was in variety in Liverpool and I used to come across her, always dressed 'like a star', and not a hair out of place, in the digs. She did tell someone a very funny story, later in her life. A lady had come to have a drink with her before going off to have dinner with someone in London, and this lady related how a man stepped out of a doorway and said, 'Give me your handbag.' The lady had very little money in her bag, so the man said, 'Give me your mink coat, then.' This poor woman handed over the coat and he sped off with it. The person to whom Dorothy was telling this story at her Baker Street flat said, 'Oh, was it dark?' and Dorothy said, 'Of course it was dark; it was a *very* good mink!'

3

Blue Skies and Dark Clouds

The Lancashire impresario Ernest Binns gave me two solid engagements during the year before war broke out. There was the pantomime *Mother Goose*, in which I played Gretchen, Mother Goose's maid, for the first time, and upset Mr Binns' sense of propriety for perhaps the last time. I thought I was frightfully smart, because I had frilly petticoats and frilly white knickers and a little Dutch headdress. I started with my bottom to the audience, as if I was bowing to them, but the wrong way round, and Ernest Binns came flying round and said, 'You mustn't show your arse like that, Miss ... Hmm ... Hmm ... I mean, it's like sayin' "come and 'ave a basinful of this 'ere" ... Hmm ... Hmm.' So I thought perhaps I was on the wrong tack; after that I started the right way round.

There was also a long tour in a show called *Blue Skies*, during which I fell madly in love for the first time. There had been crushes and enthusiasms before, but this was, for me, my first taste of the Real Thing, and I was eighteen. He was a pianist called Brian Seymour and I loved him so much that a year later I was prepared to sit up until two in the morning to listen to him doing a broadcast of that beautiful sentimental number 'Deep Purple' for the BBC. I also met and worked with a friend of mine with whom I'm still very much in touch – Olivia Jevons, who was to marry Dorothy Ward's nephew Terry. (They were responsible for christening Dimly on Page One of this book.) Now she is Olivia Ward and they live in Cheadle in Cheshire. Together I suppose we might have been thought of as the scourge of St Helen's, one of many places *Blue Skies* visited during its tour of Lancashire, because we carried on rather like punks do now. We used to buy the most outrageous hats for three and eleven, and wore a different outrageous hat every day because we wanted people to turn and stare at us. Mind you, St Helen's at that time seemed to us young people to be in need of shaking up: we had to do a Monday matinée for the miners, which was a deadly affair, because they came in, black with coal, and just sat and stared at you. But it was a good way to rehearse the opening night. Sometimes we'd even design our own hats – anything for a shock effect. When I criticize people now, Olivia says, 'Come along now – think of us at St Helen's. Weren't we awful?' And of course we were.

I recently played the refurbished theatre at Bath, which is quite beautiful. Brian Seymour, who is now seventy, lives there and I went to see him and he came to the show. His flat is covered with photographs of me when I was in my teens, which is really very touching. He has a photograph of me in his wallet which he has kept all this time. I have recently sent him, at his request, 'a slightly more recent picture', in colour, which he thought was absolutely lovely. Funnily enough, he didn't look any different to me, and, though I know I look different, he still looked at me in the same way and held my hand in the taxi. It's really rather wonderful that, through all these years, that feeling has stayed for us.

After that meeting he wrote to me, reminding me of visits I paid to him in the army. 'When you arrived by taxi at the barracks, you said to the sentry, "I want to see Brian." He said, "I don't know who Brian is." You said, "Oh, everybody knows Brian; he plays the piano, you know." He said, "Oh, him – he's up at the chapel hall, sleeping!" After that you drove round the barrack square and out of the gate, waving left and right! Another time you came over in a concert party bus to an

Ack-Ack Station and sat in the front row with the officers, who made much fuss of you, thinking, no doubt, "far too good for a mere lance bombardier". You were then taken up for a drink in the officers' mess afterwards. You were ages and we were sitting in the bus waiting to go. At last I came up and tapped on the door, and asked, "Is Miss Reid ready, as we're waiting to go?" Then you came to the door and said, "Oh, come in, darling, we're having a wonderful time. Come in and have a drink!" I had to explain that lance bombardiers couldn't drink in the officers' mess. Then you decided to help to serve out the boys' evening meal there. To each you said, "Is that enough, darling?" and gave them more. We were hysterical, because half way through you'd finished up all the food and there was none left for the others. But I'm sure you've forgotten those incidents.'

I had indeed, but they do serve to show my shame-making naïveté at the time. In the September war broke out, I was doing a summer season at Saltburn, near Redcar in Yorkshire, in the church hall, which was pretty ghastly. I had gone back to £5 a week, because it was a long run, but in spite of all that I had a marvellous time. I was riding horses a lot then and used to go to the Zetland Hotel in the morning, and go out with a groom to exercise the horses, five miles along the sand to Redcar and five miles back. He was called Herbert, and, of course, I fell madly in love with him. But when I saw him off a horse I couldn't even look at him. So that was a very short-lived romance in my head. Naturally, I was very hard up, and although there was a lift down to the beach – it's a very cliffy place – my friend Pat Cross (who was in the show with me and later become one of Hal Swain's Swing Sisters) agreed that as it was such a lovely day we ought to walk down. Actually, it was because we hadn't a penny between us. On a Friday we would have a great celebration, like buying each other a Pimms, which cost half-a-crown, and that was very 'goey'. I remember buying my brother one when he came to visit us and this very staid, quiet, beautiful man did side-kicks all along the promenade.

This season on Poverty Row was the time I used to live almost entirely on baked beans – probably the reason I can't abide them now. To me they smell of feet. Also, as we were doing self-catering to save the pennies, we used to hand our potatoes to the landlady and say, 'Don't mash them': we wanted to be sure she wasn't short-changing us!

In Saltburn also were singer Sara Gregory and her husband Richard Stone, later an agent and impresario for whom I was to do a summer season after the war. That was a nicer way of showing his appreciation than another Ernest Binns' artiste, not a frightfully good comic in the pantomime. He was so angry with me, because I seemed to be doing quite well then, that he smashed all the photographs of me outside the theatre. Not, I thought, in the best taste. But you can't have everything.

With the outbreak of war all the theatres closed and I joined ENSA. The first one I can remember opening afterwards was a little one in Scarborough, which I imagine was a repertory theatre. Flotsam and Jetsam – one sang light, the other very Deep Purple – put on a bill there in which I appeared, which took me back to my first season there with Arnold Crowther a couple of years previously, when I had put a ten shilling deposit on a caracul fur coat which was going to cost £7. Little did the poor woman who took the deposit know that she was going to be lifting it off that rail so many times, because I took everybody I knew to go and 'view' it before it was paid for. You do such embarrassing things when you're young. Albert Sandler and his Trio (whom I used to announce through a microphone, which I thought was terribly 'posh' when I was working with them) were coming to the Floral Hall in September. I had a terrible crush on Albert Sandler, who didn't look at me twice, and I thought, How marvellous, by September I will have got the fur coat, and wear it, and he'll think, who is.

this glamorous person in the fur coat? I didn't realize that he knew lots of ladies with beautiful fur coats.

On the day he arrived it was boiling hot, but I was determined to go to the Floral Hall wearing the fur coat. You know how hot Floral Halls are, they're all glass to reflect the heat; the sweat was running off my face, and my hair had gone all straight. I went round to the dressing-room, and he said 'Oh, hallo' in a terrible offhand sort of way, and I thought, why doesn't he say, 'What a beautiful fur coat'?

The fur coat may have been a disaster on that day, but not for the rest of its life. I wore it constantly. I said to my mother, 'Actresses must have furs, Mummy': I'd also bought a terribly scabby fox fur, with a twisted, thin tail. She threw it straight into the dustbin, saying, 'Not these furs they don't, Beryl!' So that was the end of that adventure.

I've always had a soft spot for musicians – I even married one, much later. But I've an especially happy memory of the ones at the Palace, Attercliff, where the orchestra stood up and faced the audience to sing a special song at the end of the performance:

> Cheerio until the next time
> At the Palace, Attercliff;
> May the skies be always blue
> And all your wonderful dreams come true.
> Health and happiness, we pray,
> May forever with you stay – so
> Cheerio until the next time
> At the Palace, Attercliff.

At this point the Musical Director, who wore white, holey Mickey Mouse gloves, leapt over the bandrail, ran to the bells which were at the end of the pit, and did a solo on them. When he came back to conduct the orchestra again as the people were filing out, he asked, 'What page are we at?' and they told him, 'Page Twelve, you bloody fool!' I watched practically every act every night. As I've said before, every time is my time for learning, and when there was a good act on you couldn't drag me away from the side of the stage. I was just avid for knowledge and 'how to do it'.

Apart from variety dates, my next job was a very small pantomime in Swindon. I had a run of two weeks, with a week's rehearsal, playing *Little Bo Peep* – totally unsuitable, but I did have real sheep. Unfortunately the owner of the sheep, having pushed them onstage so that they bumped into the backs of my knees and sent me flying, used to nip off smartly to the pub once the sheep had disappeared. But when I was saying, 'Oh, Fairy Sunshine, tell me where to find my sheep,' they all ran back on again. Desperately I said, 'Oh, they keep coming and going – I just don't know what to do with them – I'm in such a muddle.' Finally he was dragged out of the pub, the sheep were taken off and then at last I could say, 'I have lost my sheep, and don't know where to find them.'

Years before, I had won a talent competition at the Paramount Cinema in Manchester, with the prize of a week's engagement in London at the Paramount. I was to do my act in front of a band, and I got £20 for that week. So much time had elapsed that I was worried that I'd never get the chance. I went to them and said, 'But you've got to give it to me – I have it in writing that you're going to give me a prize,' so that, eventually, was that.

My mother came with me to London and found digs for me in Brixton with a wonderful Italian family called Pellegra. For ten shillings a week out of the thirty I had to live on, they threw in a free dinner of special spaghetti. Of course this was the time all the Italians were sending home their gold wedding rings and getting tin ones back to help build Italy's roads. The family were frightfully kind to me. Having collected my £20, I then got another week in Ciné-Variety, doubling two cinemas, which meant I was doing five shows a day between the Astoria, Old Kent Road and the Astoria, Brixton. We used to start at eleven o'clock in the morning and go backwards and forwards in a coach with band parts and props, and we finished at eleven o'clock at night. In case very young people think they're working hard now, that is what I would call hard work. My chums Jimmy Edwards and others were doing much the same – at the Windmill, which was, of course, terrible for comics.

My work in London then finished, but I had discovered that you could get something called a Friday night in Ciné-Variety. As I had no money, I used to walk every day from Brixton to fix the next Friday night. Then I would go to the Express Dairy in Charing Cross Road, and have what I thought would be a filling dish, like a plate of spaghetti, and hope that I would see somebody I knew who would buy me a cup of coffee. That went on for weeks and weeks. If I was lucky, I fixed a Friday night and got a matinée as well. I got thirty shillings for the one performance, but two pounds if I also did an afternoon – so I used to take all my props on the underground and go to the outlying cinemas. When I'd played Kentish Town and the other places around London, I'd used them all up. So I went to an audition at Drury Lane Theatre and did a turn for Basil Dean, who was then running ENSA. We used to sing:

> Basil, Basil, give us your ENSA, do:
> We're all crazy to do a show for you.
> According to Walter Hackett,
> The thing's a bloody racket,
> But we'll look fine, standing twelve in a line
> On a stage that was built for two!

I got the job, and – I know I'm always saying this – I met a violinist and *really* fell in love. He was twenty years older than I, I was with him for three years, and I loved him very, very much. He taught me so much about how to deal with people, how to be kind to people. You see, if somebody asked me to marry them when I was nineteen, I'd say 'Ooh – lumpy sick outside pubs!' – which obviously wasn't the way to treat people who were asking me to marry them. But I didn't realize that I was being terribly unkind. This wonderful, gentle man taught me exactly how I ought to treat people. If I did something frightful he would do the same to me, and then I understood. He also taught me one of the most valuable lessons in my life, how to laugh at myself: you know, when you're young you can't laugh at yourself, you take yourself very seriously indeed. He put a stop to all that and taught me how to have a good giggle at myself. I was totally happy with him. I also did a variety tour with him after we'd been in ENSA, because that didn't last the whole three years, but in between we used to do variety.

It was then I worked with a wonderful French Hindu girl called Koringa, who travelled with snakes and crocodiles. She was a fakir, brought over by Bertram Mills, a tiny little thing. Just before I worked with her, somebody had electrocuted all her big crocodiles in their water tank because they thought she was 'not on our side'. This was totally untrue. So she had to work with young crocodiles, and if you looked at her band parts, which the orchestra were handed every week, they warned, 'Keep out of the pit – you're in deadly danger!' The little crocodiles were much harder to control. Koringa had an inspired way with all these strange animals. She had a huge snake – one of the biggest I've ever seen – and I watched it in its little pen banging its head against the wall because it had a huge abscess on the side of its face. She said, 'He has much pain – I help him,' and she took the snake's head in her hand and lanced this abscess, and the snake didn't protest in any way. She laid it down, put its head on the grass at the bottom of its pen, and it was completely better.

She had enormous power over animals. I was once on the underground with her when a dog flew at her. She stood and just looked at it, and it backed away. Two Czechoslovakian men were working with her, and she used to lie on very sharp blades, one at her ankles and one at her neck, with nothing supporting her body at all in the middle, on two wooden trestles. Wherever we played, they put paving stones on her chest, and Joe, one of the enormous Czechs, stood on a chair to shatter them. Sometimes he would have to hit the stone with a mallet seven or eight times before it broke into pieces, and she would say, 'Oh, darling, the stone make me pain today,' but, though her body flinched, her back never gave way. Then she used to be buried on the stage: whether there was any trick to that I wouldn't know, but there was certainly no trickery about any of the other things she did.

I spoke recently about her on the 'Looks Familiar' programme with Denis Norden, and I got a letter to say that she had gone back to France and died, which saddened me, because of course I didn't know. She was very funny and always wanted to be having a party. She had something about her which was quite unusual. She looked absolutely beautiful on the stage: she had fairly dark skin and used to paint a little scarlet cross between her eyes, with two crosses over it, which was obviously some Indian sign, and she had an Afro hairstyle long, long before anyone else ever thought of it. She wore a little tiny floral bra and minute trunks and had lovely legs. She really was a lovely girl ...

The ENSA days had more than the usual share of both happiness and heartbreak. I have the tremendous gift of knowing when I'm happy, but this works both ways, as I became painfully aware. We used to stay on after ENSA performances to count the planes returning to the air bases after their missions. Sometimes it was a very joyous occasion, but it was horrendous when they failed to return.

Usually our work was very jolly and carefree. I remember playing an American base where they said, 'You must have a Blue Nile cocktail.' Being virtually a non-drinker still, I really didn't know what I was drinking – but it must have been absolute rubbish, and I was soon quite blind drunk. The man who was driving our coach apparently went over a hedge, and I woke up with a great big lump on my head. I don't remember going home at all, but I somehow got back to the digs – somebody must have known where I was staying. The next morning I felt *terrible* – I was never, *ever* going to take another drink. I thought, Oh, I don't know how I can stand it when somebody hits the drum tonight – but I had a little sleep in the afternoon, and recovered in time.

I didn't go back on my pledge of total teetotality until the road show with Will Fyffe, in which, apart from the Dagenham Girl Pipers, I was the only girl. And that was a purely social occasion involving something gentle in a glass for appearance's sake. It was a peculiar occasion, Will Fyffe, a very clever and funny man and a superlative character actor, had asked us all to have a drink in the dressing-room at the Glasgow Empire after we'd died on our feet. Even Will – and I think he'd just got his O B E – hadn't gone down very well. So he said, 'Come on, stay behind, we'll have a wee drink in the dressing-room.' Well, we did have a wee drink, and, because we were all chatting and talking and screaming with laughter and all that sort of thing, quite a lot of time went by. When we finally emerged from the stage door, a very drunken Glaswegian reeled forward, with methylated spirits leaping out in flames from his mouth, and said, 'Are you Will Fyffe?' We were all pretty cheerful by this time, and Will beamed, 'Yes', thinking he was going to be asked for his autograph. 'Well, Mr Fyffe,' said his fan, 'I've waited here for a long time – and I just want to tell you I think you're *rotten!*'

Will was anything but rotten, but on one occasion his pork pie was. All the actors were full of booze and eating cheerfully into his black-market pie on a train one Sunday, when I suddenly looked at it. It was more black mould than black market! Everyone inspected their tummies very carefully in the next twenty-four hours!

Will told me a priceless story about the time he and a friend went out one evening and, after quite a lot to drink, they both fancied pigs' trotters. Now, a great deal of glutinous fluid comes out of these when they're cooked. They got their pigs' trotters, separated, and Will took his trotters back to his digs. He cooked and ate them, and then, knocked out by the drink, he fell back on the bed without washing his hands and face. In the morning he thought he'd gone blind, his eyes were all stuck together, and his fingers and everything else was totally gummed up. He lay in a state of shock, until eventually he remembered the pigs' trotters. When he washed his hands and face, his sight was restored to him.

In that show was a man called Bert Brownbill, who used to do an impression of a bus conductress, of whom there were many during the war. I was in Manchester and there was this very young bus conductress and she was all hot and bothered and sweaty and pink. I think I was the last one to get on the bus, and I said, 'Oh, dear, you are busy.' She said, ' – Busy – I said "Full Up" to me mother!' Bert Brownbill became a great friend of mine. At that time I was still doing impressions of film stars, but he told me straight, 'If you're ever going to make a name for yourself, it's going to be by doing characters that you invent yourself. If you pursue it, your true success will come as a character actress.' I took very little notice of this at the time, but it eventually sank in. He also taught me several other lessons when we were at Newcastle. I assumed, as always, since they were all men in the company (except the Dagenham Girl Pipers!) that everybody would carry my luggage for me. I had hatboxes and boxes of dresses and carriers and suitcases, and God knows all-what. When we got to the ticket barrier at Newcastle station, I shouted, 'Come on Bert, give me a hand!' He replied flatly, 'No. You've got to learn to pack properly so that you alone can handle it.' I said, 'Oh, Bert, you don't mean that.' He answered, 'Yes, I do, because that's the only way you're going to learn.' And I was left at Newcastle station, with five hours to wait for the next train to wherever our following date was. I very quickly learned to pack properly. That was a very good lesson indeed. I remember it to this day, and always travel light, so that nobody helps me – unless I limp a bit.

Then came the next 'amazingly big' step in my career – a

summer season at the North Pier in Blackpool. That was absolutely lovely, except that the pier is very long and you have to walk to work every day. With your high heels going down those boards, right to the end of the pier, it wasn't exactly a laugh a step.

It turned out in several ways to be an interesting season. There was a coloured act, the Norman Thomas Trio, which was tremendously talented. They were father and son, and one other who wasn't related to them. I thought the unrelated one (Freddie, the drummer) was rather swinging, and I used to hold hands walking up the pier with him. I didn't see why this was wrong, but everybody in the world but me seemed to think it was, because he was black and I was white, and I hadn't learnt to distinguish between the two colours. It did cause everybody connected with me a lot of heartaches, because everybody talked about it. Later the son, who was called Sonnie, was arrested and handcuffed at the top of the pier, for peddling dope. However, the charge was completely dismissed. I knew nothing about the underworld. When one of the orchestra tried to flog me a terribly expensive watch for thirty-five shillings, I said to my friend Olivia, 'I've been offered this marvellous watch for only thirty-five shillings.' Quick as a whippet, Olivia fired back, 'Have you taken it?' I said, 'Oh, no,' and that was obviously the right answer. I was really mixing with a strange lot of people.

Dave Morris, the star of the show, was one of the funniest comics I ever worked with. He would be playing, or pretending to play, a flute and say, 'I've got this because it was made by Cammell Laird's in a moment of weakness!' He had a wealth of funny things to say: it was the time when the Jimmy James style of comedy, the very original approach, was in fashion. He apparently had rows with his wife; they had several children, and his wife used to meet him at the top of the pier with a different child after every performance, because we did a matinée every day and a show on Sunday. Whichever child won his heart round then, the row was made up.

I stayed at the Rivoli guest house where the landlord was a man called Mr Dootson. There was also a Mrs Hargreaves, and I don't quite know where she fitted into the plan, except that she did push her bust into everybody's face whenever serving the meals. Mr D. was shady – no question – the war was on, of course, and he used to open his skylight all the time, which rather worried me, because I thought he must be signalling something to somebody. He said to me, very seriously, one day, 'You see, Beryl, they've asked me to go into Parliament. Well, I know that I could never see eye to eye with Winston Churchill, and, rather than cause bother, I've turned it down!' So – I just had to take him at his word.

In the hotel during that eventful season there were six Polish officers, and I taught them all to speak English. I even got them reading out of newspapers, and, in exchange for that, I learned ten Polish words every day. So I have more than a smattering of Polish, and it's rather interesting that when I meet Rula Lenska I know more Polish than she does. Having just done a 'Minder' on television, where she nipped in to see me, it always amazes me when I say 'Gak się maszdzisiaj?' she doesn't really know the answer, which is 'Dziękuję, bardzo dobrze,' meaning 'How are you today?' and she says, 'Very well, thank you.' That is something that has stayed at the back of my head, and from time to time does come in useful.

During this period I must mention one soprano who rather hit the bottle, and I think it hit her back. To begin with she threw an electric iron at the manager, and was told to pack her bags. But he forgot about it, so she stayed. She used to sing 'Ave Maria', dressed as a nun, and standing in these golden gates at the top of the staircase she'd sway to and fro as she got to 'Ora pro nobis, nobis peccatoribus': it was just by good luck that they waited to close the golden gates until she swayed backwards on the final 'Amen', thus avoiding slicing off a nose noted in the profession for its prominence. It didn't all end there, because as we sang 'God Save the King' at the finale the lady in question chose to sing, I don't know why, 'God Save Our Bleeding King.' The chief comic walked along the line as we were all saying 'Good Night, Good Night' and said, 'You're a disgrace to the bleeding profession!' and hit her. I didn't feel that that was very good family entertainment.

I have always, I suppose, been ambitious, not enough to walk on anybody else's face, but ambitious to get on in the theatre, and to become more competent at whatever I did. So I returned to London and the digs in Brixton with the Pellegras. That was a very nice reunion. I had decided that Tom Arnold, the impresario who was a great power in the theatre at that time and who promoted the best pantomimes all over the country, was going to be my chief bid for this elusive 'fame' I was seeking. As usual I was very short of money, and I walked from Brixton to Tom Arnold's office in Shaftesbury Avenue, over Feldman's the music publishers, which was Lawrence Wright's headquarters, taking with me the piano part of my act, my Gracie Fields shawl and all my props, my Anna Neagle Queen Victoria regalia – the cape and the bits of sponge I put into my cheeks for 'plumpers' to make me look old – all these in a paper carrier. I went to the very sweet sergeant in the waiting room, and said, 'I want to see Tom Arnold.' He asked, 'Have you got an appointment?' I told him I hadn't, and he said, 'Well, he won't see you, you know.' 'Oh, yes, he will,' I answered, 'because he'll get tired long before I do. In fact, would you be kind enough, as I'm walking from Brixton, to keep my props and my music with you in this paper carrier?' He said, 'Yes, of course I will.' So I got there at about 9.30 every morning, sat till one, and then once more went off to the Express Dairy to have something to eat – probably ghastly beans on toast again.

I returned to the office at about 2.30 and the sergeant

would again say, 'Beryl Reid wants to see you, sir,' to be answered by the growl, 'I can't see anybody ... can't see anybody.' This went on for three weeks, and I did go every day. Finally, as I had been sure would happen, Tom Arnold said, 'Oh, for God's sake – I'd better see her.' I thought, 'Now's the time to get the props and the music out, and I went down to Feldman's office, where there was a pianist available. I did my prepared turn for Mr Arnold. And I worked for him for nine years afterwards.

4

Life's Richer Pattern

I was, of course, thrilled to get the contract from Tom Arnold. It was a tremendous victory – my first big heave-up. I wanted to celebrate, but really didn't know how to go into a pub on my own and order anything. So I went back to the Express Dairy and said to the waitress, who by then was used to me and my baked beans, 'I want two banana splits, please!' She was astounded, and the food was so sickening I can't tell you! But it was the best way I had of really, really celebrating.

My luck continued. My first season for Tom Arnold was with Jack Buchanan, in *Cinderella*. He was Buttons. Jean Gillie, who was absolutely beautiful, played Cinders and Adèle Dixon, Prince Charming. Nat Jackley and Jack Clifford were the Brokers' Men and Elsie Percival played Dandini. She was wonderful. When they asked her which key she sang in, she fluted, 'I can sing in any key at all,' and so she could, because she just spoke the words. If you do that, you *can* sing in any key at all. I was a little Ugly Sister and Fred Emney played Baron Hardup. He was terribly funny, and a high spot of the panto was a cod ballet he did with Jack, who was dressed as a wasp, while Fred was a fairy, to the strains of 'All the Things You Are'.

We rehearsed at Sheffield and then the bombs came: Sheffield was literally demolished. I lived in a street with three or four hundred terraced houses in it, and Jack Buchanan's understudy was killed in the next house to mine – the house was literally cut off. It was a nightmare. Time and time again I returned to my house, through all the flames and smoke, because I kept remembering new things that were precious to me, like my wireless, which I called Wilhelmina, and the little diamond ring that I'd been given on my twenty-first birthday. All my hair was burnt off, I lost my eyelashes and I myself was burnt. At about five o'clock in the morning I was walking aimlessly through the streets of Sheffield. When I did a Pete Murray Show a few years ago, a man rang up to say that he helped carry all my things past all the burning houses. I do remember somebody helping me, but I was in such a state that I can recall no details now, except that there was no water and I made my way to Jack Buchanan's hotel. The next day we were all taken in a coach to Manchester and of course I stayed with my mother and father.

In Manchester we played mornings and afternoons, because the people wouldn't come out in the evenings because of all the bombs. It was quite eerie, really. Eventually we did return to Sheffield, and Jack made a little speech at the finale, which I call 'All Down for the Who's Best'. He said, 'Your spirit's great, no one can break it – Bravo, Sheffield, you can take it!' He had that marvellous corn-crakey voice. He was a magical person. I think every woman was in love with him. He remembered all the stagehands' names, and knew if their wives were ill. He was frightfully kind to me and didn't make me feel like a non-star at all, inviting me to supper with him and 'his lot' – i.e. the stars, which I thought was grand. They were the sort of people who had supper out every night after the show, bombs or no bombs.

Cinderella was the centrepiece of my life for the next three years, with summer seasons and variety in between. Jack and Jean Gillie continued to play Buttons and Cinders, but the next year at Liverpool, 1942–43, Kitty Reidy was Prince Charming and Marianne Lincoln, who married Nat Jackley, Dandini. The following year we went to Birmingham, where, of course, I was to develop Marlene of the Midlands. Everything I learnt I was going to use eleven years later, in 'Educating Archie' on the radio.

I had a wonderful dresser, who held the door handle firmly in her hand, and said, 'Goodnight, each!' She made remarkable statements, like, ''Course, my Grandad, you know – 'e's a bugger with the women. People refer to 'im 'ere as the Balsall Heath Stallion!' I also had a landlady who made out that she never ate anything. She'd say, 'Well, I don't have breakfast, really; I just have bacon and egg – I force it down. I don't want it, you know – you don't when you cook it. I don't have another thing then till 10 o'clock, then I have a cup of tea and a few biscuits. Not a bite passes my lips then till 11 ...' In fact she never stopped eating, every hour, but she convinced herself she never ate. I found a very elderly chop-bone under the bed one day, because the bed had never been swept under in its life, and she said, 'Oh – I'll kill that Chum.' I said, 'But you haven't got a dog.' She answered, 'I know, but there's one up the road!' Obviously some lodger had had supper in bed and dropped the chop-bone, and it had just remained there.

Again, Jack was very sweet to me, asked me to supper and all that sort of thing. We were then playing in the evenings, of course: it was only in the very beginning that we stuck to day-time shows. In Liverpool we'd also performed in the evenings and Fred Emney was in his element: he used to make up little rhymes. I remember, 'I am the Fairy Have-a-Go, I'm Queen of the Fairy Nation, And as I've no more words to say – Three Cheers for Lime Street Station!' Or, 'I am the Fairy Knock-it-Off, And gladness is my Policy; I've nothing much to do today, So I'm swimming over to Wallasey!' I looked forward to every performance – there'd be a new one every day! Olivia, my great friend from *Blue Skies* days, came to see me in Liverpool and met Fred Emney, whom I described to her as 'the one with the dead mouse on his upper lip – you can't miss him!' He took a great shine to her, and she did a long tour with him as his lovely blonde lady leaning on the piano. They became great friends.

Americans were always seeking our attention, courting us and looking after us. I met a charming GI, Ray from South Carolina. He told me a lot of lies, I expect, but I must say I enjoyed them all at the time.

Broadcasts, which I had done from Manchester from my very early days with my own show called 'A Quarter of an Hour with Beryl Reid', pantomimes, summer seasons and lots of variety in between, were my daily fare. However life was changing, barely perceptibly, but still changing; and the quality of the work I was offered was improving all the time.

My next pantomime for Tom Arnold was at the Theatre Royal, Nottingham, with Douglas Byng, who was playing the Queen in *The Sleeping Beauty*. I was Trixie, her maid. He gave me three lovely books of *Byng Ballads* and *More Byng Ballads*. He was not only a superb Dame, but he brought to the part something of the sophistication of an international cabaret star. He had a great flair for lyrics. How could I forget 'In the Spring my Auntie Nelly, dusting down her Botticelli' and 'Oh, I Do Like a Little Bit of Edelweiss!' When in the pantomime we'd all been asleep for a hundred years and awoke in rags and tatters, he'd say, as soon as he got up, 'Oh – you're no sooner in bed than you're out again!' His next line was, 'I forgot to put the cat out.' We were all just the same, because that hundred years hadn't aged *us* – only our costumes. He had the most wonderful ones: one skirt he took off was a complete table, laid for four people to sit and eat at. He just unhooked something, and there it was, with knives and forks and goblets.

Dougie had just come back from the Far East, and he gave me some beautiful Indian material, with a pair of fabulous red and gold sandals. I just couldn't wait to wear them, but alas, after about three weeks they totally disintegrated: like a lot of things that look beautiful, they fell apart quickly. That's life, really, with the lid off.

At that time, blonde hair was all the go – if God hadn't blessed you with it, you gave Him a little help by bleaching it – and I used to do this for our smashing leading lady, Betty Frankiss, every week at her hotel. One day, when I'd done her hair, my mother was with me; we all looked in the mirror to see how Betty's hair looked, and there we were, all three, clearly reflected. I was in lime green – rather a nice little suit I had at the time. But my mother said, 'You should never wear that colour, Beryl, it makes your face look awfully yellow.' I looked at my face, and it was *bright* yellow and my eyes were bright orange. I had jaundice. It was only two weeks to the end of the season, so I was able to stick it out, feeling very sickly and poor, but that didn't matter. On the way home in the train, I had an offer from a man who asked me to do cabaret in India, presumably because he's never seen anybody that colour before. True to form my mother said, 'I would take it if I were you, Beryl!'

My second pantomime with Douglas Byng was at the Empire, Liverpool. It was *Mother Goose*, perhaps the best part ever written for a Dame, and I was again her maid, Gretchen this time. It was also the first time Wilfred Pickles had ever played in pantomime. At this time he had caused quite a stir by reading the news on the radio in his own Yorkshire accent. Some people were up in arms – and some people thought it was lovely and a welcome change from the ironed out 'BBC English' which was almost obligatory in those days. I was very fond of Wilfred: he was a marvellous teller of jokes. He enjoyed telling them so much. I don't think his wife Mabel enjoyed him telling me jokes, but that was another story.

A great friend of mine in that show was Georgette Bishop, who played the Fairy. We shared a dressing-room, and had one pink cushion between us. It was the Saga of the Pink Cushion, really, because if one of us didn't feel very well or was tired, we shared it, otherwise we used to have it on alternate tea hours, and if you hadn't got the pink cushion you rolled a towel or scarf round your handbag and that had to stand in for the prized cushion. Georgie is now Georgette Rose. She was married in the Friendly Isles at the Embassy there, and the most romantic wedding photographs were taken on the beach. I am godmother to her son, the actor Brian Holland. He is a wonderful young man, and when I'm with him I feel just the same age as he is. This is his gift, not mine. His mother later went into stage management; she was at the Haymarket for a long time, doing some of the great classical plays with many of the most distinguished names in the theatre.

Tessa Deane was the Principal Boy in *Mother Goose*. I remember that, because none of us was allowed to go to the loo in the interval in case Tessa Deane wanted to go, which was rather inhibiting to say the least. I don't think Mabel Pickles took to me very much: I said I could pluck her eyebrows for her, and so Georgette and I turned our dressing-room into something like a scene from *The Demon Barber of Fleet Street*, with towels and God knows all-what flung over the chair. We shoved one round her neck and proceeded to pluck her eyebrows, with vigour. I think perhaps that was the last time she ever had her eyebrows plucked.

While in Liverpool, Dougie Byng had asked me to have lunch with him at the Adelphi Hotel. I was a bit dressed up, and something awful always happens to me if I dress up a bit. There was this poor little man, sort of a tramp, with a white silk scarf, like greyhound racers have, and a flat 'at, and I knew he was going to talk to me. I thought, I'm not going to speak to him: this is my day for being dressed up, and I'm going to be a bit grand. Fatal – because he said, 'It's been a lovely day, 'asn't it?' I thought, Oh God – I knew he'd talk to me. Then sympathy got the better of me and I continued, 'I was in Manchester on Sunday, and it was raining there.' He said, 'Yes, it's no bloody wonder they call it the pisspot of England, is it? Good morning, lady.' The bus had arrived by this time and I got on, falling about laughing. I laughed all the way to the hotel. My dignity was quite squashed, and that's very good for me.

I seem to attract these strange conversations. The year before, in Birmingham with Jack Buchanan, the panto had run for ages and we had a kind of mini-heatwave. I went up Temple Street to sit on a seat and sun myself by a memorial of some sort. A road sweeper with a broom and a shovel said, 'Oh, 'ullo Beryl,' and I thought, Here we go again. He threw his shovel down, with great disregard for the Corporation, sat down beside me on the seat, and said, 'I don't know where to go for me 'olidays, you know. I shall either go to Margate or South Africa.' I answered, 'I would say a lot depends on how long you've got for a holiday.' He said, 'Yes, I suppose it does,' and after chatting on for a while he picked up his shovel and walked away. 'Decisions, decisions,' as Marlene said when she was confronted by a sign which said, 'Ring or Knock'!

Looking back, I can see I had it all on a plate in those days, with good shows with mostly lovely people and no responsibility. So for a challenge I thought I'd take a driving test. I'd actually been driving for goodness knows how long, really starting when I was seven, because I'd played at school with some very rich Jewish children. Pamela Batesh and I were both seven at Lady Barne House, and she had a five-year-old brother, Johnnie. Their father, who was rolling in money, had a model Bugatti specially made for them, with the gears at the proper side, and we'd all learnt to drive that car round their garden. Johnnie, being a boy, was the apple of his father's eye, and we all got the benefit.

My brother Roy and I bought cars, when I was about thirteen and he seventeen: we bought them for a pound or thirty bob and then sold them back for the same amount in a few weeks. They were all old bangers. We did have one very posh car, an Austin Swallow, with the bonnet strapped on. We thought that frightfully smart and drove it everywhere, though I could only drive on country roads because, of course, I wasn't old enough to be driving. But I adored my brother and followed whatever he could do that I was able to do too, and that did not include academic distinction. I always went to his Speech Days when he was at school because he won all the prizes, which was something I never did. But he was incurably shy all his life, and would advance towards the dais to receive his school distinctions looking very solemn with hands clasped together in front of him, causing our mother to say, 'Oh, look, Beryl – let us pray!' It was on these occasions that I learned to sing 'Forty Years On' lustily enough for both of us, because he was too shy to join in.

With all the touring I was doing, it was handy to have a driving licence. I now had an agent, Audrey Thacker, who was a great friend of Cissie Williams, who was much feared and sought after, because she was responsible for all the Moss Empire tours and her word was law. 'Myth Williams', I called her, because I never saw her. 'Cissie Williams is in front' had all the awe-inspiring quality of a Second Coming in the variety theatre of those days. Neither she nor Audrey Thacker are still with us, nor are the Moss Empires, but Audrey did me a great turn by booking me with Harry Benet, who used to put on quite lavish touring shows at that time, to play in my first musical comedy, called *Betty*, round all the Moss Circuit. I was cast as Estelle, a model to a French dressmaker, and I had lots of musical numbers and the most beautiful clothes. Jean Inglis, who was a lovely girl, played Betty: she had a beautiful singing voice. Mine, I think, was 'developing', because I've never learnt to sing, only to 'breathe'! That was a great experience, at a time when my great chum Reggie was also on tour for Harry Benet, in *Katinka*, another popular musical comedy.

I can remember the glamorous costumes I wore. There was a lime-green suit with a pleated skirt, which, of course, is fashionable now, a jacket with a tight waist and a little flare underneath the waist, and a white blouse. I had a white ermine muff and hat, both with bunches of violets on them. In the last scene I had a sensational long cyclamen dress, covered with ostrich feathers; I used to take the train home with trousers on underneath the dress. Then there was a pale blue evening dress, which crossed over in the front, with an embroidered pattern of dark-blue sequins going across it. In those days, of course, my hair was platinum blonde – some of my photos of that period seem almost to be copies of the styles of Constance Bennett, whom I much admired and who was Roy's favourite film star – and it was all 'up on top' as they say, swept up and very much back-combed, so it was quite high hair.

The cast was a good one and included Elsie Prince, Hilda Campbell-Russell, Betty Leslie-Smith and a boy called Jack Lester, who unhappily died very young. We were great friends. Hilda Campbell-Russell came to see me last year in the revue *A Little Bit On the Side* at Richmond, and it was a joy to see her. Through her I rode a great number of horses, which I wouldn't normally have done, because her father was a trainer, and indeed he was still breaking horses in when he was eighty! He used to say, 'You've got to hit 'em and hold 'em! You've got cork legs, girl!' Hilda always referred to me as 'Little thing on the beach', because I said, 'Oh, I can't get undressed here, Hilda – there's nowhere to hide,' and she answered, 'But you're just a little thing on the beach; nobody'll bother about you!' With her I rode around the racetrack at Cheltenham, which was quite a treat – we knew a jockey called Len Lefebve who let us do that.

I was then invited by Howard and Wyndhams to join the almost legendary *Half-Past Eight Show* at the Theatre Royal, Edinburgh. I didn't know who was going to be in it or what the programme allotted to me was. In fact, I was to work with Dave Willis, one of our greatest clowns. The only thing that held him back was that he never really learned lines. I used to seek David – which is what I called Dave Willis when I was cross with him – in the pub, and say, 'What are we doing next week?' (They changed the programme every week, you see, and every week I did between five and seven sketches with him without any idea what they were going to be.) I'd say, '*Please*, David, tell me what we're going to do next week.' And he would say something like, 'Well, you come on and say So-and-So and So-and-So and So-and-So, then I come on and we say So-and-So and So-and-So: we do some domestic patter ...' – he'd actually say 'so-and-so' – and then he'd tell me the end of the sketch. This was the beginning of my having to *make up* words, and the rather nervous experience I gained has stood me in good stead ever afterwards. He was a comic with real genius: somebody I could watch night after night and still be totally amazed.

Altogether during that season I did 427 sketches with him, and I had not one word committed to paper. You had to learn to be a very good busker. He'd say, 'Oh – don't put the costume on at the dress rehearsal, just surprise me on the night!' But it was always I who was surprised on the night. I was doing a sketch with him where I had a baby and he said, 'Is it a looney or a quiney?' and, of course, because I wasn't familiar with the Aberdeen dialect, I said, 'I think it's a bit of a looney.' He asked, 'What's its name?' and I replied, 'Isabel.' That of course should have been a quiney, which means a girl. A looney is a boy! That caused great joy to the audience – I'd made a real fool of myself!

Dave was very much in love with his secretary at that time, and I remember one occasion when his wife came round unexpectedly. He put his secretary in the wardrobe in his dressing-room – she was a very sweet, long-suffering girl – but then forgot where he'd put her. The poor soul stayed there till we started rehearsing at ten o'clock the next morning. He was often in these awkward situations: he was said to have fathered a child on a doctor's wife in Edinburgh, and people were very shockable in those times. I said, 'I really don't think you should push the pram about, Dave, because people will talk.' He replied, 'Oh, I don't think it matters, Beryl; it's a wee girl and nobody'd ever know it was anything to do with me, except that it's got a wee black moustache!'

He was quite irrepressible, but a very hard taskmaster. I didn't believe he'd ever say 'So-and-So and So-and-So' when he got on the stage, but he did. He was doing a sketch as a photographer, and he hadn't quite got the camera at the right angle. It was, as my mother would say, 'All to the one side, like Gourock' – there were lots of family sayings like that. So he went over to the family group and adjusted all their heads to the angle that he'd got the camera, saying all the time, 'So-and-So and So-and-So' as he did it, which left me feeling kind of futile: I was never any good, because he always made me laugh. He was very Chaplinesque. Once when I sang 'You Made Me Love You' he did the most terrible things, getting under the bench, with this little red nose, and saying, 'Have you got a light?' – of course I was totally unprepared.

We worked terribly hard in those days; when we finished the show at night we had lots of parties, because the work was so driving that we simply had to celebrate as a release. I remember we once went about rattling dustbin lids, and I was called the Belle of Tarvitt Street, because that's where I had digs. At a party one night, Hope Jackman from our show slid down the banisters: she thought there was a knob at the end that would stop her, but there wasn't, so she cascaded to the floor. She didn't appear at rehearsals the next morning, because she was all black and blue, and the stage doorkeeper, who was in league with us, rang her up and said, 'Hallo, Hopey, are you dopey?'

A man called Charlie Ross directed or produced all these shows – whatever one called it in those days, the terms have changed now to fall more in line with the cinema – and he taught me how to rehearse. A lot of people are very embarrassed when they're rehearsing. I was playing a Chinese servant pushing a missionary about in a wheelchair – we used to do just about everything you can think of, to ring the changes in sketches – and I said, 'I can't do this at ten o'clock in the morning.' He rapped, 'If it's here,' pointing to his heart, 'it'll come out whatever time it is.' And, of course, that's what I now know, that if it's there it *will* come out, regardless of time. That was the big lesson he taught me.

Jimmy Plant was also in the show, and he was Dave Willis's feed – a sort of comic's labourer, which I've been many times in my life. He always tried to be terribly grand. It was the time when *Dick Barton* was on the air, and every week we did a sketch called 'Dick Willis Barton', and Dave used to do incredible things like having a magnifying glass with no glass in it and putting his hand through it, saying, 'Ah – a footprint!'

At that time a man who played the piano had a crush on me. He had a boat at Musselburgh and said, 'Oh, you must come on my boat' – and that is one of the things I'm really rather bad at. I mean, even if I'm in a rowing boat on the Thames, where I live, I could be sick with the motion of the boat going up and down. I dreaded it, but agreed only if the whole company could come for the whole day. Of course, he was absolutely lumbered, because he didn't want to offend me. He hadn't told me that he had painted the boat in my honour, and when I got out of it I was completely covered in paint – my best clothes, too. He insisted, 'I'll soon get that off, Beryl,' and rubbed it all with turpentine, burning my skin to pieces – he was *certainly* not going to win.

At the same time there was a Swiss from Basle who asked me to marry him, but I told him I didn't think we really had enough in common. 'Let's go to the swimming baths this afternoon and talk about it,' he said. 'All right,' I said, 'but, Rudi, you have to promise me – *promise* me – that you won't do anything silly like pushing my head under the water, because I have the show to do tonight.' In those days we didn't have hot rollers or driers, or any of those things. And, of course, the first thing he did when we got into the water was to push my head under. I got straight out of the baths and I have never seen him from that day to this.

* * *

By the middle of the season we'd heard an awful lot about a man called Jack Tripp – and I'd had him up to dolly's wax. That's an expression I use a great deal, and for anybody who doesn't understand it I should explain that Victorian dolls' bodies were all made of cloth and the wax part started at their faces. I don't mean I'd had Victorian dolls, but I'd been interested in them, and if you were 'up to dolly's wax' you were really fed up to the neck and *sick* of hearing about *Jack Tripp*, and how clever he was, from Charlie Ross. 'He'll wipe the floor with all of you – you won't be able to hold a candle to *Jack Tripp!*'

You can imagine this poor man, extremely talented and a most outstanding dancer, arriving! I was very ungracious. 'Oh, yes,' I said, 'we've heard all about *you*, Billy All-Brains.' In my mind he wasn't going to be a winner, but, in fact, he was. It's only fair now to hand over the microphone to him, to put his own side of the case.

Charlie Ross had praised me so much in advance that by the time I arrived they had all been driven mad, and were sick of the sound of my name. Particularly Beryl, who was second billed in the show. When I met her she said, 'We've heard all about you, and I don't know whether to say "Welcome", or whether we're no good, or what, but I *hope* you enjoy it!' It was some time before we really got to know and love each other. We did three seasons in Scotland together, and I remember when we were in Glasgow, where the lead comic was Harry Gordon, he was not too pleased that she wouldn't put on a character make-up. She felt her character would come through with her style of voice and general insight into what she was portraying. He used to say, 'The trouble with her is she won't wear wigs,' and she never would. She could be an old lady, and she would just put curlers in or a hat, but she wouldn't wear a wig. It was just a thing she had, and I think she was one of the first to be able to portray a marvellous character without really going into deep make-up, which was remarkable.

She was still doing her impressions, like Gracie Fields singing 'Sally', and, talking about her act, when we were together in Ayr the next year, in *The Gaiety Whirl*, when Dave Willis was the top star and Beryl billed next, a local paper reported, 'Miss Reid did the same act word for word as she did five years ago.' She was so incensed she phoned the editor and said, 'If he can remember my act, word for word, from five years ago, it must have been a bloody good act!'

Still on the subject of acts, it really was a killer in those shows to have to think of something new every week and it got so desperate after twenty weeks you just got a music sheet, and whatever they were dressed in on the cover you'd say, 'Let's sing that song and dress like that.' It was so hard, and like rep at its worst. We got very stuck and Beryl said, 'We've got to do something together next week.' It was something I'd never done before, and I said, 'Why don't we do a thing and dress it as twenties, as a lady pianist and her partner and call it, like a sister act?' She replied, 'You'll have to tell me more about that,' so I took her out to what we've always called since, a 'plain tea', and I sort of made it up as I went along, remembering some old gags and some little bits I'd seen. So we literally threw this together in the three days' rehearsal we were allocated, we got two very funny twenties costumes and just kept everything crossed and hoped it would be all right. The remarkable thing is it really was one of the best things we've ever done: since then we've done it in pantomimes, on TV and so on – it was that strong. But I shall never forget, where we usually turn to each other and say, 'Well, here goes – good luck, or whatever,' I said to her, 'Please God it'll be all right, but don't blame me,' and she answered, 'Jack, never ask me to do this again!' And the music started and out we went.

What Jack has omitted to say about that night is that after I'd told him *never* to ask me to do it again, he gave me an almighty shove, so I'd no alternative but to get on with it and do my best. As he says, it really did turn out a winner, as *he* always did with his dancing and other contributions to the shows we were in together.

He was, however, very bad about words. There was one occasion when he was playing a slave to some Egyptian prince – we did the most extraordinary things at times – and he said, 'I'm like a dog at your feet!' which was the only sentence he could remember, and he kept repeating it like a record struck in a groove, until sheer hysteria set in. That was his only shortcoming; in every other way he was brilliant.

I must explain about Edinburgh's speciality teas:

there was a 'knife and fork' one, and a 'plain tea' (the treat he took me to at Mackie's in Princes Street), which was really rather grand. A wonderful array of goodies would come on, in a sort of three-tier thing, which was all the go in those days, with cream cakes at the top, then pancakes, which you put butter and jam on, and scones on the bottom shelf, all on those lovely white doilies. Actually, Mackie's was just round the corner from where I used to get my kilts: my brother and I had them made for us at Moore Taggart's. I am entitled to wear two tartans, that's the McDonald and the Reid-Robertson. Each tartan has three different patterns – the royal colours, the ancient colours and the hunting colours – giving a choice of six tartans. The ancient colours were the most beautiful. They were in the palest, rather faded shades.

When I questioned Jack over the 'plain tea' about the act he had planned for us, he said, 'I've got this marvellous idea: we come on, do some gags, then a number, and a dance, and then "I want – to be – happy!"' – in fact, all he'd got was the music for us to go off to! But from this abysmal start he concocted the most wonderful idea, which we called 'The Folly Sisters', taken from the famous twenties act, the Dolly Sisters. Once there was a grand piano on the stage, with a shawl draped on it, as people did in those days. He pretended to play the piano – Jack couldn't play, so it was all done on a record on the side – and, of course, he got up towards the end of the act and left the piano, which went on playing. I had been trying to jump neatly backwards, the way people used to leap onto a piano, lifting themselves up by their hands while facing the audience. But having failed dismally to achieve this, I turned to the piano and climbed up it as if it were a mountain, pulling the shawl off in the process and getting myself completely tangled up – and that was the end of *that*.

One number we rather fancied ourselves in was the Ginger Rogers–Fred Astaire 'Change Partners': he was in a tail coat and I was in a beautiful short black dress – I mean short as compared to floor length, the height that we wore then. We thought we were so glamorous, but when we got to the middle of it – as I said, Jack's strong point has never been words – he sang, 'And when we're alone, I'll get the waiter to tell him he's wanted on the sellitone.' That was the end of me, because we got so giggly. In fact, towards the end of the season we were practically prohibited from working together, though, of course, that didn't stop us.

The next season, in the *Half-Past Eight* show with Harry Gordon at Glasgow, was, funnily enough, a much less happy time than I had had with Dave Willis. Unlike Dave's saying to me, 'So and So and make it up,' I was sent for after each performance by Harry Gordon to account for myself if I said 'this' instead of 'that', or 'here' instead of 'there'. You can imagine what a terrible trial that was after all that freedom of speech which Dave Willis had chosen to give me. But my mother and aunts all came to see the show: there was Auntie Belle, my mother's next sister, who was two years older, Aunt Betty – 'Liza', as they all called her, who once said, 'You can't go down there, Anne, it's a codicil!' – Auntie Agnes, who lived at Strathavon with Uncle Jim, her husband – my mother called her Honeypaws because she always wore beautiful white gloves and also marvellous hats – and Aunt Jenny, who was the eldest. In my mother's younger days she used to let her and my Auntie Belle in 'with the milk', as they say, in the morning, because they'd gone out and Aunt Jenny had covered for them with my grannie by saying, 'Yes, they're all in.' They were never allowed to put lipstick or any make-up on in the house, or flowers on their hats. Make-up and flowers were considered very vulgar, so they had them all in a little bag and applied them outside.

They had extraordinary little pieces of paper with powder on them – papier poudré, I think it was called – and it was impregnated with that scent I used to think so glamorous, called Phul-Nana – and then they pinned flowers in their hats on their way to meet their boy-friends. My grandparents were amazing – this was when they lived in Glasgow, in an enormous flat, and didn't mind what their children did as long as they brought their boyfriends home. Anyone who they wanted could go for the weekend at Rothesay, where they had a house: the sisters slept end to end, five in a bed, to make room for the visitors, but nothing mattered, as long as all the visitors were presented to the parents.

My grandmother was quite surprising. She had had ten children and a strict Presbyterian upbringing, but every morning she had the bookmaker round and drank half a bottle of champagne and half a dozen oysters 'when available' – that was only her little morning's adventure with the bookmaker! This has only come up quite recently. I had no idea that Grannie ever did any of those things, and, of course, they were the sort of things I was taught *never* to do. But she was fairly 'goey' for that part of the century. Ten children is quite a lot to have, and she died comparatively young.

Anyway, the aunts arrived at the *Half-Past Eight* show and I watched from the dressing-room. They'd all come in one taxi, and they'd all got enormous black hats on, and if I'd been a composer or a writer of music I would have written it up as 'The March of the Beetles': there were nothing but black ants or aunts coming out of this taxi! There seemed to be hundreds of them – actually there were only five, but it seemed to me like hundreds – and at the end they said, 'Oh, that was quite nice, Beryl,' and 'You quite suited that hat.' They were so reserved in what they said, and they gave you no credit for anything, and I worked jolly hard in those shows. My mother sort of excused herself; she didn't say anything very much, though I hugged and kissed her as usual. And they still said, 'I don't think you should let her carry on like that, Anne!' But mother was quite unabashed by that time.

Then came another skinful of Jack Tripp, to my great delight. The fact that we worked together in the show was perhaps the happiest thing about it for me. I lived in very good digs in Hill Street with Mrs Walker, who was a frightfully straight Scottish lady. James Cohen, who had sold us cars in those days of childhood driving and who by now was in the war (later he was tragically killed in the Rome race) came to see me. He had no real fancy for me – I'd known him since I was three – but I felt somebody getting into bed with me. I said, 'James, whatever do you think you're doing?' He replied, 'It's all right.' I said, 'No, it's *not* all right. What if Mrs Walker came in?' He answered, 'Well, I could always say I was looking for my gas mask!' I thought that was the poorest excuse I'd ever heard, and I threw him out of my room. But the next day, because we were such old friends, we both screamed with laughter and he said how very sorry he was that he'd 'intruded upon my privacy'!

The last of my 'Scottish trilogy' was *The Gaiety Whirl* at the Gaiety Theatre in Ayr, a show I really loved. I lived at the Belleisle Hotel, because my parents didn't live in Ayrshire any longer, though they moved back later. I had got my mother a house in Shepperton, and she said, 'You know, Beryl, it's awful warm here' – she liked it when it was 'nice and fresh'.

The season was absolutely wonderful for me. For one thing I'd adopted a cat who was more like a puppy than a kitten and followed me everywhere. Cuppy used to go round the theatre on the shoulder of Archie, the stage doorkeeper: he was the theatre cat for a while. My brother Roy at that time was ill with a duodenal ulcer, so Cuppy wrote him a letter:

Dear Roy,

I believe you have a duodenal ulcer: you are very lucky – I only have a cork on the end of a piece of string to play with. I have a lovely time here, except that people rub my head too much. When I get fed up with this I go to sleep in a hole in the wall which is the same colour as me and then I am what is called 'lost'. Everybody shouts for me and I take no notice at all and then, later on when I've slept for long enough, and people shout again, and Beryl comes along, looking desperate, saying 'Have you seen my – "cat"', I think she calls me – I get up and stretch, and everybody rubs my head wildly again and I am what is called 'found'.

Love

Cuppy

Cuppy had a wonderful life. I thought 'he' was a boy, but it turned out that she was a girl when she went off on a lost weekend just before I left Ayr. In the end Auntie Belle had her for years in her little cottage in the country, and Cuppy had these kittens and was very happy indeed.

Archie brought me a bunch of flowers one day, and said, 'I don't know who these are from.' I said, 'I don't either, because there's no note on them, Archie.' A few minutes after I got a letter by hand which read, 'I don't mind people stealing flowers out of my garden, if you'll only point me in the direction of the culprit. You are welcome to the flowers, but we really have to stop somewhere, and I can't bear the thought of people ransacking my garden.' Dave Willis was back in the show with me, and so in a terrible state I went into his dressing-room, saying, 'Oh, Dave, I've had this awful letter from a woman, saying that someone has stolen these flowers out of her garden.' He seemed as deeply concerned as I was. 'That's terrible,' he said, as I went on and on. Then I looked in the mirror and knew from his face that he was totally responsible for the whole thing. He had, in fact, bought the flowers and then he'd written the letter as if from this woman to take the gilt off the gingerbread. Those were the sort of wonderful practical jokes he played on me.

We were friendly with somebody who was introduced as 'the Poacher' – so there was no doubt about what he was. His name was Tommy Robertson and he played for Ayr United. The first time they 'got' him – that is, the police – he had a chicken up his jacket, which he was bringing back for me to pluck, clean and cook when I got back to the digs. That time he got off with a caution.

I used to go up the doon with him, because he 'tickled the salmon'. One night some boys shouted, 'Who's the

Birrd?' Tommy said with great dignity, 'She's no' a Birrd, she's from the Gaiety Whirrl!' Unfortunately he got a little bit beyond himself and robbed the bank at Maybole, where I lived and quite near where my mother died. He stole £22,000 and did seven years, and we all knitted things for him. He was a riveting character, but when he came out he was hounded constantly; every time he went to the dogtrack or the racetrack or anywhere, they used to say, 'Let's see the money.' They never found it – it was obviously buried in some rich lady's garden – but he couldn't stand the strain. He died very young of a heart attack.

Tommy Robertson had a 'friend' at Minishant, and from him I used to collect five-gallon drums of petrol with Liza Lee, who dressed with me. I was still virtually a non-drinker, and my 'payment' was to get through a bottle of Portuguese brandy – me and Big Liza and Tommy Robertson and his friend. We were knocked out by this terrible bad brandy that you could get during the war. Liza had digs with someone that we called 'Ma Leg', because every time you asked her how she was she'd say, 'Well, it's Ma Leg!' She had a loo at the bottom of the garden and we used to hump these five-gallon drums of petrol until I could either use them or take them home.

Of course, I was frightfully well in with the butcher there. He'd say, 'Have you come for the "messages", Beryl?' That could mean *anything* – I got eggs, joints of meat, whatever was going – because that's what they say in Scotland; you don't go shopping, you go to do the 'messages'. So I left Ayr with half a sheep in the back of the car and several five-gallon drums of petrol and I'm glad they didn't stop me on Shap or anywhere like that, because I certainly would have been had up: it was each for his own then, and we had to fight for what we could get. If my car had ever been stopped leaving Ayr, I suppose I'd have been picking oakum to this day.

During that memorable season I met three wonderful

women who bred Highland cattle on the coast near the Bellaire Hotel at Alloway. They were old ladies then, so I'm sure they're not alive now. Their brother, who was a great horseman, had a garage opposite the stage door. One rather lovely thing at the end of the run was the dictaphone link that Eric Popplewell, the Yorkshireman who ran the Gaiety Theatre, had installed from his office to the box office. Of course, he couldn't believe this could really work, because everything was in its very early stages in those days. He pressed the dictaphone and said, 'Four seats in the stalls tonight. All right, Daisy?' Then he rushed to the room and said, 'Did you get that, Daisy?' because he was afraid that not all messages were coming through. These brothers – the other, the white-haired one, ran the dance hall along the road – had settled in Ayr and become two of its leading citizens, owning the theatre, among other things.

Jack Barton, who is now the producer of *Crossroads*, was the producer of the show. He made me do a lot of new things, just as my favourite directors have always done – including a scarecrow, which in Scotland is a 'tatty bogle' – a tatty person who frightens people. I had no confidence in that at all, but it turned out to be one of the best things I'd done up till then. He and I had a bicycle each. Somewhere there is a lovely photograph of me in my kilt with socks up to my knees and straight blonde hair, with Jack Barton, striding along the streets of Ayr. He was a tremendous help to me and wonderful to work with. He appreciated everybody's talents, and had no favourites, which is a rare gift for a director.

Another thing that constantly fascinated me about Ayr was Robert Burns' life. This was all the poet's country and I knew it inside out and back to front. We lived very near his cottage, where he and his father and Agnes Brown had walked from the Highlands: they had no shoes, and he'd built this little tiny house, which she said was like a palace. They kept the cows in the end of the house, and she thought it was all completely wonderful. I could go on about Robert Burns for the rest of this book, because I know and love his whole life – how people recognized him as a genius, how his father taught him mathematics, and how a lady called Betty walked ten miles each way to his house just to teach him all she knew, because she realized that he was a very brilliant person. Everything about his life moves me very much. He died when he was only thirty-seven. I know every farm that he and his family worked, and it's all very poor land, because they had not the money for food, and they had no horse. He had to pull the plough himself. He died of tuberculosis at that very young age, which is terribly sad. I think he had more women than hot dinners, but he did dearly love them all and wrote the most wonderful songs for them. He was going to marry Bonnie Mary of Argyll – in fact they had a marriage ceremony standing in the river in their bare feet and swore on the Bible that they would be faithful to each other, and she went to Greenock to wait for him.

She caught scarlet fever and sent her little brother to walk to Kilmarnock, where Robert had gone into the Trades and Excise and was going to go to India and take her with him, and he told him that Mary was very ill. By the time Robert Burns reached her she was dead, and that's when he wrote of the river they'd stood in:

> Flow gently, sweet Afton,
> Disturb not her dreams.

He actually finished up with a lovely girl called Bonnie Jean Armour, who had twins, and, I think, two other children by him. He was always held up to ridicule by the Kirk – the church-going people of the district – which makes me angry, because everyone there since has always made such a good living from tourists who come to seek mementoes of him. Of course there is a place called Brig o' Doon, practically opposite his house – a cobblestone bridge, about which he wrote the poem *Tam O' Shanter*. There's one couplet in it which runs, 'He yelled out "Well done, Cutty Sark" [which means "short shirt", because there were a lot of witches dancing, and he was very drunk] And in an instant all was dark.'

5

Monica, Marlene and Archie

Mother Goose was always flying into my life, but never more notably than in the season at the Royal Court, Liverpool, when George Lacy played the part. He's one of the greatest Dames I've ever worked with, and I grew very fond of him. He was reputed to be a very difficult man, but I did not find him so because he was so clever: if you're as clever as that, you're allowed to have your little ways, which often add up to wanting to get things exactly right, and not suffering fools gladly. One line of his – 'Oh, dear, I should never have had that hot soup on top of those liquorice all-sorts' – is something I always think of when I eat the wrong thing!

I remember the old lady in the goose skin having great difficulty laying those golden eggs, but she managed, helped along, I'm sure, by the Good Fairy, a young Geordie named Victoria Elliott. During one of our moments waiting to go on, she told me, 'I'm going to be an opera singer, you know.' I said, 'Oh, I'm going to be a star.' She did go into grand opera. I can't speak for myself.

But I *was* seeing the country. This was the last time I played Gretchen in *Mother Goose*: the other two occasions were at Brighton for a very short run which came to an end due to an epidemic of smallpox, which meant we all had to go into quarantine, and the year before at Bristol. During the Brighton epidemic I remember we had to queue for inoculations – 'Principals First' were the instructions! On both occasions George Gee played the Dame and Jill Manners was Principal Boy: what I remember best about the production was the friendship I struck up with Jill's son, a marvellous little boy of about ten.

He used to put his hands on my bosom and say, 'Ah – Bosomeo – would you like to join me in a steaming love dance?' He was a very strange little boy, brought up by his grandparents because, of course, Jill was away a lot. He said to me one day, 'Say something terrible to me.' I tried, 'Smelly lavatories.' He said, 'No, no – much worse than that!' I went on, 'All right: a man hanging from a tree, with his eyes pecked out by the crows and the smell of death all round.' He said, 'Oh, yes, that's more like it!' He would lift the lid of the piano half an inch and say, 'Look – have you Macleaned your teeth today?' I found him absolutely riveting. We invented a man called Succalini, and we wrote a little song that went

> I'll buy you for Christmas a Succalini's baby,
> Old Pappa Puchi's got one. You get them from
> Woolworth's,
> They're worth tuppence ha'penny –
> A Succalini's baby, a Succalini's baby for me!

We got on really wildly well. He spent a lot of his time in my dressing-room, and called himself 'H. Lime, Junior', because the 'Harry Lime Theme' and *The Third Man* was all the go. He was one of the most fascinating children I ever met. I long to know what happened to him when he grew up.

I did a lot of broadcasting during these years – dozens and dozens of 'Variety Bandbox' shows, and even more 'Workers' Playtimes', in which I met my future husband, the producer, Bill Worsley. I got to know him gradually and our relationship was, in a way, very slow to develop. But I did fall in love with him and realized he was a person that I could marry. When I went to the New Theatre in Newquay in the summer of 1949 I was engaged to Bill, an engagement that lasted for two years, which, I suppose, was pretty old fashioned, but that was the way you did things then.

The banns were read at the beautiful Quantock

church. But I wished the vicar hadn't sounded so bored when he read them. During the prayers he'd say, 'Oh, *Christ*', as if it was a dirge, and turn over the page. That is enough to put you off religion, because it's not like that at all: it should be a jolly thing. But I expect I reacted in that way because I was in a state of romance.

The Newquay season was wonderful. I had found a boarding house facing Fistral Bay, where I surfed every day. It was matinées if wet, so we had to assemble at the theatre at 2 o'clock, just in case there was a sudden spattering of rain. As it was a perfect summer, there usually wasn't. It was a very matey company; Clifford Stanton, a brilliant impressionist, was in the show, and Mary Brooks was the singer. We used to say, 'Which beach shall we go to today?' all with our surfboards – those who hadn't got one used to pay a ten-shilling deposit to hire one. We'd chorus, 'Oh let's go to Treyarnon Bay, let's go to Fistral.' It was really a lovely summer. Bill Footer, one of my friends in the show, was very short-sighted and one day he took off his glasses and came surfing with us. Now, if you're doing lying-down surfing, the board bends upwards: Bill Footer saw a wave but didn't notice that his board was bending downwards. He got on the wave, and was doing quite well, until suddenly he shot to the bottom of the sea. He just couldn't let go of his surfboard, because it had a ten-shilling deposit on it! We all had to dive down and get him. He wouldn't let go, and quite right, too!

This was at Bedruthen Steps and it was there that I gave Bill Footer and my mother the worst fright they'd ever had in their lives. The cliffs there are very high and I shouted to them, 'Oh, come on', and ran, looking backwards and not at the edge of the cliff. I thought I could go straight across but I couldn't, because there was a great V across the cliff with a six-yard gap, which I hadn't seen. They didn't dare to shout to stop me, they just counted on me looking forwards for a second – which I did. I came to the most terrible, skidding halt, like you see in cartoon films, right on the edge of the precipice.

For about five months I dreamt of falling over and I think that moment put years on my mother.

During this season I became extremely friendly with a young man called Peter. At Cambridge during May week he'd got completely broke, so he had to earn some money during the summer. He took a job as a lifeguard. He was a magnificent figure of a man and gave me confidence to go out far in search of a big wave, for the surf (if you ride a really big one, you can come right in onto the beach). As long as I was swimming with him, I felt really safe.

I began to get very fond of him, then thought, 'No, no, no, no; you're engaged to Bill Worsley, so stop all that nonsense!' I can be quite strict with myself occasionally. But Peter took me out on wonderful waves – the currents are very treacherous on that coast – and we'd come whizzing in. I don't think there's anything more exhilarating, and certainly nothing nearer to perpetual motion, than surfing. As soon as you've got in on one wave, you're out looking for the next.

I said to him one day, 'Peter, what would happen if the yellow flag was up?' Yellow is for caution. He answered, 'Well, I suppose we'd come and save you.' I asked, 'What if I went in when the red flag was up?' He said, 'You know when you wave?' 'Yes.' 'Well, I'd just wave back!' That rather tipped me the wink that I mustn't go in when the red flag was up.

When my step-daughter-to-be broke up for the school holidays, she and Bill came down and we stayed at a wonderful place, Rose Cottage. The name of the lady who lived there was Rose Juniper, and she was a fabulous character. She cooked on a fire oven – not an Aga Cooker, or anything grand like that, it was just a black-leaded fire oven. She worked all day, because she had lots of people staying. They put electricity in, but she had only one electric light bulb in the middle of the kitchen. She was always used to working in all the kitchen heat, but she would say, 'Oh, my love, this alectricity – oh, 'tis so 'ot, that lamp.' She would describe how some of the people who ran boarding-houses in Newquay were doing their customers out of everything: 'Sometimes, they do have 'alf egg, 'alf egg each.'

She told me, 'Sid's done the lavatory at the end of the garden' – it was a sort of dry toilet, with newspaper in it, and she said, 'He's put a chain on it; they like to pull, dear, because people do like to feel they've gone. Nothing happens, but they do like to pull it!'

Describing to me her previous Christmas, she said, 'Oh, my love, the table was groaning with food, groaning with it. We had rabbit, we had turkeys, we had Christmas pudding, we had ... didn't we, Sid? There was twenty-four of us – so many people – no, you was 'ere, Sid. That makes twenty-six.' This conjured up a terrible vision of Sid with two heads.

While I was there, I was on the beach by about 9 o'clock in the morning. One day a telegram arrived for me from the BBC, and the man who brought it also sold a few rabbits. He waited all day for me, until 6 o'clock in the evening, and by that time Rose had given him three meals. She said, 'Oh, my love, there's a telegram waiting for you.' I asked her what it said. She answered, 'We've been waiting for you to come home to open it, dear.' They'd been sitting there all day, holding their breath. All it said was, 'Will you come to London on such-and-such a day to do such-and-such a programme?' They said, 'Oh, that's all right then.' But they'd waited all day, because a telegram in Fiddler's Green was something totally unheard of.

I called on her eleven years later, to return a plate. I said, 'Rose, I've brought it back,' and she replied, 'Oh, I knew you'd bring it back, my love, I knew that, because, you see, I've not been very well.' She had a colour television, which she kept on all the time I was there, and the garden was totally unkempt, which it had never been before. Dear, lovely Sid had died and I said, 'What's wrong, Rose?' She answered, ' 'Tis as if I'd got a butterfly in my heart.' That was the last time I spoke to her.

We had a special night when Rose and Sid came to see the show at Newquay. I thought, stupid me, that she was going to look a bit of a fright and it was going to be rather a giggle, because she said, 'We've hired the Fiddler's Green flyer,' the huge local taxi. But she was so dignified and beautiful when she came to the theatre that I felt very ashamed. She was a large lady and wore her white hair in a bun. She had a dark coat on and a dark dress and was a great credit to everybody – a marvellous woman, a very strong, good Cornish character.

I had several funny experiences of the Cornish way of life. I started looking for a drink called Cornish mead, but couldn't find anybody who knew about it. When I went into one shop, I had a conversation I had to write down as soon as I got outside, lest I forgot it. I said to this woman, 'Have you got any Cornish mead?' and she looked me straight in the face and said, 'Well, it's been very popular, but up to now we've had no demand for it. We sold out!' That left me absolutely floored. I went into a pub to get some rough cider, with a chap I knew there. I was wearing the lowest cut neckline you could imagine, and he looked straight down my cleavage and said, 'I'm very sorry, sir, but we don't have that here!' They rather defeat me, the Cornish people, but I do adore them.

I have been back several times to Newquay, just to go surfing, and to wonder how many goes I can get in before my first meal. But, as I've got busier and busier, I haven't been able to have any holidays. My surfboard's still in the bathroom. I hope it'll come into good use again.

My mother, who came with me one evening to the Cosy Nook Theatre at Newquay, gave one little piece of accurate forecasting: 'I think I've seen somebody awfully promising, Beryl', she said. 'His name's Benny Hill.' Well, she was right.

Almost immediately after that, I got married to Bill Worsley. Georgette Bishop was my bridesmaid and Olivia, by then perhaps my longest-standing friend in the theatre, made my wedding dress. The ceremony had to be postponed for a couple of weeks because Bill's brother Francis, who had directed 'ITMA', had died. This put everybody out of gear more than somewhat and was said to be very unlucky. But it was a lovely wedding, shortly before I had to leave for panto in Bristol – a more than usually full life for me at the time, because I had then started to paint landscapes in oils. I didn't find it as relaxing as it was supposed to be, because I was a total novice and had no technique. I knew a bit about colours and how to put them on, and I just had to keep on and on at it, so that when I saw the result I thought, 'So that's how you do it!' It was a constant sort of Eureka – finding out exactly how one should make water move, or cliffs look as though they were fading into the distance, and all that sort of thing – things that one would normally have learnt at an art school, only of course I hadn't. But I did go to an art college at Bristol, armed with the pictures I'd done while I was there. I asked the art master if he'd let me come to any of the classes. But he refused, saying, 'If I were to let you do that, your sort of natural flair and lack of fear would disappear entirely, and you'd become inhibited by perspective and technical matters, which you're not inhibited by at all now.'

Bill came up to see the pantomime, which was a big success – it was the *Mother Goose* I've already mentioned, with Jill Manners. And life was great.

Bill had a house in Amersham at the top of a hill, but as he'd had his previous marriage there and he was mad about sailing, we moved to Sunbury-on-Thames, to a bungalow in Willow Way, which we bought from Janet Hamilton-Smith, the opera star.

At that time I had a housekeeper, because I was away practically all the time. It said on her birth certificate: Father a chimneysweep. I began to miss things in the house, but I know I'm careless, and at first I didn't take a great deal of notice. Then the day came that my brother-in-law, Cuthbert – T. C. Worsley, theatre critic for the *New Statesman* for a long time and then for the

Financial Times, a sweet man – visited us. He hadn't any money on him, so Bill cashed him a cheque for £5. When they came back, there were only £4 left where the fiver had been. They waited for me to drive home from Peterborough, I think it was, to ask her if she'd taken this pound.

I said to her, 'Well now, come on. Mr Cuthbert had five pounds and since they went out on the boat there are only four left. Have you taken the pound? It doesn't matter if you have, because it's something that we will overlook. You're very good to us and your work is very satisfactory, and all that sort of thing.' She answered, 'Oh, Madam, oh, no Madam, oh no – I couldn't do a thing like that.' After about an hour of trying to persuade her to admit the theft I got so desperate that I said, 'If you don't tell me the truth, I shall have to ring up the police.'

So the CID man came – 'Sid', as he's always been known to me. He said, 'Come on, then, where is it?' She answered, 'Under the meat dish, sir,' and she lit a cigarette – and I'd never seen her smoke – saying, 'You write it all down, and I'll sign it!' When she was taken away, I went into her bedroom, where I'd never been allowed before. Everything that I had lost was in her chest of drawers – scarves, bits of jewellery, money, rings, everything – and the space underneath the bed was cram-packed with empty gin bottles. This solved the mystery of Matthew, our tortoise, and his strange behaviour one day when I came home. Matthew was attached to a string – we'd got the vet to drill a little hole in his shell where there was no tortoise – and I used to tie this string to different trees in the garden. When I returned, the housekeeper said, 'Oh, Madam – that Matthew – he was right up at the top of Willow Way, and I had to go on my hands and knees to find him!' In fact she was blind drunk. I discovered, when I went into the off licence, that I owed something like £190, because she'd had it all on tick; also, she'd had a fence living in while I was away, and she'd flogged my expensive wedding presents – silver entrée dishes and so on. They don't really come into my life anyway, so I didn't particularly mind, but in addition, I'd given her money for her Insurance Stamp every week, and I owed nearly £200, because she had never put one stamp on her card.

So that was the end of the Great Adventure of my housekeeper: happily she hasn't, to date, come to visit me backstage.

By this time I had discovered that Bill had a kind of gipsy in his soul, and he could get rather sulky and like a U-Boat Commander. As soon as we'd really settled in the house in Willow Way – it was called Norock – and I'd done all the decorating, he thought it wasn't at all suitable, and we found another house, Ripple Cottage, a little Regency house next to the Magpie in Sunbury. The front of this house was actually on the main road, and then you went down a lot of steps. It was a narrow, tall house and I rather loved it, but since I'd lived in a bungalow for quite a while, I really did prefer living on one level. I've never liked stairs, and I'm always falling up and down them when I go to other people's houses. But Ripple Cottage was quite beautiful. And then, of course, he began to be very discontented with that.

In the meantime, I was working *all* the time and getting ready to go to Yarmouth for the summer. This provided a few months of relaxation. I was kind of comic's labourer to Roy Barbour, a lovely funny man, and I was beginning to do the schoolgirl act again. I think we did five programmes, so that wasn't tough at all: you can find five acts quite easily. I was then painting all the time, and I got one picture into an exhibition at Yarmouth. I went to every exhibition of landscape paintings that I possibly could and at one I met a most wonderful man called Mellon: I still have a painting of his. He died towards the end of the season, but I had one marvellous day with him and enjoyed myself more than any five other people in Yarmouth. He showed me all his first sketches, and talked about how he'd started on paintings. His paintings were wonderful – if I'd had the money then I could still have my favourites now.

One of these was *August Bank Holiday on Yarmouth Beach*, and the other *Old-fashioned Bathing Tents on Yarmouth Beach*. They cost only £5 each, because he was totally unknown, but he was really one of the most gifted landscape artists I have ever seen. I learnt a great deal from studying his painting, and I was very, very grateful to him for all his patience.

But, you see, I gave all my own pictures away: as I painted them, I just gave them away. One or two have come winging back to me in the fullness of time. I now have three of my own. And, of course, I will paint again when nobody wants me to act.

Every Saturday night a gang of us, including the Burt Twins, used to drive back from Yarmouth to London. I drove on to Sunbury, and we were like a lot of children going home, with lots of wonderful made-up names for the places we passed. Six Mile Bottom became Six Mile Bum, and Staples Corner was Mattress Corner of course, and that was how we whiled away the journey. Both the Burt Twins drove, so we used to take it in turns, miles at a time. The Burt Twins did a piano act and they were super boys. They used to shout at each other in the car, 'Oh, don't go on the Cats' Eyes, Tim!'

As I was married to a BBC producer, I was allowed to do only six broadcasts a year. But then I had a real stroke of luck: I was asked to do a 'Henry Hall's Guest Night', and I thought, now shall I do 'The Schoolgirl'? I did indeed do 'The Schoolgirl' (who hadn't been called Monica yet), at the Playhouse Theatre on the Embankment, and Henry Hall stood on the side of the stage and laughed like mad. I was in my school uniform – my gymslip, my original school gymslip, and boater (it says on the hatband 'Temperet omnia veritas' – 'Truth governs all things'). People were screaming with laughter – the audiences for the broadcasts weren't used to artistes in costume, but I can't do the characters unless I dress up. Then the Head of Light Entertainment switched on, didn't know who I was, and said, 'Whoever that is, we've got to use her all the time!'

So of course I did several other 'Henry Hall's Guest Nights', and I actually got Henry to play in sketches, including the Herbert Farjeon sketch called 'Snaps', which he'd written for Dorothy Dickson in revue, the one about a girl showing her boyfriend terrible holiday snaps, and ending with, 'Oh – there's that bloody chicken again!'

I was then asked to do a series as 'The Schoolgirl', and now, of course, she had to have a name, and so Monica was christened. This series was to replace 'Monday Night at Eight', and it was called 'Starlight Hour'. Janet Brown was going to do it, but unfortunately fell ill, and I was offered the spot. Janet was a smashing girl, and of course I loved her husband the late Peter Butterworth, who was terribly funny. Somebody said to him when I was there, 'Have you seen Fellini's 8½?' and quick as a flash Peter answered, 'No, I saw the first three inches and left!'

In 'Starlight Hour' Brian Reece played my uncle, and he used to come to school every weekend and take out this terrible schoolgirl called Monica. Of course I had to have a different spot every week, and Ronnie Wolfe started to write for me. My dyslexia meant I had to have the scripts in plenty of time, because, though you could read them on the radio, I always had to part-learn so that I could look away and do a lot of 'acting', like pulling up my knickers and getting out my hankie, all that sort of thing.

Monica, by this time, was becoming really quite well known, and I was asked to go on a tour with Max Wall, an absolute genius. He was excruciatingly funny, and he also wrote the most beautiful songs. This roadshow ran for a year, and was called *These Radio Times*. Also there was a man I was later to marry, Derek Franklin of the Hedley Ward Trio.

Max Wall used to sing his songs and accompany

himself on a guitar. One was called, 'All This I See in a Baby's Smile', and another, 'Ginger'. When I met him for the first time, I said, 'Good evening, how are you?' and he replied, 'I'll let you know later.' So I said, quick as a flash, 'Then through a solicitor, please!' Of course, from that time on we were great friends.

He could be quite a frightening person. Sometimes he had the people laughing even when they were buying the tickets – they'd be rolling about in the aisles, and he could not go wrong. But the very next week we'd go somewhere where he'd not get a titter from the audience, and as he got more and more aggressive, they liked him less and less. He was almost (and it seems a funny word to use, but I can think of no other which sums up what I'm trying to say) a schizophrenic performer. Some people just adored him, and others couldn't stand him. He was an acquired taste. Now, as we all know, he's become a cult figure; he has come right back into his own, and is the star he should always have been.

During this tour I began to realize that, because of Bill getting more and more like a U-Boat Commander, I was happier when I was away and amongst actors and pros and having a laugh than when I was at home. I found the situation increasingly impossible to cope with. So, when I'd finished the tour, I remember very sadly, sitting in the garden and saying to him, 'I have to speak to you, Bill.' He went bright white when I said, 'I don't want to come back.' We agreed to be separated first, and then we started divorce proceedings. I was terribly sad about it, because it meant I had failed in what I set out to do. I can't bear sulking: he wouldn't speak to me for perhaps four days at a time and in the end I'd say, 'What have I done? Why? Why? Why?' You see, I wouldn't leave it alone, because I wasn't used to not being spoken to. He had to invent something, like, 'I've got a pain in my big toe,' because by then he'd forgotten why he wasn't speaking to me and didn't want to speak to anybody. If he had said that I would have understood; but he couldn't bring himself to say it.

We were married only three years and during the last year *These Radio Times* was not the only show to give me the chance to broaden my experience in the theatre. In Festival of Britain year, 1951, I was offered my first season in intimate revue at the tiny Watergate Theatre in the Strand. This horrified my agent, really, because I was beginning to do well, and at the Watergate we got only £1 a show and a slight petrol allowance.

At the Watergate I suddenly realized – This is what I want to do: I don't want to be a variety act any more, I want to be working with other people. At that time they did write about me as a 'comedy actress'. I didn't take a lot of notice of it in the beginning, but in my four seasons at the Watergate I kept learning, learning, learning. It was there that Ronnie Hill, who was in charge of those shows, mentioned a number to me called 'Cowslip Wine'. While he was reading it to me (because, as always, reading was difficult), I said, 'Oh, Ronnie, I've got just the shoes for that!' This was the first time I really understood that, for me, characters started from the feet. If you got the right shoes, then you were three-quarters of the way to doing the character.

My first revue at the Watergate Theatre was called *After the Show*. We had to move our clothes out every day for the other people to come in and do their show during the first part of the evening. There was a lot going on at that tiny theatre in those years, including the last play ever written by Bernard Shaw, called *Far-Fetched Fables*. I was given a peg, because I was rather late coming in: though it was a late night show I was doing several other things at the same time, to make up the pennies. After the normal six weeks' run at £1 a show and petrol money, we transferred to the St Martin's Theatre – the West End, at last!

I had to do a television programme during the day of the night we opened, and I was installed, happily, with all my clothes hung up, in number one dressing-room. But unfortunately one actor who I thought was my greatest friend, took all my things out of number one dressing-room, threw them into the corridor, put himself in there, and I was relegated to number two. This was terribly unimportant to me, because, as I said to him, the audience don't know if you dress in the lavatory – it doesn't matter a damn to them. It was rather sad, and the management bought me a great pot of flowers and said, 'We're terribly sorry that you've been upset like this.' But I did have a success there on the first night. Unfortunately we ran for only six weeks. My dear friend Reggie came on the last night and loved the show. Everyone sympathized, but that was neither here nor there: what mattered was that I was at last doing what I really wanted, revue.

With a great deal of radio and theatre work in between, to keep the wolf from the door – mind you, I'd by now managed to build some fairly effective netting to keep him out – I was able to go on to the next Watergate show, *First Edition*. People involved with this now read like a roll-call of radio and television talent: James Gilbert, later a BBC director of note, did several numbers with me; the music was by Francis Essex; the lyrics by Richard Waring; also in the company were Petra Davies, Robert Bishop (who was to become a lifelong friend) and Nicholas Parsons, with whom I did 'Spring Song'. He was an American and I was a terrible, be-ringletted, awful lady in what turned out to be a very sunny number. I sang, 'Spring in Hyde Park, how exciting!' and he went on, 'Spring in Hyde Park, how *sublime*.'

There was a wonderful number, 'The City on Sunday', by Diana Morgan and Robert McDermott, which caught to perfection the spirit of the city, totally deserted. In all, there were three revues in 1952, all devised and directed by Ronnie Hill. We went on to *Second Edition*, staged by a very young Lionel Blair.

During rehearsals there was a phone call for me and I said, 'Do you mind, Lionel – may I take this telephone call, please?' because I'm very respectful to directors. He answered intensely, 'Yes, but *come back soon*!' So I left my shoes right there, in the centre of the stage, where of course I happened to be standing at the time (and if I'm not, there's something radically wrong) and walked off barefoot.

Nobody wanted to play old men, because they were all young and attractive. Ronnie Hill got fairly desperate, and said urgently, 'You don't realize how useful it is to have an old man up your sleeve.' I must say they didn't, and neither did I until that moment. Anyway, everything went very successfully.

The *Autumn Revue* was staged by Jimmy Browne. There were people like Bill Pertwee in his first professional job as a writer, Robert Gould, Douglas Argent (who went on to become a television producer-director), Barry Sinclair from the Ivor Novello musicals (who was really quite a snip for the Watergate, as we'd got so little money), Pamela Charles – the list went on and on, and I became more and more obsessed by the fact that this was the sort of thing I wanted to do. The first seed had been sown by the press in those words 'comedy actress', though the term had never come into my life before. I'd never been to a drama school, or learnt anything much, except how to dance.

I first came into contact with Ian Tucker, who ran the financial side of the theatre when I went to him to seek permission to do an impression of Margaret Rutherford. She gave it readily, with the words 'Yes, your little friend can do an impersonation of me – providing, of course, she doesn't make me look eccentric!' But at the end of this last season, Ian Tucker called me to one side, rattling all the change in his pocket; he was highly nervous, and so tall that he had to bend down to speak to me. He said, 'I'm terribly sorry; I think the show will have to come off the week after next, because there is no movement on the sheet.' I had an immediate picture of fleas jumping over bed-linen, but of course he was on about the box office sheet. The Watergate had to come to a fairly grinding halt.

*   *   *

After the break-up of my marriage to Bill Worsley, I decided to buy a caravan. It was a beautiful thing, called Country Life, and it was all hand-made. I got it onto a site between Windsor and Maidenhead, the Willows Caravan Park. This is now crammed full of caravans, but in those days there were very few. Funnily enough, it was on the river again, and life there was wonderful. All I had to do when I got home was just shut the door, put the gas poker in the fire, and it was alight again. The only slight drawback, which made life rather difficult, was that I had no telephone, but Mr Capon, who ran the caravan place, was very friendly to me and took telephone messages.

One day a message came: would I like to do a radio show called *Educating Archie*? 'Yippee – Yes!', was the answer. I was going to do Monica, exchanging gags with Peter Brough's cheeky dummy, Archie Andrews. When I first joined the show, everybody was in it: Harry Secombe, Max Bygraves, Hattie Jacques – you name the stars, they were all there at one time or another; Julie Andrews had been in it, and so had Graham Stark; Dick Emery, James Robertson Justice, Benny Hill, Alfred Marks, on and on. Peter Brough had this extraordinary gift for getting people just on the crest of the wave. He and his assistant Wally Ridley gave us all that extra push that we needed to become well known. I think, perhaps, that I was the very last person to make a name through radio.

Eric Sykes was very fond of Hattie Jacques, and so of course was I. Eric, who was writing the show at that time, might have thought that I was trying to put Hattie's nose out of joint, but of course I wasn't: I admired her totally, but we were nothing like each other. Because Eric guarded Hattie so closely and was so devoted to her, he didn't think I was really funny – and humour is a purely personal thing. So he didn't write successfully for me.

We sorted this out years afterwards, and we're now great friends and I've done several shows with him. I said to him the last time we met, 'Oh, I do miss Hattie', and he agreed, with deep feeling. Anyway, at the time I went to Peter Brough and said, 'Now, look here; I'm wasting your money and time and my own time if I haven't got somebody who thinks I'm funny writing for me.' So I asked Ronnie Wolfe to help. The spot was five minutes long, and I said, 'I do want twenty laughs in five minutes, Ronnie.' 'Oh, right-o,' he said, and although I didn't know it till later, Warren Mitchell, who was barely known then, also wrote some Monica jokes and got £1 for each one. Ronnie Wolfe is, of course, still in my life. He has written a good deal of material for me recently.

Using my head a bit, I thought that after two years of Monica I really ought to find another character from another class. I started racking my brains, and thought perhaps I'd try a posh cockney character. When I tried that, people said, 'Oh, it's lovely – just like Joyce Grenfell.' I thought Joyce Grenfell was the most talented person in the world, but it's no good being *like* anybody: you've got to be an original. And then suddenly my mind went back to Birmingham, to the Jack Buchanan days; I asked Peter Brough, 'What do you think of me doing a terribly with-it, real, tough Birmingham dance-hall girl?' He said, 'Well, let's try it.' So I explained the character to Ronnie Wolfe, I did the voice for him and repeated some of the things I've said in this book that came from that part of the country. He said in his usual deadpan voice, 'Oh, yes, I think I'll be able to do that.' It was always up to me to say, 'No – she wouldn't say that,' or 'No – she wouldn't do that,' because I understood the characters. Though I've never written scripts for myself, I follow them very closely as they're being written and I can tell the minute something is out of key.

Marlene had actually first seen the light of day back at the Watergate, though like Monica in the beginning, she had been nameless. It was when a dance called the Creep came out. The show was staged by Ian Stuart, who like Jimmy Browne was then a spectacular dancer in the Reg

Dixon musical *Zip Goes a Million* at the Palace Theatre, and we performed the Creep together in *First Edition*, crossing the stage once, with me in Teddy Girl zoot suit, droning in Birmingham accents, 'This is my night for dancing ...' Ian Stuart is now called Marc and is a television director, but it was he who first piloted Marlene into the limelight.

It took a while for me to realize just how much she had taken to that limelight. When I first introduced her to Archie and Peter Brough on the air, I received a few letters from people saying they'd been in Birmingham, and, yes, it was very funny; but I had absolutely no idea of the success I was having until I went to Dudley to do a pantomime. *Goody Two-Shoes* was the first time Marlene as a character had been actually written into a pantomime.

This is quite in order, because pantomime was made up of contemporary people, and Marlene was a contemporary, put in that setting. All the clothes, although they were frightfully modern, had to have something about them that represented the character. So every time I made an entrance I put on a different set of earrings. I had telephones, Christmas trees, beer buckets, earrings that lit up when I had a striped black and white jacket on and said, 'Ooh, look, I'm a Zebra Crossing!' Marlene even had red high-heeled shoes made into earrings, and I had to be very creative about this, because the audience started to expect something more spectacular dangling from my ears every time I came on stage. It was an absolutely splendid gimmick.

Of course, I met some wonderful people there, particularly Emily, my dresser, who was an absolute gem. She referred to everybody by their Christian names, except her husband, who she always spoke of as 'Mr Newey'. 'Bob and Maurice' – the Kennedy Brothers, who owned the theatre – were called just that, but Mr Newey was 'Mr Newey' and that was that. There was the Yellow Dwarf in the show, and I was trying to think of some funny name of the time to mention when he came on –

you know, like 'There's So-and-So'. I looked at the television in my dressing-room (a luxury I don't allow myself now, because I have to concentrate much harder!) and said, 'Emily, have you ever heard of Sir Mortimer Wheeler?' She replied, 'I don't know, Beryl; I never mess with the nobs at the back – Mr Newey does that!' I don't know what she thought I meant, but I never questioned it.

Emily was absolutely devoted, and if I said, 'I don't want that person to come into the dressing-room,' they'd have come in over her dead body. I did say to her, 'Do you and your husband have a nice holiday in the summer?' She said, 'No – me and Mr Newey just have a nice walk round the pithead. He's got silicosis, you know.'

The following year, she came to the Coventry pantomime ball with her apron on and her curlers in. I took her up to my room at the Leofric Hotel and said, 'Let's have that apron off,' and combed her hair a bit. She enjoyed the ball just as much as everybody else and thought it was wonderful.

I made so much money for the Kennedy Brothers that year at the Dudley Hippodrome that they were able to run the theatre practically at a loss for the next two years. Sadly Maurice Kennedy committed suicide some years later, but Bob is still helping Harry Secombe with his work, and has been with him for a long, long time.

6

Changing Gear

My interest in music and musicians introduced me to two of my dearest and longest-standing friends, Terry and John Hacking. Actually the introductions were made by Derek Franklin. John was in the Hedley Ward Band, and then bought a retail stationery business, fell in love with Terry Newman-Solloway, who was helping her mother in the catering business, and brought her to see *These Radio Times* on their wedding night. Quite why, God only knows, but He's a funny fellow and must have had His reasons. So Derek introduced us, and by that time, which was September 1952, he and I were very fond of each other, as Terry remembers quite clearly. Terry told me about what happened on her wedding night:

When we went back to the theatrical digs after the show at the Chiswick Empire, Derek came to our room and sat on the bed, telling us of his great love for you. It was so funny, when you think about it: it was officially our First Night. John and I were sitting up in bed, listening to his declarations, and in the end I said, 'Oh, Derek, you must be so cold: get into bed. So he did, and the three of us sat up in bed whilst he went on about his great love for one of the stars of the show he was in – well, the female stars, I hasten to add! This was our first inkling about the way he felt for you.

The feeling was mutual. We were married in Blackpool and had what was called a honeymoon for a day and a half in Southport, because we were both working. By that time I'd found my Shangri-La, having decided the time for the happy gipsy existence in my lovely caravan must come to an end. The reason was, basically, a practical one. I had a great friend in the Willows Caravan Park and her name was Sue Stauffer. I was to become godmother to her marvellous little daughter Verity, who came to be nicknamed the 'Boring Rotter', for reasons to be explained later. One day I told her, 'I can't stay here any longer, Sue, because I cannot live without the telephone.'

I asked her for something to look at on a Sunday evening, because we had no television, and she lent me the *Eton, Windsor and Slough Gazette*. In it was an advert: 'Unique riverside cottage for sale'. I made my way to Wraysbury and realized at once it was not only unique, but absolutely beautiful. Eric Monro, who built it, must have had the most fantastic imagination, because he brought bricks from the seventeenth-century village Colnbrook, which is just near here, and made rough plans from which he worked. All the rooms are round – he was crazy about circles – and nothing has the same measurements, which drives builders mad in this day and age, because they're not very skilled or patient. Nor did everyone share his love for his creation.

My immediate reaction to Honeypot Cottage was, 'Oh, how wonderful!' The people who were then renting the place thought I was obviously a nutcase – they had put navy blue velvet over the door, so that they couldn't see the river. They didn't like the look of it. I find it terribly hard to understand that attitude. There was a cooker on bricks, a sink on bricks and wet rot in the kitchen, but to me that was absolutely nothing: I'd found a beautiful place that was like a caravan or a boat, anything that I loved the look of, and it was near the water and perfect for me.

I became very friendly with my nearest neighbours, Jean and Alan Batham, who had a little yawl at the end of the garden. I was sorry to lose them when they sailed away to start a yacht club in the Friendly Islands. They came in to tell me they were going and said, 'I expect you think we're very silly.' My immediate reaction was, 'No,

I don't think you're silly at all. I think it's absolutely great.' They asked if their son and daughter could come and see me whenever they wanted to, because they were quite young and not going with them. I said, 'Of course': I was frightfully fond of them, because they'd been very good to me. They were, however, mistaken about one thing. They had told me, 'You know, nobody can grow any flowers here,' which I've proved to be totally untrue. I grow everything here.

There was, of course, a lot of work to be done on Honeypot Cottage. There was dry rot in the bedroom where Eric Monro's first child had been born, when he'd torn some willow trees down and made a round cradle for the baby. But it was all lovely: he had built three circles; a round kitchen, a round dressing-room, and the living room has the back of the three circles in it. So unless I'd lived in a caravan I couldn't possibly have furnished it, or known how to use the space.

I bought it for very little, because property then was much cheaper. But Eric's love for the house he had created was so strong that he said, 'If ever you're going to sell it, will you promise me you'll give me the first refusal?' Of course I did willingly. But he went on to have several children, and this is not really a family house.

Derek, who also had a streak of the nomad in him, loved Honeypot, and it was the ideal place for us to start life together. But, during the first crisis there, he was missing; unfortunately pressures of work often kept us apart, but that's all part of life if you're married in show business. The first winter, the river came up alarmingly and I remember getting out of my car, because I couldn't drive to the house in it: the whole of the driveway was flooded. I had a rather sweet little ermine coat, and I held it over my head and walked in my high heels through this ice-cold water, tears running down my face, saying, 'Who'd buy Honeypot now?' Actually, for all the money in the world I wouldn't part with it: since then, of course, they've dredged the river, and it's much more unfloodable. But at that time my two friends John and Terry were on to this thing about the floods, and they thought it was really a bit of a giggle. In fact, it wasn't if you had to come home by boat every night. But John had sent a parcel inscribed 'Wraysbury flood victims' with red, white and blue sellotape round it: the whole thing was obviously a huge joke to them. The postman, Sid, came in his boat to bring me this parcel and said, 'My word, Beryl, it's got about, this flood, you know.' When I opened it there was an extraordinary conglomeration of things: a string vest, one lacrosse boot, a sun hat – linen, with machine stitching round the brim – an honorary fisherman's membership card for 1933, a 1921 bathing costume made of Celanese with a flared skirt and a V-neck, which was called a 'modesty vest', and some very elderly recipes for Skippers' sardines.

I thought, 'Ah – now I've got you' (because when the flood had subsided a bit they were going to come to me for Christmas), 'I'll have all this on when you arrive!' So I was cooking for them, and it was a big cook, because this was Christmas Eve, when there was a knock at the door. I thought, 'Oh – good' – I had all the clothes on – and I threw open the door, wearing all the gear they'd so thoughtfully sent. But it wasn't them at all – it was Sid the postman. I suppose one lacrosse boot and a 1921 bathing costume *is* a little eccentric on Christmas Eve. I tried to explain what I was doing to make them laugh, and he said, 'Oh, I know – you theatricals!'

Eventually they did arrive, and John Hacking started taking photographs of me in the outfit. He backed and he backed and he laughed and he laughed – and he fell into the river. So it was sort of tit for tat.

But Terry and John had the laugh on me on another occasion when they were staying at Honeypot, when my mother was there too. John, Terry and my mother were watching me refacing the bricks with plaster of Paris, and she said, 'It's a pity Beryl is so undomesticated!'

In fact, my home affords me so much pleasure it is

always a wrench to leave it. It really is quite beautiful: I've got this great big river frontage – water is wonderful to me – and when I look out of my window, every day of my life, I think, How lucky I am to live here. Of course, it isn't everybody's cup of tea: round rooms would surely worry some people; myself, I just adore them.

After Derek and I moved in, little cats began to come into my life again, and now I had an ideal home for them to share. The first one was a wild cat whom I called Ella, because she had rather a sexy walk. We used to have a shed, which has now been made into a spare bedroom, and we had left four of her kittens in there after Derek and I had climbed the ladder to the roof when we heard crying, to find that Ella had had her kittens in the straw surrounding the water tank. There were these teeny weeny fur balls, but we didn't at that time know if there was a mother coming to feed them, so we brought them down and put them in the shed. I didn't realize then that if anyone touches kittens at that very early age the mother will kill them, and we left them there for the day. There was no door, because the shed had been intended to be a garage, but you couldn't possibly drive a car in there because the angle was too acute. I was talking on the telephone that Sunday evening, which is the time that people know I'm in – Sunday is a very sacred day for me for being at home – and in the meantime Ella had appeared and taken away three of them and destroyed them, leaving just one, which was the most advanced one. And that was Footy: I called her that because she wanted to sit on my feet all the time – I mean when I was walking about – which made life very difficult.

I thought one tiny kitten was going to be very lonely, so I acquired another little black kitten, who was called Fred. He grew to be enormous and weighed eighteen pounds. I thought he was going to be a puma or something, nobody had warned me he'd be so big, but he did stay to be a cat and lived very happily to the age of seventeen, while Footy lived to be twenty. In the meantime, of course, lots of cats came and went.

Eric Monro carried his passion for circles into the planning of the garden. There are five little paths that go down to the river, and at the bottom, right on the river level, he built a quarter of a circle, with a pillar down the front of it, and a little seat. I said, 'Why did you build that, Mr Monro?' He explained, 'If you sit here you get the very best view of the sunset, because this faces west.' No fool he – he's absolutely right: you can catch the best of the day practically all round the house.

Since then I have had a dining room built on, which is practically all glass, and there's another most wonderful view from there: I'm really opposite Old Windsor Church and near the lock. I rehearse in the dining room, because I can shut the door, and it's a place where I can be on my own. In the summer, though, that isn't so easy, because every time they open the lock the boats come past, and I have to turn the rehearsing into something like dusting or tidying up, so that the people in the boats don't think I'm absolutely dotty if they see me leaping about acting. I suppose it does look a bit silly if you're on a boat having a lovely holiday and you see this daft woman learning some part – complete with actions.

The purity of the air at Honeypot was very precious to me in those days. During that exciting season in Dudley I realized I was going to be subject to bronchitis. I was not used to working for long stretches at a time in industrial areas, and the Kennedy Brothers, who were very kind to me, used to have friar's balsam burning on top of a radiator, so that I was able to breathe to get onto the stage. But Honeypot was the best restorative of all.

That was the start of ten years in the Midlands for me – and ten successful years – as Marlene in pantomime, when it was brought home very forcefully to me that I didn't respond well to industrial fumes, because there was no such thing then as smokeless fuel.

Also at this time Grace Sargeant entered my life, a devoted soul. She left some very lovingly wrought embroidery (with the stitches pulled close together, like children do) on the front steps of the theatre, with 'To

Beryl with love from Grace'. When eventually we did meet, Grace said, 'I come every day to the pantomime, because you smile at me.' In fact, of course, I was smiling at the audience, but Grace took it very personally. One day I saw her and she had a petticoat on, some four inches below her frock. I said, 'What a lovely petticoat, Grace,' and she answered, 'Ah, yes, well I bother with myself, you see!' I haven't heard from her for some time now, but we did exchange letters for about twenty-five years.

Then came my first real brush with the medium which was to become so very important later – television. Of course it was then in its infancy, but I was involved in a series called 'Vic's Grill', produced by Bill Lyon-Shaw. He had a secretary called Anna, and we put a notice on his door saying 'Anna – And the King of I Am', because he was a little powerful. I laughed about this years later with his daughter, who made me up to do a commercial for Bird's Eye, where I was a mother superior. It was a non-speaking part, because it said on my desk, 'Silence is Golden' (I really must try and learn that), and there were lots of jolly nuns singing 'Congratulations!' to promote 'Stir and Fry'. They'd made a wonderful set at Ealing, in a barracks which had lovely light coming through beautiful stained-glass windows. Anyway, Bill Lyon-Shaw's daughter got me ready for that strange scene, thirty years on from 'Vic's Grill'.

Norman Wisdom was the star, and he was at the peak of his career. Vic Wise took the title part, and Norman had a straight man, who was the king of exaggeration. We realized this and played on it, because you only had to mention Wimbledon for him to say, 'That's funny, when I was playing on the centre court! ...' Or, 'Of course, I did some spectacular falls in a show and the King came to me and said, "I wish you'd teach my two gils to do falls like that!"' You could get him on anything, and he just used to play into our hands.

Norman Wisdom was very endearing. He'd been a

poor little thing, and he and his brother had lived in a demolished building for a while. He went into the army, where he was a bugler, and of course one day he was late, and there he was on his bicycle, cycling wildly and blowing Reveille as he headed for the barracks. He had some wonderful stories about his life in the army and how poorly off he was; in fact, he was that Little Man he portrays – that is the story of his life. I didn't know him later in his career, but he was absolutely enchanting at that time, when he told all those very funny stories about himself and being so poor.

On top of all this, another gear change took me into movies. In 1954 I was asked to make a film at Shepperton. This was absolutely great: it sounds extraordinary, I know, but though I love the theatre and the audience and their nearness and warmth and their immediate reaction to what I'm doing, I have to say that I think my favourite medium is filming. Television is a cross between the two: you haven't got the joyous thing of being lit properly, as you are in films, because it's all top lighting in television and it's a cross-medium. I love and enjoy it, but I would say it's the most difficult to do, because it's a one-chance thing. In films there is much more than one chance: you can do takes till the director feels that he has got what he wants. I like to see the 'rushes' every day (that's the work that you've done the day before, produced on film), and I think it's the only way you can really keep in touch with the characters that you're playing. You soon know if you are doing too much or too little. But some directors unfortunately don't want you to see the rushes, although others encourage you to. If you're filming every day you can nearly always see them: if not it's not so easy.

My mother and father were at that time in the house I'd bought them at Shepperton: they didn't take to the 'warm' climate, as I explained, so they quite quickly went back to Ayr. But at the time I was doing *The Belles of St Trinian's* I could always call on the way home. It was a truly carefree film. Alastair Sim was the star, playing the headmistress and 'her' crook brother, and he was such a wonderful actor. *The Magistrate*, at Chichester, the last thing I saw him do, was one of my most wonderful evenings in the theatre. In *St Trinian's* George Cole played the spiv, and he was Alastair's adopted son: when I worked with him this year on 'Minder', he did say, 'It *is* thirty-one years since we met!' To me it just seems like thirty-one minutes.

There was a galaxy of star people in this film. Renée Houston played the art mistress and was an outrage in her own right and very, very talented; Irene Handl was the English literature mistress using that lovely cockney voice she does, but of course she hasn't got in normal life at all – she's Austrian really and has written some outstanding books; Hermione Baddeley was the geography mistress who, because she was rather plastered most of the time, only knew the wine-growing districts all over the world; and I was the maths mistress who was mad on golf and had a monocle and hair that had to be greased down straight every day. She wore a very butch suit and was always swinging a golf club when there was room. Joyce Grenfell played the games mistress and was absolutely idyllic, and Betty Ann Davies, in a sort of Mrs Danvers outfit with a long black wig, was, I think, the science mistress. She was very beautiful, and a sort of forerunner of the people who played on television in 'The Adams Family'. Unfortunately, like Renée and Joyce Grenfell, she is no longer with us. I didn't have any scenes to do with her, but she was a joy to meet. There was no sense of responsibility involved in making this film at all: it was one jape after another! We had days of throwing soot at each other and the girls, and days of throwing flour.

Ronald Searle's little daughter came one day, and in films you don't always get filmed at the time you're expecting to be. The poor little thing was only four at the time. She came in the morning with her father, who, of course, created the characters on which the film was based. We all had lunch together, and she was sick all over us immediately we got out of the restaurant. She said to me, 'I say, do you think anyone noticed that I was sick?' I said, 'No, I shouldn't think so.' It didn't matter, as we were all filthy dirty anyway!

That wonderful film was followed, quite quickly and also at Shepperton, by one in colour called *The Extra Day*, starring France's most glamorous Simone Simon and one of the most loved pop stars of the day, Dennis Lotis, a South African who has made his career here. With my side-kick Shani Wallis I was the leader of the Dennis Lotis Fan Club, and we kept mobbing him. I did it as Marlene, with the earrings and all the gear. Another very enjoyable experience – and near home. Thirty years later, while I was preparing this book, they replayed the scene of me chasing Dennis, froze the frame and cut to us still running after him in the BBC TV show 'The Time Of Your Life'. Both he and Lita Roza, whom I'd not seen for donkey's years looked and sounded in great form when they sang together like they used to do in the old Ted Heath Band days, and Lita reminded me of our first meeting, during the war, when *Cinderella* was in Liverpool, her home town. She was a twelve-year-old juvenile dancer in her very first job and said to me, 'I say, kid, where do we get tights for the first scene?' There I was, flushed with early success as an Ugly Sister, all done up like a fourpenny rabbit. I said, 'I really don't know, I'm a Principal. I speak lines.' Talk about airs and graces...

New experiences in television were also happening thick and fast. I was asked to do a play, which was terribly exciting as I had never done a TV play before. All I can recall about it was that Hugh Sinclair was the star, and I played a maid in a Kensington hotel: it was a whodunnit, and, in fact, I was the only person who knew who'd done the murder and I promised Hugh Sinclair that I wouldn't tell anyone. My first television series for ITV, 'The Most Likely Girl', concerned one of those competitions where you send in a photograph, and I'd sent one of somebody quite different, with my name on it, Arethusa Wilderspin. I was pretty plain, and wore a kind of sailor hat. I won the prize of being The Most Likely Girl (to succeed, I suppose) and Noele Gordon played a very smart, beautifully dressed newspaper reporter. The shows that we did – there were only four – were hilariously funny. In those days I used to do what they call the 'warm-up' for the show, which means getting the audience in the mood to laugh; explaining what it is all going to be about. I really enjoyed that. The series was written by Robert Bishop, whom I'd met in one of the shows at the Watergate, and sadly that's the reason why the season was so short. He was in Midhurst Hospital with TB, at the same time as Malcolm Allison the football coach, whom I got to know quite well. He was frightfully handsome then (as indeed he still is): the girls who served the meals were running about and back in half a second with whatever he asked for. He'd say, 'What kept you?' which I thought was rather lovely.

The difficulty over Bobby being in Midhurst was that we couldn't be constantly in touch with him about the script, which made it impossible for him to continue writing the series. He had set times to rest, to sleep and so on, which, I think, accounted for the disappointingly short run of such a promising idea.

During this time the Queen Mother visited Midhurst, because I believe one of the Bowes-Lyon family was in there: she's smashing – she really enjoys what she does. She was very well aware that everybody in the hospital knew she was coming and she had this slightly fluorescent lipstick on. She got out of the car, and stood there, looking up at every window where every patient was hanging out. She said, 'Oh, isn't it a *beautiful* building,' so that everyone had a lovely look at her. This is one of the things I admire so much about her: she never stops giving herself.

At this time I went to see Lord Grade, then in charge of ATV and plain Mr Lew Grade. He was on the telephone when I arrived, and said, 'You must excuse me for a moment, but I'm on the telephone to New York.' Well, of course, I'd never known anyone who'd been on the telephone to New York, and I was frightfully impressed. He put his hand over the receiver again and said, 'I've got a series here that's going to make 'Robin Hood' look bloody ridiculous!' In fact, it was 'Ivanhoe' which, even with Roger Moore, *didn't* make 'Robin Hood' look bloody ridiculous.

As long ago as 1950 (as Olga Lowe, now a National Theatre player, reminded me in a letter when I was preparing this book) I had a chance to extend my theatrical career beyond variety. Her late husband John Toré asked me to play Mabel, the full-blooded saloon-keeper in Johannesburg in a musical about the Gold Rush called *Golden City* which was due to open at the Adelphi in the Strand, with an imposing management list under Stephen Mitchell – director Michael Benthall, choreographer Robert Helpmann, no less. I was very excited, but explained that I was already contracted to do a summer season at the Wellington Pier Pavilion at Great Yarmouth. They said, 'No problem, darling – they're bound to release you for a West End show.' But they weren't and they didn't, and, though obviously disappointed, I fully appreciated their attitude. A contract's a contract, for a' that. Eleanor Summerfield, wife of Leonard Sachs with whom I was to work a lot in the future in 'The Good Old Days' from the City Varieties, Leeds, played Mabel, and got most of the notices.

Mention of life in Yarmouth suddenly brought back to mind two very dreary ladies I overhead walking along the front. Their husbands had obviously got rid of them and gone off to the pub. They were shambling along with bitter faces, and one said to the other, 'We only live two and a penny, you know, from Blackburn.' The other replied, 'Do yer?' The first said, 'Yes, but we never go in. We're not much for life!'

I was given opportunities in the legit. theatre by John Counsell at Windsor, and Melville Gillam at the Connaught, Worthing, where, with excellent companies, I appeared in two new plays. In one with Bill Owen, *The*

Dream House by Philip King, author of *Sailor Beware!*, and Faulkland Cary, I played a fortune teller, and in the other, *Witch Errant*, by R. A. Dick, with Gerald Flood and Angela Browne, I was a Scottish governess. Both were well received, but I was especially delighted when Ronnie Hill, who had so encouraged me to spread my wings at the Watergate, and John Counsell, who runs the beautiful Theatre Royal at Windsor, asked me to be in a revue, devised and directed by Ronnie, called *The World's the Limit*. Julian More and Jimmy Gilbert, also old friends from the Watergate, helped write a lovely story and music, with myself playing a woman who has come into a lot of money through winning the pools and who goes to a travel agency, run by Patrick Cargill, and grows so weary and over-excited she falls asleep and dreams her way through all the countries she wants to visit.

This, of course, gave me great scope: I was cleaning the Russian steppes in Russia, in Spain saying 'Give us the rock, cock' as a Spanish folk singer, I was Monica in Germany and Vera Lynn singing a song called 'Snowballs'. My present agent, James Sharkey, and his wife, Isabel George, were in it as a young couple appearing on a motorbike in every country we visited. Peter Graves was the leading man; I was later to play with him at Windsor again in Noel Coward's *Nude with Violin* – so I really was among friends.

It was a show that almost went to London, but I had other commitments; I couldn't make it. And it wasn't quite right; it should have had some more work done on it. But we'd all fallen in love with the revue. It was like Bernard Shaw's saying, 'Be sure you like what you get, or you get to like what you've got.' We were absolutely in love with it at the time, but my commitment, I know, would have made a space between leaving Windsor and starting again, so it never did get to London.

Patrick Cargill was among the contributors. One number I remember very well was in Russia, 'The Red Square Dance': he was the Caller. One of the lines was,

'Step to the left and you'll go far; Step to the right, Siberia!'

That was the year that Ascot was cancelled. The Queen had, I think, twenty-eight guests staying at Windsor Castle, so perhaps they had nowhere to go that evening. Anyway, they chose to come to the theatre: I think that was the first time that the whole royal family had been to the Theatre Royal. When the curtain went up we were absolutely blinded by the flashing of diamonds and tiaras – you name it, they had it on – and it was quite beautiful: the first two rows of the raised part were totally occupied by the royal family and their guests.

Three of the company – Peter Graves, Patrick Cargill and myself – were presented to them at the end. But there were so many of them that *they* had to file past *us* while we stood still. I know they always do walk past, but there are usually a great number of people waiting to meet them, and that seemed very funny, with so few of us being presented. But it was wonderful for the theatre, because I think the royal family now make it a habit to visit their 'local theatre'. I did say at the time to the Duke of Edinburgh, 'It *is* coach trips, you know, that keep the theatre going!'

Nearly a year at the London Palladium, with Harry Secombe in a show called *Rockin' the Town*, accounted for most of 1956. I know that for sure, because there's a brass plaque in my dining-room to prove it: if you played the Palladium you were allowed to take away the name plate from the dressing-room door. Harry, of course, is a dear sweet friend now. Alma Cogan was in the show, and we got on terribly well; she had great joy in coming into my dressing-room and trying on the props and wigs. I suppose it was because she always dressed for glamour on stage, while my way of dressing was fairly terrible. She was at that time always near the top of what they then called the Hit Parade, and so was Winifred Atwell, the honky-tonk pianist who had had a training in classical music and was to stun her admirers – and others

– later with a marvellous concert at the Albert Hall. She was a charming person, whose smile lit up the auditorium, and who died only recently in Australia, while Alma succumbed, tragically young, to leukaemia.

There was a man with some chimpanzees, one of whom was called Candy, and if she hadn't done a very good performance, she used to limp all the way to the dressing-room, to show how sorry she was. She loved Coke: we always had a Coke for Candy. There was also a wrestler in the show, who had his ways of getting secret supplies, so we did get one or two perks, like beluga caviar for two shillings and sixpence a jar, and bottles of cherry brandy, if you liked that sort of thing, for knock-down prices.

Harry and I did sketches; one was called 'Buying a Husband', and they were all hanging up on a rail in a shop. Another was called 'My Son, My Son', where I was dressed as this awful old crone, the possessive mother of an almost simple son, played by Harry, and based on the hit film of the time, *Marty* with Ernest Borgnine. Harry had his hair parted in the middle. I always 'called for' him – it was like going out to play, really – and if I didn't go to his dressing-room he'd say, 'Why didn't you call for me?' He'd got this caviar and some champagne in cups, and I said, 'You know, Harry, there is only one way to eat caviar, and that is off a shoehorn!' As I happened to have two I could lend him one of mine. We had this fabulous caviar, dressed in these awful costumes with the hideous make-up, and he looked at me quite seriously and said, 'Oh, we've never had it so good!' To top it all, when some friends of his came round to see him, he introduced me to them as 'Val Parnell's mother!'

We did two shows a night and three on Saturday, and I always took lobsters and Chablis to the theatre. This all sounds terribly grand, but everything was so inexpensive in those days, compared to now. I didn't have a fridge, so I put the lobsters on the fire escape outside my dressing-room. Harry would say, 'I'll yodel up your canyon when it's teatime!' He had an icebox – and I used to say to him, 'Now I'll just keep doing it until you tell me to stop,' because with three shows you lose all count of what you're doing, and you've no idea what comes next.

But we had a marvellous time. I did Marlene and he played my boyfriend Perce, and I kept looking at my watch and saying, ''E'll be 'ere in a minute, will Perce,' then we did a great rock 'n' roll dance, and he had those thick crepe soles, because he was a Teddy Boy, which were then all the go. It was an extremely successful show and I treasure the little brass plate from my door. It's a great landmark in your life, a season at the London Palladium, and I'm sure everyone will understand that whatever I've done since or before, it was absolutely wonderful to be appearing there with the people I've named.

What Val Parnell and, later, Leslie MacDonnell were to the Palladium, S. H. (Sam) Newsome was to the Midlands, and I went on to do several shows with him, three at his lovely theatre at Coventry, originally called the Hippodrome. That was when I first met Pauline Grant, his brilliant choreographer-director and later his wife. Eve Boswell played *Aladdin* and I was, as usual since Dudley, Marlene. Eve had been there the year before, when she had things very much her own way, and was obviously not happy about sharing her solo star billing with anyone, least of all another girl. I remember her being very, very temperamental, and my personal success in the pantomime did not make for the best of feeling. One day Eve said to me, 'I suppose you're not talking to me.' I said, 'Of course I'm talking to you, Eve; it's just that I've got absolutely nothing to say to you!' I enjoyed Aladdin, nevertheless, because it was highly popular and the business was wonderful. And I remember the lady doorkeeper, which was rather unusual, called Nan. She died very recently, as I learnt from her daughter, who sent me a cutting of Nan having her photograph taken with Harry Secombe. She was a lovely lady and will be sadly missed.

Bron, who dressed me, was also absolutely super. I haven't heard from her for many years, but she used always to cook me a chicken to take home with me for the weekend, because I drove home on Saturday nights. It was referred to as 'Bron's chicken', as though it was made from bronze, and we all got on exceedingly well together. Joe Church was Wishee Washee, the late Sonny Jenks a very good Twankee, though, he, too, had his moments of temperament.

The other pantomime I did for Sam Newsome at Coventry was some four years later, when I appeared with Ken Dodd in *The Pied Piper*. In the scripts there were great spaces vacant, where it said KEN DODD, and a lot of empty pages.

Ken Dodd had had an enormous success there the year before and so, of course, was the principal comedian: I was the Grand Duchess of Dresden, again as Marlene, with a lot of very funny earrings and some grand garb, but the humour about the part ended with the ears. Not to put too fine a point on it, it wasn't a very funny role. I was really only allowed on while Ken Dodd changed his clothes. He was extremely funny; he drew the crowds and had the people in stitches and he used his tickling stick and he had a state-registered nurse, who was his girlfriend, and used to sit and clock the laughs he achieved. They lived at the Leofric Hotel, but moved out every weekend. I used to keep my room on, because I only stayed away Sunday and Monday morning, but they used to check out, lock, stock and barrel, every weekend and go back into a room, which I found rather eccentric, with a dog in a dog-basket and a carful of things. But that was his way of living. I called the show 'Waiting For Doddo'.

The other show I did for Sam and Pauline was the Coventry 'Spring Show', which was to go on to Manchester and Liverpool as an 'Autumn Spectacular', copresented by Leslie A. MacDonnell, who had then taken over the Palladium from Val Parnell. The constant factor in these shows was Jimmy Edwards – 'Big Jim' –

of whom I was very fond, but he was not always very good at knowing his lines. In one of the sketches we did together there was a quite lovely horse called Tunis, who all too obviously took a shine to me, because he would always get a great erection as soon as I climbed on his back. We had to carry on with the scene in front of him as best we could. It was often a case of Jimmy placing his bowler strategically in front of the horse, who, mercifully, wasn't around when we went into our Twist – the dance of the moment – together. Coach loads of women came to see this sketch and they screamed with laughter as it got about.

At Coventry the singer was Joan Regan, a lovely girl with a great sense of humour, with whom I did a TV show, her 'Be My Guest' programme. Joan gave me a tip about eye make-up for outdoor photographs, which I've used ever since: she puts on very small false eyelashes which photograph a treat. She lives in America now and sadly I never see her, and that's the way it so often goes.

When the show went on to Manchester the leading lady was opera singer Adèle Leigh, who came into my dressing-room on the opening night and said, 'Oh, I sang *gloriously* tonight.' I replied, 'What a pity *you* had to say it!' But, indeed, she did have a glorious voice and that was just me being rather naughty. Otherwise the show was the same mixture as before: the same horse – the same everything.

One day Jimmy Edwards and I went to lunch at a place called the Shambles, which is in a very old part of Manchester, and you climb up these narrow stairs to a wonderful restaurant. There was an old chap sitting there, with a rather poorly dressed lady and a very flashily dressed one. I thought, the poorly dressed one's his wife, the other's his mistress. When he saw me he said, 'Nay, bloody 'ell, it's Beryl.' He turned out to be Mr Kruschen and, at ninety-three, a very good advert for his Salts. I asked, 'Are you celebrating something special?' He said, 'Just being alive, that's all. We celebrate that every Wednesday!'

At Liverpool – same show, same Jimmy, same horse – I stayed in one of the last of the great theatrical digs; they really don't make them like that any more. The landlady was Mrs Ellison who, the first time I peeped around the front door and saw there were no carpets, said, 'I don't let them in in stilettos, you know!' This time my father came to stay with me for six weeks, and he and Mrs Ellison got on very well indeed. She was an excellent cook, and made lovely rice puddings and things for him. I planted her garden with rose trees because she had nothing growing, and I thought they would grow anywhere. I heard from her daughter recently that she is now in a home, but still watches everything I do; it is nice to think that she's still in my life.

Anyway, Jimmy and I had to attend some mayoral function in the city, and when I got back I felt jolly tired. I'd got a cupboard full of different alcoholic beverages but Mrs Ellison asked, 'Do you want a cup of tea?' I said, 'No, but I'd love a Pernod.' She replied, 'Shall I peel it for you?' She really was a gem, and she looked after me very well indeed.

By this time Jimmy Edwards and I had a TV series together, 'Man O'Brass'. My friendly horse was no longer with us. Jim, of course, played his euphonium, and I was his wife Bessie, who didn't share his enthusiasm for brass bands. But I did find very funny the line he said before playing the instrument: 'I must take my bicycle-clips off, otherwise I shan't feel the benefit when I go out!'

We had a very good time during the series, though I sometimes had some difficulty making him learn the words. I think that's perhaps why they had me, because I was frightfully strict with him; I would say, 'No, you can't go and play polo, you've got to learn your part; we can't have you here not knowing the words ...' There was a sequel, 'Bold as Brass', with me still hating Jim's music as much as I had in the first instance. I'm not crazy about brass bands anyway, except for the one that played 'Give My Regards to Broadway' after I got the

Tony Award in New York. That, I must say, moved me to tears, but I was in a very emotional state then, with Kirk Douglas' arm around me, walking across this red carpet which went straight across the street. That *was* lovely.

Out of all the summer shows I used to do, some of the most enjoyable were those connected with Harold Fielding's 'Music For The Millions'. They were really variety bills and entailed a great deal of travelling, but luckily Derek and I were touring together at that time, because the Hedley Ward Trio did so much work for Fielding. We got a caravan and used to pull it with the car. We always did a hundred miles on a Saturday night towards the next place, then we'd pull up at the roadside and have breakfast in the morning before driving on to the next venue. We had a budgerigar who used to travel with us and his name was Humdummock. He'd fly about the car and sit on my head. 'D'you know you've got a bird on your head?', Derek would say, and I'd say 'Yes.' If I pulled up for petrol the bird would say, 'Hullo, my darling,' because they can only imitate voices they know. At that the man putting the petrol in the car would look round quite suddenly, and the bird would say, 'My name is Humdummock, and I've got a fat stomach!' Those were very happy days with the caravan, because it meant you weren't dependent on finding digs, and maybe eating what you didn't want to eat. You just cooked and ate what you wanted when you wanted it.

We went to some lovely places, which you don't usually get to play, like Harrogate and Knaresborough – the old Mother Shipton country. Derek bought me a lovely topaz ring. I have in my car to this day a glass walking-stick that I got at Knaresborough's miraculous market, to keep witches away. So, if any witches are following me – beware!

For two years I played Margate in the summer, and the first year, 1959, was really fun. The show at the Lido was produced by Eddie (E. Kelland) Espinosa, and there was Gary Miller, a romantic singer and a very beautiful chap, and Derek Roy, with his beautiful, enormous St Bernard, who used to fill the tiny dressing-room when he flopped down, for preference on one's foot. Hattie Jacques had a house in the square, and we used to have a great time, because Hattie would bring her children to the dressing-room. Kim was then four and Robin just a bit older: one day Kim had a glass of red wine and went very red, made a lot of rude noises then stood on his head. He'd gone a little too far!

Hattie and John and the two boys came to the caravan at Birchfields, a beautiful site where I had bought the caravan, and I could cook everything in the oven there and entertain any number of people. It was like the loaves and the fishes, though it was quite a small caravan. But I did have the telephone laid on, and also had a dear friend in the greengrocer's shop across the road. She gave me the beautiful roses which now grow over the shed in my garden; they are so lovely – there's one red rose that runs through a yellow rose – and they give me such pleasure every year.

It was a good summer and we had a terribly easy life, except that the theatre we were working in was rather like an aeroplane hangar. It was then that Jack Tripp came to the opposition theatre with *The Fol de Rols*, and I said, 'Oh, Jack – you're so good, you're marvellous; leave at once!' I remember one day Hattie and I were walking along the cliffs together and the boys were running on ahead and John was about half a mile behind, and she said, 'Look at him, dear – the Father Figure!' John was an absolute treasure because he always did lag behind a bit, and was very slow in speech, but when he said something it was really worth hearing, and *always* made me laugh.

The following year, at the elegant little Regency Theatre Royal in Margate (a greater contrast to the gaunt Lido could hardly be imagined), I had another opportunity to work again in revue, still one of my favourite things, though I hadn't made any money out of it. My agent felt disgusted that this was the line I wanted to follow, and for *One to Another* we all got £25 a week. The show had twenty-one authors, including Bamber Gascoigne, Harold Pinter and John Mortimer, all writing their first revue sketches. N. F. Simpson, Dorothy Parker and John Cranko were among the others, and virtually everybody who could contribute to revue contributed. It was directed by Eleanor Fazan, who didn't look old enough to direct anything, but she was absolutely lovely and a fabulous worker. One of the pieces was adapted by Stanley Myers, whom she later married. It was 'Spanish Folk Songs', and had been written by Robert Benchley in 1923. We found it in a glossy magazine and adapted it for the stage.

Sheila Hancock and Patrick Wymark were in the company, which included 'Introducing Joe Melia', Barbara Evans and Tony Tanner, who has since done so well in Canada and America. Patrick Wymark, another talent to be nipped in the bud at a cruelly early age, had come straight from Stratford-upon-Avon and revue was entirely new to him. He said to me, 'You have to establish the characters very quickly, don't you?' because he'd been used to being on all night, with perhaps a few lines here and there, at Stratford. I said, 'Well, yes you do, Patrick darling – five seconds flat, or you may as well just get off!' He also said, 'Aren't the people funny who come and fit you for the clothes? They came and looked at me yesterday and they said, "Oh – I see ..."' I tried to comfort him by saying, 'They do the same to me, Patrick. When they were fitting me for the Spanish folk singer they said, "Satin isn't a very flattering material; it makes you look fatter." I said, "I don't care if she does look fat"' because I was fatter in those days than I am now.

We went through all these hassles together, with things being constantly cut out of the show and re-instated, or thrown away, which happens all the time in revue. Patrick remarked, 'The clothes disappear, as if by magic, and it isn't mentioned that you're not doing it, but there's a new running order on the noticeboard!'

We went on to do a highly successful run at the old Lyric, Hammersmith, which (like the Theatre Royal, Margate) was also owned by J. Baxter Somerville, and then we transferred to the Apollo in Shaftesbury Avenue, where I said to Disley Jones, who did the lighting and was partner to Reg Cornish, the producer, 'You see, dear, we must have some more light. It might be very artistic to do it in the dark, but, as far as I'm concerned, I may as well be in the dressing-room.' He protested, 'But this is an authors' show.' I said, 'Well, let the authors get on and do it! Unless we can be seen there's absolutely no point in it.'

We did get more light, but they chose to put quite the wrong notices outside the Apollo, like quotes saying, 'This is a highly intellectual show,' which on that Golden Mile in those days was absolutely no good at all. So we had a fairly short run, and I was desperately sorry, because it was one of the best shows I did. Sheila Hancock was brilliant in a wonderful sketch in Italian with Roddy Maude-Roxby, all about whether he would eat the spaghetti or not. Roddy loved appearing in the show, and couldn't care less what he did – he was a truly enthusiastic performer.

Patrick Wymark took me across the road to the Bricklayer's Arms at Hammersmith, and again started me drinking Guinness because that was his drink. We became the greatest of friends. I was delighted at Joe Melia's success; he said to me one day, 'I don't know, Beryl, I've been in this business ten weeks, and they're still telling me what to do!' He'd just come down from Cambridge!

This was the show in which I first met that lovely actress Dorothy Dickson, whom my press chap Eric Braun brought backstage to see me. She said some awfully kind things, and I couldn't help saying, 'Oh, I think you're really beautiful' – because I used to say everything that came into my head: I'm a tiny bit better now, but not much. She said, 'Why don't you keep your

big trap shut!' and that was our great meeting. That's
been our sort of communication all through the years: we
send each other little cards with variations on that theme
occasionally.

Despite all this work in revue, pantomime – and Marlene
– were still very much part of my life, and so were the
Midlands during the late fifties and early sixties. Smog or
no smog, I loved playing there. *Jack and the Beanstalk* at
the Birmingham Hippodrome was the first time I worked
with Reg Dixon, whose gentle style, I thought, was ideal
for pantomime. He was so lovely singing 'Confidential-
ly'; he was a very nice chap and that was how I first met
Eric Braun. We've been together now for twenty-six
years – nothing trivial, you understand. He has what
strikes me as a tremendous knowledge of the entertainment scene and has helped me to remember, because I
have no memory of things past until I'm given a little jog.
I also had the great pleasure of meeting Audrey Jeans,
who played Jack. She was a wonderful girl and came to
be a very good comedienne. We had a great time
together. Both she and Reg are, sadly, now dead: he died
while this book was in proof, and Audrey was killed some
years back in a car accident in France while on her
second honeymoon. There was a rather 'getting-on' – not
exactly in the bloom of youth – Principal Girl, and my
mother was well on the scene there. She became very
friendly with the young manager of the theatre, who
adored her. So did everybody because she was such a
very quiet but, in a way, very witty person.

When she saw the heroine in the giant's lair, which
had some bars going across the front of it, she said,
'Beryl, in the name of God, what is she doing in yon cash
desk?' She was remembering the little things they pulled
and how the change whizzed along from the cash desk, as
in H. G. Wells's Mr Kipps's apprenticeship days, in big
stores. She was going to see the pantomime again and
her friend the manager said, 'Where would you like to
sit, Mrs Reid?' My mother, thinking of the Principal

Girl, whose act consisted of flashing mirrors in everyone's face as she sang to them, said, 'Actually, John, I would like to be awfully near the front, because I would like a close-up of the Ancient Mariner!'

One of the real pleasures of working in Birmingham was Anne Venus, who became a very great friend of mine and who had a beautiful dress shop in Temple Street. She was absolutely marvellous; she took things from all the French magazines and I got the very first replicas. I don't know how she did it, but she had Princess Margaret's wedding dress in the window, cut out, made and on display by six o'clock on the day that she was married. She was a very clever cutter and designer who kept me two years ahead of fashion, which meant I got the very best wear out of everything, because I wasn't so much on television as myself in those days, so outfits could be kept for private functions, like the one I wore at the Coventry pantomime ball, of black, very, very fine shot silk taffeta, with a low round neck, sleeveless, and a balloon skirt caught in below my knees with a band of the same material and a bow of white ermine and a little diamanté buckle, and a similar bow and buckle in my hair. It really was beautiful.

Anne featured very prominently in my life in Birmingham, and I often stayed with her and her husband, Gordon. Once she did something very funny, and really made me laugh. I'm always swanking about how my flowers invariably come out *first*, before everybody else's: I must say all my friends are sick of hearing about it, but I do seem to have very early flowering things. Well, I went to Anne's house one day, and I don't know how much it cost her, but she'd filled the garden with plastic flowers – tulips, delphiniums, everything out of season, and said, 'You see, we're very advanced in Birmingham: they do come out very early!'

That was the year I started dealing with Smithfield Garage, where I met Bill Winkley, who sold me all my cars for years, and Malcolm, his son. Bill took me to the Motor Show and it was the first time I could say, 'I'll have that one' when I saw a car that took my fancy, because I happened to have a little money at the time, but that, of course, is getting away from Birmingham. Bill Winkley died very suddenly. He hit a ball on a golf course and they said, 'That's a rotten shot.' When they looked round he was dead – a marvellous way to do it if you can, but very distressing for those you leave behind. He was just fifty years old.

Anne, whom I loved so dearly and was so inventive, had been to a dinner and dance with her husband one wintry evening. She'd just said, 'Do you know, I think the dresses are going to get shorter and shorter: you know, in the end we're going to look like Principal Boys with long boots and very short skirts' – this was a few years before mini-skirts came in and, as usual, she was right, because she was able to foresee what fashion was going to do – and at that moment, while they were both laughing, the car, which he was driving, skidded on black ice and went straight off the road. Anne was killed instantly: they were both taken to hospital and it had to be broken to him that she had died in that car crash.

With all this sadness, I was fortunate enough to make friends with a wonderful man called Alan Rook, and also Dennis Woodford, one of Irene Handl's greatest friends, who helped her with the production of her remarkable novels. I'm a great admirer: she does so many brilliant things, and I chose the sketch she wrote for *Swinging Sellers* on 'Desert Island Discs', the first time round. It's the one where she's a coy old tart, picked up in Hyde Park by Peter Sellers as a Frenchman, and it is called 'Shadows on the Grass'. I took it to Hollywood with me and played either that or Tony Hancock's 'The Blood Donor' every morning before I went out.

7

Of Boring Rotters – and Proper People

Hattie Jacques was responsible for many happy things in my life – none more so than unknowingly nicknaming my dear god-daughter Verity 'the Boring Rotter', as Sue Stauffer, her mother, reminded me. When Hattie and John LeMesurier had their sons, Robin and Kim, they were over the moon, the more so perhaps because when they first married, they were not over-blessed with the riches of this world. Warm-hearted and generous they were, and they loved to entertain their friends, so they hit on the idea of installing a small vending machine that supplied drinks. Bottles of spirits in those days cost pennies, in comparison with what has happened to prices since – but they still *did* cost, and pennies were hard to come by, especially at the BBC. Hattie was a much-loved radio star, but love alone doesn't pay for many of the luxuries of life. John was a respected actor and together they lived a happy life, but without many of what you might call perks.

Hence the drink machine. They put in half-a-crown and out would come a small gin or whisky or whatever, for their friends. I thought of a way to help without creating offence, and being a gardening nut, I popped along and put in some vegetables for them, so that at least in that way they could become self-sufficient.

Anyway, Hattie was talking one day about her children, when suddenly she stopped herself in midstream and said, 'Oh – I really mustn't talk about them any more, because it's so boring.' So when Verity came along Sue kept this in mind, and when people asked about her little girl she'd say, 'She's absolutely lovely, but I mustn't talk about her, because it's very boring to hear people talk about their children,' and that's how she came to be called 'the Boring Rotter'.

Actually, I don't think it *is* boring to hear people talk about their loved ones, whether they're children, cats or dogs – so long as the people doing the telling aren't boring themselves. But that's another story. So I'm going to hand over to Sue, who's fairly 'goey', and anything but boring, to talk about Verity in her own way. She's an animal lover too: when she was going to have Verity she said, 'I wish I could have a cat instead!' But Verity turned out to be absolutely marvellous. In the summer she'd be playing in the garden wearing a sort of life-jacket. But let Sue go on with the story.

That's right: Verity would be wearing no shoes, no knickers, nothing. So if she fell in the river nobody cared – we'd go a few houses down, and when she floated downriver we'd fish her out. She also used to ride her bike with no shoes on – a tiny little bike about eighteen inches high. It was Beryl's fault that she went to school in the first place. She gave her a satchel for her second birthday, which she wore round her neck, and it used to bonk along the ground, because she was so tiny. As she had a satchel, that meant that the next thing was she should go to school, and there used to be violent ructions because she couldn't go to school at the age of two. She used to 'leave home': she filled her satchel – she had no clothes – and cleared off on her bike, wearing her satchel. There was a little bridge over the road with a stream underneath and she used to sit under the bridge till her dad had to go and fish her out and she came back protesting. This was just upriver a bit from Beryl's.

When Verity was old enough to go to school I took her down to meet the principal – it was just in a little house – Verity was three and pushy and about nine inches tall. She was introduced to the headmistress, Mrs James. Verity said, 'And is there a Mr James?' This girl – my daughter, I mean – is now a partner in a firm of solicitors and it's Beryl's considered opinion that she's 'brilliant'. We then decided that as she was going to be a hooligan and probably go to live with the gipsies, who then lived in Welley Road, we were going to put her in the convent school in Windsor, where at least they spent their time trying to make girls into something like ladies. So when she was four we took her to enrol. It was a lovely great big mansion which had belonged to the Duke of Marlborough's family.

There was a long flight of stone steps up to the front door, where the headmistress and mother superior were waiting to welcome us, wearing those nuns' uniforms which had put Sister George in mind of albino mice, with just eyes and a little bit of mouth showing, dressed all in black, right down to their feet. They were standing at the top and we took this little mite up the steps and said, 'This is Verity,' and she said, 'Oh, I see; you all wear men's shoes here!'

Beryl took her when she was about three to a cat show she was judging in Bexhill and Beryl's father went along too; he must have been, perhaps, seventy-five, but really they were the same age, and they quarrelled all the way, with each trying to be 'top dog'. They tried to outwit each other with jokes – everything to be 'king pin', because Mr Reid used to say, 'Everybody in my club calls me the King Pin!'

Now it's my turn to outdo Sue, as Verity did my father at the cat show, because she'd quite forgotten the garden party at the convent, where the one colour they weren't allowed to wear was red. When the mother superior said, 'And what are you wearing at the garden party, Verity?' she outshone Bette Davis in *Jezebel* by saying, 'Oh, I shall be all in red!' She sprang it on them, just to cause a bit of a stir: I don't think she had anything red. She hasn't changed at all, and that's why I love her.

There's a lovely little quote from her in David Creaton's charming book *Suffer Little Children*. She came to see me when I had a cold and said, 'Now, Beryl, do you think you've got cancer?' I said, 'I don't think so this time, Verity.' She answered, 'What you really need is a good roast dinner!' Now in her mid-twenties, that's still her cure for everything.

When we were talking, Sue reminded me of her visit to a pantomime when my dresser, Angie, who had taken a drama course at the Central School of Art and had quite a penetrating voice, knocked at the door and said there were two fellows to see me. She barely pushed it to while I asked who they were. 'Oh, it's a coloured man and a fair-haired pouf!' she said in her clearest School-of-Speech-and-Drama voice. In fact, it was an up and coming West Country management on their way to offer me a job. Needless to say that was one firm I never worked for. I told her, 'There's such a word as gob-shut,' and she gave me a china gonk at the end of the season, which lives on my mantelpiece to this day, and is called Gobshut.

Sue also clearly remembered her visit to the Palladium when the late Lou Levisohn, manager–husband of Winifred Atwell, said, 'Look at my poor Winnie, working like a bloody nigger!' That was the night Sue rushed in to tell me she was going to have a baby, and I wasn't sure whether she wanted me to say, 'How wonderful!' or, 'How bloody awful!' Anyway, Harry Secombe, bless him, made it all right by coming in with tooth-mugs of champagne to toast the occasion.

Finally, she recalled a visit by my father one fine summer's day. In fact, all of his visits were memorable. He needed to be lifted and carried all the time, unlike my mother, who would say, 'Don't worry about me, Beryl – I can manage quite well myself' – and meant it. His attitude was, 'Never mind about me, Bee: as long as I have three cooked meals a day and enough to drink, don't you worry!' I was working all day and every day and had to send him off to Sue at times for his dinner.

When Mr Reid was here, it was a beautiful afternoon. There were about five of us and Beryl was there in a floaty, romantic dress – olive-green flowers on a cream background, with a sort of flared skirt.

We were all there listening with rapt attention to King Pin, and a cat, Footy, I'm almost sure, had strolled out along the trunk of the willow that overhangs the river. I was vaguely aware of a splash and a yell and a carry-on, and I didn't even look round, because I had to attend to King Pin, like everybody else there. A bedraggled figure, the steam of pure fury surrounding the head, emerged from the river and a voice that was unmistakably Beryl's roared, 'I've fallen in the river with all my clothes on – look at my hair, it's like a Mars Bar!' as she squelched onto the bank, by which time Footy, totally unconcerned, had strolled back along the branch from which Beryl was trying to rescue her and dropped onto the lawn, in search of more rewarding games. Her hair was sopping wet and she was completely saturated. I think one or two people glanced round, but nothing else, and her father didn't even draw breath. I think it took us about fifteen years to live that down.

It was the time Beryl was going to see Bobby Bishop in Midhurst Hospital, which brings us to 1957. I fancied myself as a cook in those days – ever since Beryl had come to see me, prostrate with some ailment in bed in the caravan in Willows Park, and produced a cheese soufflé out of the air, later demonstrating just how simple it was with a recipe of Hattie's: 'Start with a thick cheese sauce . . .' I'd made a whole big tinful of chocolate éclairs and I was putting them away, to store, when Beryl arrived, whizzing off on her way somewhere. She said, 'What are those?' I explained, 'Chocolate éclairs.' 'Oh,' she said, 'I'm just off to see Bobby at Midhurst – I'll take some of those,' and she was gone. I was left with three. And my final word on Beryl and cooking – she was, I suppose, my original inspiration to be venturesome – was when she was telling me how to make a pie and ended, 'And you do like Derek's mother does: you fluke it with your double hands.' You don't need to say any more, do you?'

One thing I envied Derek was his ability always to get a good night's sleep. It's one of the things I don't achieve without sleeping pills: I've been taking them for years, always under strict supervision from the doctor, and they've done me no harm whatever.

Derek was able to drop off the moment his head touched the pillow. But he was the most active sleep-talker I've ever known, and that could be alarming. One night he said, 'Oh, you're the woman from the farm who's got the gun!' and I shot out of bed, holding the clothes up to my throat. Another time he shouted, 'Chris!' I said, 'Chris who?' 'Cross,' he said. When he shouted, 'Women and children first!' I was almost out of the door before I realized where I was.

Work was separating us more and more, but we did make great efforts to be more than ships that passed in the night between engagements. For instance, when I flew off for a short holiday in Palma, Derek motored all night back from Aberdeen to see me off. That time we were more ships that passed in the morning, because he couldn't come with me as he was going straight on to another job.

Terry Hacking who, with her husband John, had played such an intimate part in the early stages of my romance with Derek, was my companion on several pleasant holidays abroad, which had their moments, as Terry recalls:

We were out walking one evening near Torremolinos when Beryl had a call of nature and I waited by the roadside while she disappeared into the dusk. Suddenly an impassioned Spaniard rushed up out of nowhere, babbling ten to the dozen and attempted to hurry off in the same direction Beryl had taken. I grabbed hold of him, saying the only word I knew in the patois – 'Filthy idiota!' When eventually I let him go, he hurried off in disarray, shrugging his shoulders and still rambling on. I waited and waited and waited, getting increasingly worried, and then I went to investigate and saw Beryl, literally on all fours, crawling up the side of the gravel pit; her dress was ruined, her stockings were ruined. The man had been trying to warn her that she was heading for a sheer deep drop. She was a mass of bruises, and that night I wasn't going to get any Oscars from her for my performance in trying to save her from a Fate Worse than Death. She was, in fact, lucky to escape with her life!

She came into her own, though, during a flight to Malta, where we were going to spend a couple of weeks. There was a strike, so it was a case of no food and carry your own luggage to the plane. They landed in Naples to refuel and to get food for the first-class passengers. We were travelling Tourist, and they announced that first class only would be able to eat. Beryl went mad and stormed onto the tarmac, which was literally No Man's Land, because then you had to have passports to set foot in every country. She stood her ground and refused to move until they promised that food and drink would be prepared for Tourists also. Unfortunately she made me go with her and I was terrified. I quite expected to be shot at dawn.

Well, I'm happy to report that Terry has survived to

face several thousand dawns since then, and I was spared to be able to accept an offer to play in South Africa. At that time, which was the end of 1961, my life demanded in some way that I should travel – I don't know why, because I really have no inclination to leave here, but I suppose I'd got a bit mixed up in my marriage to Derek, and perhaps I wanted a little escape route. I went at the beginning of their summer, in November, and of course it is the most exciting place at that time.

When I was packing to leave, Fred and Footy were quite demented by my luggage, because there was so much of it. Some had to be sent by sea and the rest came on the plane with me, and the press came to take some pictures of my wild attempts to get ready, with the cats 'helping'. The *Evening Standard* and other papers used a photo with the caption, 'Fred (left) and Footy help Beryl to pack for South Africa'. I don't think Fred ever quite recovered; it went straight to his head!

I arrived at Johannesburg and changed from my winter clothing into a beautiful summer dress, a white accordion-pleated hat that I'd been lent by my friend Anne Venus, which was really rather stunning, and that was how I stepped out of the plane. I know the Queen changes on her flights, but I don't expect she does it in the tiny little loo supplied on the aeroplane.

South Africa was fabulous. The jacaranda trees were just losing all their flowers, making pale mauve carpets under every tree; poinsettia, which we buy in little pots every Christmas, formed hedges to make you catch your breath. The great flower was the protea – I think there are six hundred and fifty varieties of the protea species, and, like the swans here, they are protected: you're not allowed to pick them. But you can buy them at the airport, so somebody is allowed to pick them, under strict control.

The company were wonderful in South Africa: they were mainly English people who had gone there to live and I re-met Anne Ziegler and Webster Booth, with whom I'd become friendly during our days in variety. They were giving singing lessons and also had a decor business: since then they have settled back home in England and I am told picked up the threads of their old life and went on singing as blithely as ever until Webster's death in June 1984.

On arrival at Cape Town, I was whizzed around by the press and met the people with whom I was going to work. There was so much entertaining that in Johannesburg I said to Leonard Schach, who was presenting us in the show *Something New*, 'You must really make up your mind what you want; are you going to have an actress who's able to go on at night, or are you going to settle for her being a stupid lolling person who's not able to do what she was brought over for?' He wanted a great social life, because, of course, there is all that out there: he used to take me to the ballet and the opera and everything every night. I just couldn't keep up the pace if I was going to be able to remember the words.

I took a selection of the best material from the revues I'd done in London to date – the best from each, so they had the pick of the bunch. I was taken to the first night of the South African version of *Beyond the Fringe* and for the occasion Anne Venus had made me a fringed dress in white. A lady who didn't like me very much accidentally-on-purpose threw a glass of red wine over it, and it was never the same again. But it had served its purpose and I'd worn it for that particular show, so there was no point in crying over spilt, or rather thrown, wine. That was an unhappy incident, but the ladies in South Africa have so little to do, because they have so many servants, that they become much more involved in social things like 'tea on the lawn in the morning' and all that sort of thing.

It was not a life that appealed to me, but I wouldn't have missed it for anything. We opened in Cape Town at the Hofmeyr Theatre. It's such a beautiful city: Table Mountain is so called because there's always a cloud over the mountain that looks like a tablecloth, with pale pink cliffs going up to it, which reminded me of Glencoe.

I did go in a cable car up to the top of Table Mountain, which was very exciting. The company were so marvellous to me; they would never let me alone in case I was lonely. We rehearsed on the beach when it was 105 degrees: I was the only one who could possibly put up with it. All the people who lived there hid in the shade, but in those days I absolutely loved the heat and didn't even wear a hat. We'd go for a picnic every Sunday, and we'd all contribute something, such as a water melon with the centre taken out and soaked and filled with rum, put to cool at the edge of the sea. That was the pudding! There were so many lovely things to eat, and we all became the most devoted friends.

I went once to a vineyard which had made Bellingham Rosé, the wine the Queen drank on a train, and we sat at a round table and ate off gold plates and drank from gold goblets – real gold. They spoke about trivial things, like two servants killing each other during the weekend over a box of matches. That upset me greatly; to live there would be unthinkable. We had a footman behind each chair and at the end of a very grand meal the hostess got a tin of Nescafé out and put it into the cups. That made me laugh!

In Johannesburg I lived in a hotel, and met a very beautiful young man with whom I went on lots and lots of picnics; the weekends I would spend at my leading man John Boulter's house. This was not the singer in 'The Black and White Minstrel Show', but an Englishman living in South Africa who became one of my dearest friends while I was there. His house reminded me very much of Honeypot, because rondarvels, the round rooms with the thatched roofs, actually come from South Africa, which I hadn't realized until I'd been there.

Letty was his servant, and she was also a servant to BBC producer Cedric Messina when he was out there: it was he who introduced me to Shakespeare on radio, broadcast while I was in South Africa. She asked me, 'How's my Ceddie: he said he was going to send me a bed.' I hope he did remember, because Letty was rather marvellous. Then one night, some burglars came in the early hours, and the wonderful Letty, stripped to the waist, went out with a knobkerrie, which every African carries, and laid about them until they were utterly routed and bloody and ran away. I didn't know anything about it till the next morning, because I was fast asleep.

I still use the recipe that Letty gave me then for a superb fish pie: you steamed or boiled the white fish with onion, flaked it and put a layer of fish, a layer of tomato, one of grated lemon rind and one of cheese, then chopped hard-boiled eggs. You repeated this in layers all the way up the dish, then you put white sauce over it and cooked it in the oven, and, of course, it's absolutely delicious. If you want to add a covering of mashed potato on the top that is beautiful too.

One weekend I made up my mind I wasn't going to stand the agonizing gnat-bites any more: I was bitten to pieces. So I sprayed the curtains wildly with what I took to be fly-spray, but it turned out to be my hair-spray and the curtains all went stiff. I think John could have killed me.

I did give a return party at John Boulter's house for all the fantastic entertaining to which I'd been treated: thirty or forty people came and we had what they call in Afrikaans a *Braaivleis* (burning flesh). I bought half a sheep, had it cut up, and we had baked potatoes in tinfoil, and salads, and all the exotic fruit salads that I'd made, and lots of drinks in the world. The company came at 2 o'clock and we opened with a cricket match, which was all the go – we were always having cricket matches on the beach – in John's huge garden. The party went on until 3 o'clock in the morning. They drank and they ate and they drank and they ate: there's no twilight there, and it goes from being daylight to immediate dark, when all those 'mozzies' come out and eat you alive. But it was wonderful, and the whole thing, I think, cost me £35.

The things that upset me were notices in butchers' windows which said, 'Servants' meat six pence a pound' (which meant all the bits they'd picked up off the floor) and that in one of the big stores there were two lifts, one for non-Europeans and the other for Europeans. In the one which said non-Europeans there was no lift installed, meaning 'You bloody well walk.' And they had to step off the pavement if there were white people walking on it.

I must say I did do a lot of things that some people considered silly. Blacks were not allowed to go into liquor stores and I used to buy large bottles of gin for them. Drink was very cheap then. Brandy was about twelve shillings a bottle and the enormous bottles of gin cost very little indeed. Some thought I was marvellous, to others I was a fool. One black girl became very ill in the hotel in Johannesburg: I rang the manager and said, 'I will pay for the doctor to attend to her, because I think she's very, very ill.' She was, maybe, twenty-seven. She said to the manager, 'Thank her very much and tell her I don't want to go to a doctor, I am seeing the witch-doctor tonight.' That made me realize that there were very clever blacks who struggled against all odds to become doctors and so on, and others who were very little removed from mud huts.

In Cape Town it was the same thing. They used to sit in groups on the corners and jeer, 'Oh, pretty white lady,' but I never felt afraid of them. The only time I was nervous was when I was alone in John Boulter's house in Jo'burg: the theatre in South Africa is so poorly paid that every actor has to do two or three jobs – at least that's the way it was in those days. A lorry-load of militia came with rifles. Of course the servants had all fled to the hills when they saw this lorry coming, which I hadn't, and I opened the door and asked what they wanted.

They said, 'We want to come in and look at his house.' 'I'm sorry,' I said, 'you can't come in.' They asked me who I was, and I told them, 'I'm an actress from England.' They said, 'We believe he is mixing with the coloured servants' (who lived in an adjacent bungalow-garage). I said to them, 'One of you can come in and ring John Boulter at his business address – but only one of you – and if he says you can all come in, then I will let you in.' My knees were knocking; I was absolutely terrified but fortunately none of that must have showed on my face. I shut the door, and there was a quarter-of-an-hour pause while they talked it all over, then I said, 'Well – is one of you coming in to ring Mr John Boulter? That's fair, isn't it?' They said, 'No, no, we go; we go away.' They drove away and didn't come back.

It was untrue that John or any of us were 'mixing': but I used to go and watch the blacks dancing, because they were marvellous to watch. They made their own Kaffir beer, and in the streets of Johannesburg there were wonderful little groups of children: one had a tea-chest, with a one-string thing which was a double bass; another played a penny tin whistle, and a couple of them danced, or played made-up musical instruments. They absolutely captured my heart every time I saw them on the streets. I always used to give them something like half-a-crown, which sent them berserk, because they didn't know what that sort of money was about.

I did do shows for black people and coloured in both Johannesburg and Cape Town, but they were not given the best show, because I wasn't allowed to have white musicians or even white stagehands.

One night we got back from the show late on a Saturday – and not only was it a very hard show to do, but they'd omitted to tell me that Jo'burg is 9000 feet above sea level, so the dancers and I in a number called 'I Shall Hate Myself in the Morning' had to use oxygen masks on the side of the stage, because we couldn't get enough air into our lungs until we'd become more accustomed to the climate. Anyway, on the Saturday in question, Letty had cooked this leg of lamb for us and the two cats, Anthony and Cleopatra, had chosen to take it away and devour it entirely. There was no question about it – just a bone was left, and we were, naturally, fairly ratty about it.

John didn't tick Letty off at all in front of me, but the next morning I saw him walking round the garden with her explaining what a disaster it was. She came in with her form of apology: 'Mr Boulter says I have to say I'm a little bit disappointed,' which was quite funny really, considering a whole leg of lamb was involved. I'm sure she was; I was more than a little bit disappointed myself!

She would come shopping with me some Mondays; you could buy sweet corn and mangoes all the way along the side of the road, as cheap as dirt. Biltong was another thing I got to like; it's dried fillet of beef, cut off in tiny slices and sold in stalls by the roadside, all costing practically nothing, on the way to the capital, Pretoria. I was paid in rand – one rand was about ten shillings at that time but everything's bound to be much more expensive now.

As we walked to the nearest shopping centre Letty would say, 'Now you carry the basket till we nearly get there,' so I used to carry it, empty unless we bought anything along the roadside, then when we got near the shops she'd put it on her head, which looked absolutely spectacular, and walk with it with the great dignity which only these African women have. Then she would say to all her friends, 'This is my friend, you know, an actress from England.' We would do the shopping, and she'd walk back a short way with it on her head until we were out of vision, and then I had to carry it again. That was Letty's little exercise of power.

I was introduced to a great friend of John's, who'd had the same servant for twenty years. But things were, as usual there, pretty dicey, with a bloodbath always liable to be lurking around the next corner. She told me she'd said to her servant, 'Now you wouldn't kill me, would you?' He answered, 'Oh, no, Missus; I'm going to kill next door's Missus – he's going to kill you!' That was the reassuring feeling of loyalty that they had for one another!

I came home to my biggest movie chance to date from James Hill, who was planning to direct a film called *The Dock Brief*, written by John Mortimer. There were just

four of us in it. I played the wife of Richard Attenborough, a bird lover who wanted a very quiet life, but I
screamed with laughter all the time – at the radio, at
everything. So he got me a lodger, who was David
Lodge, funnily enough. We got hysterical together and
my husband planned for us to go off together. In fact, we
didn't: I thought the lodger was getting far too forward
with me and said, 'I don't want that sort of thing in my
house,' as I went into peals of laughter before making
him pack his bags and leave. So there was nothing left for
'Mr Fowle' to do but to murder me, which is how Peter
Sellers got his first brief. It was hilarious because he was
absolutely useless as a lawyer or barrister or whatever,
and he and Richard Attenborough were brilliant together.

I didn't get a chance to see the film until much later,
when I was playing Worzel Gummidge's mother, with a
carrot nose, for a television film just outside Southamp-
ton on location a couple of years ago. James Hill was the
director of that too, and I told him I'd never seen *The
Dock Brief*. He said, 'I'll try to get a copy sent down,' and
it was there the next night. After we'd seen the daily
rushes he got drinks and sandwiches for us all and we sat
and watched *The Dock Brief*. I was thrilled because I
realized what a very big chance he'd given me.

A summer show for Richard Stone opened in Hastings
and settled down at Weston-super-Mare with another of
the most personable young pop stars of the day, Craig
Douglas, and Billy Burden as the comic. This was a time
when I really was in a pit of misery. My mother was very
ill indeed in Ballochmyle Hospital in Ayrshire and she
died the morning I left to drive to Weston, but, as
always, she would have expected me to go on working;
she wouldn't have wanted me to stop to go to her funeral.

Actually, my husband Derek was in Scotland, doing a
season there, and he said he would attend. He did say
that he thought my family were a terribly funny lot,
because they weren't there at all. In fact, he'd gone to the
wrong funeral, and, of course, nobody would have

laughed more about that than my mother. Auntie Belle, the next youngest to Mother and her great friend, said, 'We were rather shocked when Derek didn't appear at the funeral, but when we realized that he was subject to that sort of thing, we all had a good laugh!'

In that season at Weston I repeated what had become one of my favourite numbers, 'The Spanish Maid', written for me by Paul Dehn and which I bought for future use after *On the Avenue*, the Arthur Macrae revue for which it was devised, closed at the Globe Theatre. My great friend William – Billy – Chappell directed *On the Avenue*, with a cast that included Joan Heal and George Rose. Arthur Macrae was extraordinary: he used to come to me with a new number every day, which made everybody else absolutely furious, but he'd just got into the way of writing for me. I'm afraid nearly all of them worked, so people did get a little bit cross about it. We did a tour first and then we came into London, but by this time *Beyond the Fringe* had made its mark, and people didn't expect beautiful clothes, having been turned on to something more casual by the new undergrad type of revue. I suppose we looked dated, because we were well-dressed, and the notices were, in some cases, vitriolic. It didn't have a long run, but it was extremely successful as far as I was concerned, and also extremely happy. I don't know how my mother had found her way round to the stage door so quickly on the opening night, but she almost kicked the door open and said, 'Beryl, what a triumph. Could you not bow decently to the people!'

My last revue for many moons was *All Square* at the Vaudeville in the Strand. I think it was the last of the really glamorous, well-dressed revues. It was written almost entirely by Alan Melville and directed by Charles Hickman. The company included Naunton Wayne, Joyce Blair, Lionel's witty and talented sister, Robin Hunter and the sons of two great theatrical names, Nicky Henson, son of Leslie, long-time partner of my friend Dorothy Dickson, and Julian Holloway, whose father was Stanley Holloway. Nicky and Julian were always starving, and we used to call them Grumbleguts and Rumblebelly. We all had to supply them with food, because they were terribly poor. They were lovely, lovely boys, both of whom have done very well; Nicky, particularly, has done very well in the theatre. And Naunton Wayne was a wonderfully dry and funny person to be with. There was a witty sketch for him and me as two tramps philosophizing on a couple of dustbins.

From the sad to the sometimes sublime, I did several of the charity shows called *Night of a Hundred Stars*, which usually started after the show had finished at the Palladium. We had to rehearse all over London. Once I appeared in a sketch with Hermione Baddeley, in which we were two bus conductresses, and we had to rehearse at the Theatre Royal, Haymarket. When I went into that theatre I had the most wonderful feeling about it and I thought, This is one of my ambitions; I have got to appear in this theatre. And, indeed, so I did, nearly twenty years later, in 1983, with Donald Sinden in *The School for Scandal*. I wasn't disappointed. I had a lovely dressing-room, where the theatre ghost lives. But I found it a very friendly ghost, who did nothing vicious, never threw anything – just lived quite happily. But things did move sometimes in the dressing-room. I suppose they would, if he got tired of them being in one place.

From 1961 another dear friend, George Evans, had taken over writing Marlene for me, and at the Alexandra Theatre, Birmingham, it was yet another *Mother Goose*, a story in which I must have appeared more than any other. This was for Derek Salberg, who put on the best. Frank Ifield was in it, so were the Dallas Boys and Ted Rogers, with Jack Tripp in the title part. It was a very star-studded cast, but a little unbalanced. Frank Ifield had his pop fans, who I don't think had ever been to pantomime or even knew what it was about – he'd got off on a slightly wrong foot with me the year before when at a press party he'd told me he thought pantomime was a 'lumber' – they shouted and cheered whenever he came on but didn't want to know about the comedy. But there was another part of the audience who *were* interested in what I was doing and didn't just want to hear Frank Ifield sing 'I Remember You' and a continuous stream of pop songs.

When frustrated I used to say to Jack Tripp, 'Come in the dressing-room and have a drink,' which sounded as though we were having an awful lot of drinks, so I suggested we changed it to the secret password, 'Come in and have a sandwich!' Since then he and I have always called it 'having a sandwich' and when we ring each other up, Jack will say, perhaps on a Sunday evening, 'I'm on my second sandwich,' and I'll answer, 'Oh, I'm only on my *first*!' The trouble was, I really was eating far too many sandwiches, as far as the company were concerned.

It's funny how musicians and singers do make an awful noise all the time, and it was very difficult to have a rest in the tea hour. We did do twice daily all the time and I think we were there for sixteen weeks, so it was a jolly hard show, and frustrating, to say the least, at times. But I'd got my lovely friends from Birmingham, Anne Venus and John and Terry Hacking, so I wasn't short of friendly company and I did drive home every Saturday night, except twice when the AA rang up and said, 'Don't let her go,' because once there was going to be a blizzard, though I defied them and went through, and the other time it was very foggy but again I paid no heed to their warnings. But I should have done: at the time of the blizzard my car was snowed up when I got home and Bob and Joan Bissett helped me dig it out; Joan was with me for nearly twenty years. I hadn't returned until about 2 in the morning and I had to leave again at 9, to make sure of getting back to Birmingham, so it really was silly of me.

Next Christmas *Mother Goose* alighted again, this time at the Grand, Wolverhampton, and again with Jack Tripp, Ted Rogers and the Dallas Boys for Derek

Salberg, but without Frank Ifield. This was, in every way, a totally successful season – even more so, financially, than the Birmingham one had been. Jack made me do lovely dances and things which I didn't think I would be doing, but we worked so well together, and his friend Allen Christie, a very good singer who has been his partner in shows for many years, was the director. I had a lovely flat there, and a man called Peter Pankhurst had slithered into my life. I had met him at Birmingham the year before and decided against him, but this time he seemed to have won.

The flat which I rented for the season was quite luxurious, and lots of my friends came to stay with me, including Terry Hacking, who had a little holiday there, but I was still finding it very hard getting used to not having my mother around. Jack reminded me of the thick pea-souper fog that hung about Wolverhampton during that run and caused near chaos at the theatre one night. He recalled an incident I personally can't remember, so I'll let him tell it.

We were doing twice daily for ever, and then the fog came. There was the worst pea-souper ever – pure smog – and we couldn't get the company there, we couldn't get the people into the theatre, and the coaches broke down, so by ten past seven there was only Beryl, Al [Allen Christie] and about two other artists there – nobody out front and the curtain due to rise at seven thirty. Still no movement at seven fifteen and Beryl said, 'This is bloody ridiculous. Let's have a meal.' Great; we sent for the menu from next door, because the show, we thought, was definitely going to be cancelled and started to choose what we would order. Just before seven thirty Allen rushed in and said, 'I don't know what you think you're doing, but a couple of coaches have just arrived and the curtain is about to be rung up!' One by one the company had drifted in, but only one of the Dallas Boys had made it, the little tiny one, Peanuts, and he had to go on and do an act for all of them. His opening number was 'You'll Never Walk Alone', and it was this poor little guy who'd never sung melody before, singing on his own – ill with fright. Bit by bit they all arrived and the audience arrived and by nine o'clock it was almost like a decent second house. It was quite an amazing evening.

My last pantomime for Tom Arnold – in fact my very last pantomime of all on stage (to date!) – was *Dick Whittington* at Golders Green. This show was with Gary Miller and Tommy Cooper, who has died so suddenly and so recently and really touched everybody's heart. He was a total clown, who couldn't have a serious moment. He brought itching powder, and that sort of thing, to rehearsals, which I wasn't quite accustomed to, but I had to take it in my stride. He didn't understand the jokes, either. As Marlene I said something like, 'Give us a kiss.' He was supposed to say, 'What an effrontery,' and, as I turned away from him, 'Not a bad backery, either.' He said, 'What an effronterer,' and 'Not a bad back, either!' I said, 'I don't think we should do that, Tommy; I don't think it's your type of humour.'

Gary Miller played Dick Whittington, and I had some numbers with him which I really enjoyed. He is no longer with us – a very, very handsome, beautiful blond young man. He used to pay me visits in the dressing-room, but he rarely looked at me: he more or less addressed himself in the mirror.

The Dame was Billy Whittaker; he and his wife, Mimi Law, were very old friends of mine. I remember being in digs with them at Norwich, and he said, 'Oh, d'you know, during the war, the one thing I used to dream of was tea in digs in front of the fire and us all sitting together talking.' He was very funny, and his wife Mimi was a very good comedienne. We have been in lots and lots of shows together and enjoyed them so much, and, of course, they are still going strong.

Old Time Music Hall took me to the City Varieties at Leeds, and this was the first time I sang 'Burlington Bertie'. I know I did another song, possibly 'Poor John', in a lovely evening dress with a train and a high Victorian hat. The thing about the City Varieties is that the auditorium is absolutely wonderful and they had a two-year waiting list for tickets, and people dressed up and came in hansom cabs and had all their fancy dress things on – which, of course, was beautiful on television; but the back stage was absolutely abysmal. I remember the first time I went I was dressing with some pigeons – sorry, doves, I've been corrected – and the lady who worked with them. I think her name was Edna Squire-Brown and I did work in variety with her too. She was awfully grand and I assumed the whole family was too, but I remember being on a train-call in variety, when the birds were in the guard's van, and her father was saying, 'Come near those bloody pigeons, and I'll kill yer!' so I realized perhaps hers was a little affectation of grandeur. It was quite spectacular – they were white doves, really, and they flew from the back of the circle and landed on rather strange places – all over Edna Squire-Brown. I dressed with the birds and a sort of cracked mirror and a Bentwood chair and three other acts in the room, so we all had to keep turning round to let each other get a look in the mirror and do our make-up. It always seemed, when I did the City Varieties, the longest day of my life. I'm sure it wasn't and it did turn out quite well.

One absolutely disastrous thing happened to me there: I was going to do a number in one of my long dresses – something like 'I'll Be Your Sweetheart' or one of those beautiful Old Time Music Hall songs, which I revel in. (I made a record of them with coachloads of people from the East End, who came to be the audience and were given wine and food! Norman Newell produced it for Music for Pleasure, and it was called *Beryl Reid Music Hall Singalong*.) Anyway, back in Leeds, I was going for the final run-through before the performance, and I caught my high-heeled black shoe in the train of my dress and fell down about thirty-five stone steps, which were very well worn and dipped in the middle. There was no rail – it was a single staircase – and I went over and over and over and over until the bottom, where I had to pause to find out if I was alive. Surprisingly I was. Because nobody could get there to help me, I got up and just stood and cried. In fact, I would have liked to have gone on crying, but as it was the penultimate run before the television, and I was still alive, what I wanted to do next was sleep, but I wasn't permitted that until I got home after the show. Finally I did, but it was a pretty horrendous experience.

At Leeds Jack Tripp and I resurrected the Folly Sisters with great success. We couldn't do it in the twenties' dresses, it had to be in the period of the music hall, so we wore different costumes, but it was still a joy to work with him and to hear these enormous laughs, even though I'd said in the first place, 'Jack, never ask me to do this again!'

The Theatre Royal, Windsor, is just up the road apiece from Wraysbury, and I was able to travel there on my bicycle. I did Old Time Music Hall there too, called 'Victorian Music Hall', with Henry Hall's son Mike, and Ronnie Corbett. I remember that he and I did a super number in very old-fashioned bathing costumes, which was:

> You can do a lot of things at the seaside that you can't do
>   in Town;
> Fancy Mother with her legs all bare, swimming in the
>   fountain in Trafalgar Square,
> Bobbing up and down in the water, 'Twould make a
>   policeman frown;
> You can do a lot of things at the seaside that you can't do
>   in Town!'

Those are the sort of things that you can't do anywhere else but in Old Time Music Hall.

I sang 'We Live in Trafalgar Square' with this wonderful lanky actor John Heawood. Violetta was in the show too, and because the theatre is so near where I live – we were there for, I think, three weeks – they all came back here after a matinée and we drank four gallons of red wine. I lost practically all of my knives and forks because everyone leapt up trees and into the river and so on. I'd cooked steak and kidney pie and pigeon pie – oh, I can't remember everything. Like Mrs Juniper, 'The table was groaning with food, my dear!' and everything was consumed. If you don't know actors well, they do always eat as if it's the very last meal they're ever going to have and quite right too! It's not that we're greedy; you see, we have no real security.

That was, again, a very gay, carefree time. You don't feel much responsibility when you're doing those sort of numbers. But, although I didn't know it then, a very big change was about to happen in my life.

8

The Killing of Sister George – and Taboos

Right at the back of my mind those critics' words 'comedy actress' had taken root, and I thought, That's what I want to be. All the people I'd worked for, like Binkie Beaumont and all the other managements, had said, 'Oh, darling, you must do a play,' but they had never found a play for darling. Then out of the blue came Michael Codron, who I think had been to see everything I'd ever done. I had the reputation of being rather strait-laced: this is absolute nonsense. It was only when people used to write in revue, 'If you want flagellation, try Charing Cross Station, Just ask for a porter named Len' – I didn't think that was good enough, or funny enough, just because it rhymed, so I wouldn't perform it. But in fact I'm totally unshockable. I mean, if somebody said, 'I'm having an affair with a goat,' I would say, 'Oh good, what colour is it? I hope you'll be very happy.' Anyway, Michael Codron didn't know this, and he'd heard that I complained about words in revue. He said, 'I want you to see a play called *Entertaining Mr Sloane*.' He had even tried to get me for the 1964 production of this play, but I was engaged with Big Jim in the television series at the time, and quite unable to do it.

Now, nearly a year later, he asked me to Joe Orton's play, which was still running successfully. I thought it was the most wonderful thing. The next day I rang him up and said, 'Oh, I think it was absolutely marvellous.' 'You weren't shocked?' he said. 'In that case, I have a play for you to read. It's called *The Killing of Sister George*.'

Well, I read it, and I thought, I don't know – I really

don't know. There were two chaps in my life at that time and I got them both to read it. One said, 'Don't touch it, it'll ruin your' – that silly word – 'image.' I've never understood that, because I don't really think I've got one. Then I gave it to the other chap to read, and he said, 'Well, you love challenges; you must take it.' I really was torn again, the ball was back in my court. But I thought, Yes, I *do* love challenges; if you're going to do a play, then jolly well get in at the deep end, so I said, 'Yes, I'd love to do it.' Val May, the director, and the author, Frank Marcus, had no idea of what I did, and said I would have to audition. My agent said, 'Oh, she doesn't do auditions,' but I said, 'For this she bloody well does!'

I was given the extract, and I just went and read to them – and I was 'in, Meredith'. It was, of course, the greatest turning-point in my career, because I had suddenly – not really suddenly, it was a very slow and painful process – become an actress.

I had already done *Twelfth Night*, for Cedric Messina, the radio producer. That had been three years or so before, with Jimmy Edwards and a lot of other noted actors. I was cast as Maria. Surprisingly, it was awfully easy to learn, because it's so well written. If something is really well written, I find it much easier to learn. I was enchanted by the play. I also did another Shakespeare soon after, again for Cedric Messina, *The Merry Wives of Windsor*. I played Mistress Quickly, with Big Jim playing Falstaff. I didn't enjoy that so much, because I found it rather muddly, but I had been so sold on *Twelfth Night* that I was delighted to be asked to act again, and I did that on radio too.

The Killing of Sister George opened at Bristol. Val May was absolutely marvellous; he taught me that you don't speak to the audience, you speak to the other people on the stage, which I hadn't realized. I'd always walked on and said, 'Good evening, ladies and gentlemen,' and done whatever I had to do for *them*; except of course when I did those little television plays and the little plays at Worthing and Windsor – I suppose I'd learnt from those – but I was still far too outgoing. So he took me to one side and just told me. I knew exactly what he meant.

While we were in Bristol learning the play, Eileen Atkins and I used to go over to a wonderful pub with a super landlord, who took rather a shine to me. He was really extraordinary; there were lots of stiff-looking dirty socks all over the stairs, where he kept his bicycle and things like that. He had the habit of taking these two layers of false teeth out. I used to go in and say, 'Now what have you done with all those beautiful teeth I bought for you?' And of course he'd got them under the counter and would quickly turn round and whip them in, so that he looked more attractive to me. I said, 'If we have a glass of red wine at lunchtime it should be slightly warm, not ice-cold.' The next day I went in he had it sort of boiling in a saucepan; it was absolutely useless. But anyway, Eileen and I always went over there at lunchtime, and one day we did, I must admit, have a few glasses of red wine. She said, 'Can you dance?' and I said, 'Oh, yes, can you?', and we came back with the marvellous idea of the Laurel and Hardy thing. We did a little soft-shoe dance, which we'd made up during the lunch hour, and we did it for Val May and said, 'Do you think this can go in the Laurel and Hardy bit?' So of course it was in, and it stayed in, and that was a little invention from the lunchtime session in the pub. Which was wonderful.

The cast consisted of Eileen, Lally Bowers and myself, apart from a slightly eccentric lady, who, on the last night of the three-week run at the Bristol Old Vic – the historical Theatre Royal – tried to set fire to the theatre. She was rather hurriedly replaced by Margaret Courtenay, so we had to stop for a minute and re-rehearse before we started on the tour.

The tour was a disaster. We were path-finders. In the British theatre nobody before had spoken about Lesbianism, and this really destroyed the people we were playing to: in Bath we were deafened by the old chaps in their bathchairs being wheeled out by their nannies, their urine bottles rattling as they went, saying, 'Disgusting, disgusting'. Cambridge was another disaster; Oxford – terrible, but a friend came and said, 'Do you know, you four ladies have got an enormous success on your hands?' This was Robert Bishop, who went right back to the Watergate days, and was still in my life. I thought, You must be batty.

Hull was the biggest disaster of all. The people of Hull would barely serve us in the shops, they were so horrified. I thought it would never succeed anywhere, and I dreaded going into the theatre there, but there was a fascinating shop that sold second-hand false teeth, and I used to stand for hours trying not to go into the theatre, looking at these false teeth, thinking, How do you choose them, How do you try them on, How do you see if they fit you? What if there was some seed-cake left in some of them? – all sorts of terrifying thoughts; *anything* to keep me from the theatre, where it was huge and empty, really delaying the disappointment of it all. The Thursday matinée at Hull was the absolute D-Day – something to remember for ever: it was deserted, and there was stony silence throughout the performance. In London, if anybody started showing off, I used to say, 'Remember the Thursday matinée at Hull!' *That* brought us all to our senses again.

Eventually Michael Codron decided he *would* take the play to London: he was brave – very brave indeed. We did two previews, one for nurses and one for policemen. They hadn't a clue, so, apart from the fact that it was full because they were previews and the tickets were cheaper, the silence was still deafening.

But then, on the opening night at the Duke of York's, the most amazing thing happened: the audience started to scream with laughter. I thought Eileen was doing something terrible, like taking her knickers off behind me: of course she was doing nothing that she hadn't done all the time during the tour. It was just that this was a play for London and not, at that time, for anywhere else. It has been done by practically every company now, all over the country, even by amateurs, though whether it's been successful I couldn't tell you: it's a very difficult play to do, because you walk a knife edge the whole time. I think even the people who came into my dressing-room on the first night in London, and there were many, had slight doubts, and hadn't got the courage of their convictions. They'd had a jolly good evening, but they didn't want to say so, in case they were totally wrong.

But the next day the notices were raves, and the show was sold out for the next five months. I had said to Joan Bissett, who helped me then, 'We'll only run one night, Joan, and this time I won't be disappointed, because I know it's not going to be so hot, so it doesn't really matter. Don't worry, I won't be sitting crying' (as with some failures I'd done, that I'd had great faith in). Then there was this great sell-out, and we just went from strength to strength, and during that time Eileen got the *Evening Standard* Award for Best Actress in London, and we were then asked if we would like to go to New York with the play which had started its touring life with the banner headline 'BATH NOT READY FOR SISTER GEORGE!'

Jessie Matthews had come round on the opening night at the same time as Dorothy Dickson (who had opened her trap with some of the warmest praise I'd heard up to then) but Jessie obviously disapproved. She was playing 'Mrs Dale' on the radio at the time, and because *Sister George* is about the leading lady in a soap opera getting the sack (as had indeed happened some years before with 'Mrs Dale's Diary'), she thought the whole thing was pointed at Mrs Dale. She was fairly disgruntled by the whole thing. Later in her life, she herself played Sister George in one of her last stage parts, so eventually she had clearly come to terms with it.

Everything about that opening was amazing. I had done thirty-eight different endings to the second act, which we just could not get right. Frank Marcus and Val May used to invent new ones every day, and I rehearsed them every day, and had them written on my hands or anywhere I could see. I'm glad all this isn't happening now, because I couldn't read the writing! They even gave me a new ending for Act II for the opening night in the West End! I said, 'Oh, good, because then it won't seem like a First Night; it'll just seem as if we're going on doing it!'

My mother would have appreciated *Sister George* very much. But when my father went to see it he said, 'Now, look here, are they sisters, or are they just good friends?' My friend who accompanied him said, 'They're just good friends, Daddy' – and he enjoyed it on that level.

I had said to Val May at Bristol, because I needed help, 'Could you give me one word to keep me on this very thin line with this character?' It's a tightrope walk, because if you play for sympathy you never get it. He said, 'Yes, I can give you one word exactly – "indefatigable".' And that's the word I stuck to all the time I did this part; even at the end, which is so sad, when she is offered the part of a cow in a children's show and she finishes up alone on the stage, going 'Moo, Moo, Moo', you realize that she will be a success as a cow.

Michael Codron's decision to take the show to New York was very, very exciting. I'd never been to America, and the prospect of going there to play in a successful show was wonderful. It was presented by Morton Gottlieb. We flew over in great style, Eileen Atkins, Lally Bowers and me, but the Equity contracts insisted we had one American artist, and so Polly Rowles took over Margaret Courtenay's part. When we got to Kennedy Airport, somebody was waving wildly from the observation platform. It was Jonathan Miller, who happened to be in America, shouting, 'Welcome, George!' with no inhibitions whatever. It was *very* exciting.

I then met Warren Crane, who was to play a great part in my life. He was what they call there the stage manager, but what we would call the company manager, i.e. a higher-up job than stage manager here. Warren was confronted by these three dotty birds, as he thought, because he'd never seen us near-to, but for him and me it was love at first sight, which was wonderful. He said, 'Would you like to go out to dinner tonight?' I said, 'Oh, no, I'm going to bed.'

When we got to the hotel, the Algonquin, where lots of famous authors used to stay, we all decided our bedrooms were wrong and we kept changing them. I can't bear a bed that hasn't got a bed-head. If it's just a wall at the back of the bed, I don't get on at all well, and I think I changed three times. Eileen changed bedrooms five times, and locked herself out every time she went into a new one, so we turned out to be a terrible hazard on the afternoon that we arrived in New York.

Eileen and Lally did go out to dinner with Warren, but I stuck to my guns and went to bed. But I couldn't live in the Algonquin for long, because I saw no daylight: there was only electric light all the time, and I didn't find that right for me. Hotels aren't right for me: the only time I'm really happy is when I'm buying food and cooking it. So eventually I found an apartment.

Lally was, I think, bitterly unhappy in New York, but while we were rehearsing I said to her one lunch hour to cheer her up, 'Now, come along' – it seems I'm always saying that to people – 'now, come along, we're in America and we must live like the Americans do, and I'm going to have a dry Manhattan.' I don't drink gin at all, and dry Manhattan is solid gin, with a tiny dash of dry vermouth in it, ice-cold, so you don't know you're drinking solid gin, and an olive in it. I had one of those, and fell off the stool. I said, 'I'm very sorry, you'll have to tell them at the theatre that I'm not very well and had to go to bed.' It was disgusting: I'd only had one drink!

We got used to those signs which said 'Walk!' – 'That means "run" across the road,' I said to Eileen. 'Stop! – Walk!' – there are absolute commands about New York, which was so busy and so much tattier than I'd expected.

Times Square was a bitter disappointment. It's a kind of triangle, covered with lots of dirty paper and some signs which go round with all the news as it comes out. I'd thought 'Times Square – it's going to be absolutely fabulous,' but frankly, just to me, it was a bit shabby.

We were taken out to a lot of very grand restaurants during rehearsals, and I asked Morton Gottlieb how he thought the show was going to go. 'It's going to be a nervous hit!' he said, and he was absolutely right: it *was* a nervous hit. A lot of the ladies in New York found it far too close to them. Eileen and I had a favourite quote. We often took a taxi to the theatre, and once, as we paid our fares, we overheard a wife saying to her husband as they walked past the front of the theatre, 'I don't care what you say, Eddie, we are not going to see *that play*!' I have a feeling that Eddie sneaked in by himself at a matinée, and watched '*that play*'. There were always a lot of Eddies in the audience.

We certainly provoked a few positive – and mixed – reactions; like the friendly cab driver who said, 'Can I kiss you? I have never kissed a lesbian before.' I said, 'Well of course you can, if you like, but you still haven't, you know!'

My apartment was in West 72nd Street. It took me three months to make the butcher smile at me. He was lovely – jet black, and if you said, 'I want a chicken,' you had to be terribly quick with, 'And don't do anything to it!', because if you didn't, it was all cut to pieces before you knew where you were. But we became great friends, and when eventually I'd done the film I went back to see them, these lovely shopkeepers that I'd met, and I think they were quite amazed. They had been astonished that I had smiled at them every day, and thought I was a bit batty. I'd say, 'Get off that phone, dear, *I'm* here – I need you,' and at last they got the message that this was my way, and I was never going to be any different. The same at the supermarket, the same at the drink shop, the same at the vegetable shop, the same at the fish shop; all of these things had to dawn on them gradually.

Eileen also took an apartment four floors above me, at 72 West 72nd Street. The streets in New York run eastwards; it becomes very easy to find your way about, as the avenues run crossways to the streets. I used to walk to the end of my road, turn left or right, and I was in Columbus Avenue, where all the wonderful Puerto Rican shops were. If you walked a little further along West 72nd Street you came to Broadway and if you had the strength to walk along it, because it was a long, long way, you would come to West 44th Street, where the Belasco Theater was, where we appeared.

If you had the money there was nothing you couldn't buy, and you became a little bit spoilt. I was a little bit spoilt when I came home, because I wasn't used to things being unobtainable. I said to Eileen, 'Now, come along, as we're living here we should try public transport.' If I can possibly avoid public transport I always do: I've always driven a car. But I hadn't got a car there, and, of course, there's a great difference in the language. I said to Warren, 'Will you lay on a car for us?' and he was totally foxed by that, because he thought he had to lie on top of one instead of ordering it. So one day I decided we were going to go to the theatre by car – by taxi – and then get Warren to put us on the proper bus to go home. After we got on the bus I said to Eileen, 'This man keeps leaning up against me, Eileen: there's really something the matter with him – I'm going to move.' We moved to another seat and, of course, he fell flat on the seat. What I didn't know was that he was dead. The bus conductor got off the bus with all the money – this was before we had the money taken at the front of the bus in Britain, but they'd had it there for quite a long time – and he got a policeman off his horse. The policeman lifted the man onto the back seat, pulled his eyelids up and said, 'Oh, yeah, just drive him to the depot.'

Of course, we couldn't believe that the man was really dead. But he was – he'd been attacked by somebody, and everyone had turned a blind eye, as some people do when confronted by disaster or violence. He was laid out on the back seat, and when all the posh people in evening dress got on at the Lincoln Center, which is the great centre of culture in New York, because they couldn't get a taxi at that time of night, they sat next to him. Eileen and I couldn't wait to see what would happen. But it was inevitable. As they discovered that he was lying there dead, they all moved away rather hastily. It was really sad and terrible, but it was such a shock to us that it became almost jokey. I said, 'I think I was wrong, Eileen; perhaps we won't use public transport in future.'

In fact, we did once more. It was when *Hello Dolly* was on, and all the theatre people were on this one bus when the bell broke. When we wanted to stop, we shouted 'Ding! Ding!' and the bus conductor had to pull up at the next stop. We also once went on the subway, which is really very, very seedy, and slashed and dreadful and, I suspect, highly dangerous. I normally have very little fear of anything, but I was pleased that Warren took us home, as we both lived in the same block of apartments.

I was appalled to hear that the night porter, who'd become a great friend of mine, was shot dead about a month after we left New York. I can't think of any good reason that anybody could find to shoot him. It seemed to sum up one aspect of 'public' New York for me.

After we'd run about four months, both Eileen and I were nominated for the Tony Award. We had notifications in advance, which made us absolutely furious, because it meant we would have to wear long dresses and we didn't have such a thing between us. We astounded people in our mini-skirts, and Eileen said, 'Do you know, if someone tried to undress me quickly, it would take them a full sixteen minutes to do it!' There were so many latches and buttons on her fur coat and boots to unlace, that she'd worked out that it would take that long.

We did go to a lot of parties and in the end I said, 'I think we're wasting our time, Eileen – what we really are is poufs' molls.' We were always a sort of excuse at a party: they could get us, because we were four women and had very little opportunity of meeting any men. So we got invited to these quite extraordinary parties – well, not extraordinary, they were perfectly normal, really, but they weren't doing us much good. We weren't meeting any real chaps.

There seems to be some confusion among gay people over my use of the word 'pouf'. I use it only because I haven't got the right word. You see, 'gay' for me means the show that Cicely Courtneidge did, *Gay's the Word*, or that book written about Robert Burns, *Wonder of All the Gay World*. I can't bring myself to use it to mean homosexual, which isn't right either – it's so clinical. I haven't really got a proper word. My mother got the nearest to it: if she saw a rather masculine lady, she'd say, 'Oh, look, Beryl, I think that's a collar-and-tie job.' Of a rather effeminate gentleman, she would say, 'Oh, Beryl, I think – "What if I am?"' These were perhaps the least offensive ways of saying any of these things. Certainly I would never be uncomplimentary about anybody's sex or emotional life.

Anyway, Eileen Atkins insisted we go to these parties, and one evening Warren took the three of us, Eileen, Lally and me, and I kept playing with all the gadgets on the side of the car. It was a limousine with a glass partition; we three dotty birds were sitting in the back, and Warren and the driver were in the front. I pressed one button when Warren was turning round to talk to us and I very nearly cut his head off, because the glass partition shot up and I didn't know how to stop it – I'd forgotten which button I'd pressed!

As the day for the Tony Awards grew nearer, we accepted that we'd have to do something about dressing for the occasion. We said to Warren, 'Now, come on, we're going to the sales at Bergdorf Goodman's.' We were determined not to spend a lot of money, and we went for all the cheapest rails. Eileen got a beautiful yellow dress, which needed no alterations. I bought a black dress with a long black petticoat and what looked like just skin you saw through the top, and a high black collar. Net with spots on it formed the covering for the dress and the skirt as well, and it was really very beautiful.

But, of course, you weren't allowed to try the dresses on – mine had cost something like twenty-five dollars – and when I got home, I had to take it all to pieces. I had nightmares, because I thought I'd never get it together in time to wear on the big night. But I did, and my lovely dresser in New York, Alma (who appeared in so many mink coats and arrived in so many beautiful cars that she was obviously much richer than any of us!) got us ready to go off to the Tonys. Warren came with me.

I got the Tony Award. It was the first time it had been televised on one of those coast-to-coast hook-ups, and Kirk Douglas presented me with the award. When we got out, there was red carpet from pavement to pavement, right across the road to Sardi's, and I couldn't believe *that*, for a start. I've already mentioned Kirk Douglas' arms around me and the brass band playing 'Give My Regards to Broadway'. It was so unexpected, so overwhelming, that the tears were just running down my face. I was an absolute push-over. Kirk Douglas was wonderful, and one of the finest American actors. One of my favourite films (which a lot of people don't like because it's so sad) is *Lonely Are the Brave*, which is practically just him on a horse, trying to escape.

I had to share my happiness, and after that unbelievable evening and its excitements were over, I rang Terry and John Hacking at their home in Richmond. Terry had been very close to the play, and in fact had helped me during the London run when my regular lady fell ill. She came on with me when we moved to the St Martin's, and she had stayed with me in New York only a few weeks before the Tony Awards ceremony. She had her own special memories of *George*, and I'd like her to tell them in her own way.

One night Barbra Streisand came backstage at the Duke of York's and was so knocked out by the performance that she invited Beryl to her birthday party at the Prince of Wales, where she had made her great hit in *Funny Girl*. The party was in the circle bar, and Beryl was really the guest of honour, because I think there were only about six of us at the table. The rest were all in the Streisand company, including Michael Craig, who later was to be in a film with Beryl. The cake was brought to the table, which was part birthday cake, and the other half had the stork bringing a baby: it had just been announced that Barbra, who was then married to Elliott Gould, was leaving the show because she was pregnant. It was a marvellous evening: Beryl admired Streisand's talent so much, and they met up again in New York when another party was thrown, again in Beryl's honour.

But, to get back to the night of the Tony Awards, she rang to tell us her great news. And before she rang off, she said, 'And now, darlings, to the washing-up!'

After I received my prize – and before this we had been playing to what I would call quite good business, a nervous hit, as Morton Gottlieb had said – three people were injured trying to get into the next Wednesday matinée. Which meant really, you see, that I had to get a badge for doing it.

In the meantime Noel Coward had come into my life again, and 'intervened'. Julie Andrews was about to play Gertrude Lawrence in *Star!*, the film story of Noel's greatest friend. Noel said to the producers, 'There's only one person who can play Rosie, and that's Beryl Reid.' In the film we were a sort of variety turn: Bruce Forsyth was supposed to be Julie's father, I was his mistress, really, because they were never married, and we toured the halls. This was almost the opening shot in the picture.

My lovely big hat, which started off so beautifully, was absolutely squashed, because Rosie did drink rather a lot. When the director Robert Wise asked, 'Now, I suppose she'd drink gin, wouldn't she?', I said, 'No – Arthur would buy her a Guinness, and she'd keep it in the dressing-room. Underneath the dressing-table, behind the little curtain, she would have a bottle of port, which she'd bought very cheaply, because of course drink was extremely cheap in those days, and she'd top up the Guinness with the port. She'd drink port and Guinness.'

They really got port and Guinness for us. During the scene where Julie Andrews is telling me she's going to leave the act, and she's trying to get the fare from me, we both sat drinking port and Guinness. She said, 'Oh, it's *ages* since I've had port and Guinness!' and I said, 'It's ages, Julie, since *I've* had port and Guinness.'

The film was made by Twentieth Century-Fox and we had three and a half weeks for the music hall scenes. The choreography was done by the wonderful Michael Kidd, and I arrived a week late, because I'd had, as it were, to work my notice out on Broadway. I was perfectly entitled to leave *The Killing of Sister George*, and I really felt that after a year and five months in London and seven and a half months in New York, I wanted to do something different. It may have seemed rather disloyal at the time to Morton Gottlieb, but it was never meant to be.

I was a week behind with the dancing: Bruce Forsyth is a wonderful dancer, Julie Andrews is a wonderful dancer, and I kept saying, 'Wouldn't you like me to do an excerpt from *The Killing of Sister George*?' because I was lagging behind so far. But eventually I caught up with them all, and we did this lovely routine to 'Piccadilly – Piccadilly, the playground of the gay ...' in the music hall setting, and of course I enjoyed it immensely. Another English actor, handsome Michael Craig whom I'd met at Barbra Streisand's party, was in the film, but we had no scenes together.

Would I enjoy being in Hollywood, would I like it? I was very curious. I was at the Chateau Marmont on Sunset Strip, a relatively old building, and I stayed in an apartment where Greta Garbo had lived, and Boris Karloff had stayed – not together though. I found it totally agreeable and discovered a lot of friends who had lived in England and gone eventually to America and settled there.

My treat was going to the Farmers' Market every

weekend – four and a half miles of the most luxurious and luscious food from every part of the world. Again, if you have the money, you can buy anything. Saturday mornings were great. I didn't work on Saturdays, and I used to go round with my pram – the kind you push in the supermarket. Mind you, mine used to have one rotten wheel, which always sent me off at a tangent and I kept hitting people. You could have Mexican food, Chinese – anything you wanted. I decided that if I was ever offered a big part in a Hollywood film, it would be lovely.

It certainly didn't occur to me that I might be offered *The Killing of Sister George*. Admittedly Bette Davis had been to see me after one of the performances, and had said, '*Nobody* must do the movie but you. You're the *only* person to do it.' She didn't know me, and had no other reason to come round. Then, in every paper the next day, it said, 'Bette Davis to play George in *The Killing of Sister George*.' I blame this totally on the press, because I found Bette wonderful, and don't think she would ever have behaved like that intentionally. I thought, Right, well I'm not going to get this part, but I might get offered something else in the future.

I did also have the great pleasure of meeting Barbara Stanwyck, who came round to my dressing-room. She is a most beautiful woman, so slender, so elegant, and that was like a dream to me. A lot of it was like a dream to me, because I was meeting some people I'd never thought I could possibly meet in my life. (I was delighted to read, when I started on this book, that she had won the Golden Globe Award for her performance in *The Thorn Birds* on television.)

When I returned to England I suddenly had a few film offers, and the first was *Inspector Clouseau*. *The Pink Panther* had, of course, been done before that, but this time Alan Arkin was going to play the Inspector, the only time, I think, that Peter Sellers didn't take the part. I played Mrs Weaver, and amorously pursued Alan Arkin, though I was married to Police Inspector Frank Finlay, who turned out to be the villain. I remember appearing suddenly behind Clouseau in the final scene in a plane. I whipped down my mourning veil and said, 'The Widow Weaver, at your service!' In the meantime I'd done the Highland Fling in my kilt and even indulged in a little light caber-tossing. Foolish, but fun. The film was directed by an American, Bud Yorkin. It was also the first time I worked with Clive Francis, the handsome son of Raymond Francis, whom I was to meet again, just before I began writing this story, in *The School for Scandal*. Clive played a glamorous young man who appeared to be the baddie, but, of course, he wasn't.

There was also a film called *Assassination Bureau*, which starred Oliver Reed and Diana Rigg, with a lot of guest stars including Patrick Cargill, Telly Savalas, Warren Mitchell, and Jess Conrad as a singing gondolier. On a lot of these films, though, you don't actually meet the people, because you're not in the same scenes as they are. *Assassination Bureau* was directed by the late Basil Dearden – our first encounter since, believe it or not, the George Formby film *Spare a Copper* at the beginning of the war, when he was associate producer and helped write the script. I'm afraid I found him a fairly unsympathetic director, so I made my mind up that I was going to do it rather quickly: I was engaged for seven days, but I did it in three.

The film was set in Paris at the turn of the century, and I was Madame Otero, a brothel-keeper, wearing a jet black wig – quite a fun part, on paper, but I had nothing much really to get my teeth into. But it was all grist to the mill and all part of how I've learnt to do other characters, developing them as I've gone along and always starting with the shoes. Eleanor Fazan, who'd directed *One to Another*, did all the choreography for the Clouseau film, when I had to do the Highland Fling, so these two films were full of echoes of the past.

A much more rewarding offer was a television series – my first, apart from the times with Norman Wisdom and

Jimmy Edwards since 'The Most Likely Girl' – called 'Beryl Reid Says Good Evening.' This was with Hugh Paddick, who I think is wonderful, and perhaps one of the most underrated performers in the world. He has such a superb flair for comedy. I was to do a record with him, again for Norman Newell, in which he sings something like 'With a Flourish and a Flair' from the Disney film *Bedknobs and Broomsticks* – and that's exactly what he's got. We got on terribly well together, and had a marvellous relationship.

When we were talking about this show it was suggested I introduced a guest singer every week, but I said, 'No, I don't really want a different singer every week: I want that man I saw in a television show from Leeds, when he sang a song about Joseph being in the shed with Mary.' He had stood like something that you knock down at a fair, because he didn't know what to do with his hands when he wasn't playing his guitar. 'I want *him*,' I said, so it's really my fault that Jake Thackray gave up being a teacher and came into the theatre. I think his songs are superlative: he is like, if I could say such a thing, a north country Noel Coward, because he writes all his songs himself, he plays the guitar and he has such a way with words. If you have the patience to listen to them, the words are fabulous – songs like 'Lah-di-Dah', 'Leopold Alcocks' – they're all my favourites. He came into the show, did one number with the guitar, and then, in a sort of interlude, while everybody but he had a rest, he would do another. I used to sing at the end 'Every Time We Say Goodbye', which is one of my favourite songs, because it's the story of our lives in the theatre: we meet people and love them and then you have to be parted from them, because of the way of the work.

I have seen Jake Thackray do a great recital absolutely on his own – just him and a guitar, and his black polo-necked sweater. And he'd have the audience enraptured. So I think encouraging him was really worth while.

My life then really became quite crammed with television. I did another series with Hugh Paddick, called 'Wink To Me Only', which developed from a Comedy Playhouse called *View by Appointment*, a really funny situation comedy about a couple trying to sell a house which they didn't want to sell. It was written by Jennifer Phillips, who also wrote a wonderful series that Patricia Hayes and I did on radio called 'The Trouble With You, Lillian'. This was much more successful than the television series, because she writes so much for your mind. Patricia Hayes was Lillian and I was Madge and rather stodgy. I said, 'What about my legs – I've got bad legs, you know – what if anything happened to me? I mean I don't want the vet coming round 'ere.' Lillian bought a toaster, an electric toaster, from a lady that Madge didn't really approve of ('She wears 'er curlers, and 'as 'er bedroom slippers on after twelve o'clock in the morning – that can't be right'). This conjures up a wonderful picture of when Lillian gave it to her and they'd tried two lots of toast, because these two old girls didn't really know how to use it. Lillian said, 'I hope you like it, Madge,' 'Well, I suppose if you like scrabbling about on the floor for a bit of burnt toast with a crash helmet on, it might be a very nice present, Lillian!' Jennifer Phillips always writes things that capture the imagination.

I met Aimi Macdonald in a Max Bygraves show and really became very fond of her. I remember once saying, 'Can I give you a lift anywhere?' and she replied, 'Oh, no, I've got a car. My boyfriend gave it to me; it's ever so safe – it's called a Daimler!' I loved working with Max Bygraves, too. I had worked with him before in 'Educating Archie', and had a lot of very good sketches to do in his programme, finishing up with a thing as Mae West, which nobody had ever seen me do, and I didn't know I could do. And we did a lovely sketch together at the beginning of the show, drinking champagne, when I got a bit tiddly, singing 'Auntie Mary had a canary, up the leg of her drawers'.

The first time I worked with Ian Holm was in a straight play called *Edward the Confessor*. Alfred Burke was also in it and a splendid actor he is too, but Ian Holm I felt very much at home with – no pun intended. I had actually met him in New York. He was in the Harold Pinter play *The Homecoming* – it's all 'home', here – and he told me about his wife, who was having a baby while they were there. They got a taxi and asked the driver to take them to the hospital and this taxi-driver said, 'Is she pregnant?' Ian Holm said, 'Yes, she's just going to have a baby.' He said, 'Get out, then,' and made them get out. They had to go back to their apartment and call an ambulance to take them to hospital, which they were both a little shattered by. But I did begin to get to know him there and realized that one of his ambitions was to play Napoleon, which eventually he did do, most successfully. *Edward the Confessor* was an excellent idea: he was a character who was dying to be noticed and confessed to every murder that there was. In the end he did commit a murder and, of course, the police wouldn't believe him. I was his landlady and he was my little shy lodger of whom nobody could believe anything bad. I still don't; every time I look at him I know he wouldn't do anything bad, because he's a very gentle soul.

I was one of David Jacobs' guests in his Sunday night chat show, when I was delighted to meet Mary Tyler Moore and to see again Alfred Marks, another Archie Andrews survivor to distinguish himself in the theatre, and Frankie Vaughan, who offstage is as courteous and charming as he's dynamic on – another gentle soul. My clearest memories of David Jacobs are of doing several sessions of 'Any Questions?' with him on radio: I think the most riveting one was when I was with Enoch Powell and Jack Jones – a fairly frightening combination. I mean Jack Jones the union leader, not the singer. Jack Jones said to me, 'What are you 'ere for?', and I said, 'I'm here for the charm; what are you 'ere for?'

At dinner before the show, I said to Enoch Powell, 'How wonderful that you speak and write Greek, both ancient and modern. How did you start?' He said, 'Oh, I learned the grammar first.' On another occasion we were appearing at a borstal in Dorset, and I made quite a performance because I wanted to go to the loo just before the show. Enoch Powell said, 'Oh – don't go: personally, I always speak so much better on a full bladder!' I did remind him of this at a later stage. When I said, 'Have *you* been to the loo yet?' he laughed and remembered what he'd said to me before 'Any Questions?'

Jim Dale had shortly before won the award in New York for writing the song 'Hey, There, Georgie Girl' – his talents seem always to have received more recognition over there than at home. Much later he had a big part in the film *Joseph Andrews*, playing the gipsy wanderer. In New York I ran out of people to go with to see *Georgie Girl*, which of course was all 'Londonish'. Lynn Redgrave was in it, and one of my favourite cats is named after her – so I was pleased to go on the show with Jim.

Restoration comedy was absolutely new ground for me, and the television director Basil Coleman gave me my first chance to grow into it, with Cedric Messina again the producer. I played Mrs Malaprop, and, as the reading of a part is difficult for me, I got a great friend of mine, an Oxford don, to coach me: unless you yourself know exactly what the words mean, you can't expect the audience to follow what you're talking about.

The cast was a marvellous one; it included Andrew Cruickshank, Jeremy Brett, John Alderton, T. P. McKenna and Jennie Linden. Andrew Cruickshank said, 'Of course you know, Beryl, when I come to these sort of things, the classics, I'm always worrd perfect, worrd perfect!' Actually, when we came to do it he would rattle out a cascade of Scottish syllables and consonants until he came to the words 'Mrs Malaprop', when I realized it was my turn to speak. He was a joy to work with. The play was valuable experience for me. It was the first time I'd ever worn those tight corsets, and they made me feel very gripped at the knickers – and gripped at the chest as well. I don't know how ladies managed to exist in those days.

My last actual pantomime to date was for BBC Television. It went out on Christmas Day 1969 and was produced by Freddie Carpenter at Golders Green, which the BBC had taken over. Jimmy Tarbuck played Buttons, Anita Harris was Cinders, and, of course, Jack Tripp was my other Ugly Sister. During rehearsals I took a real shine to Jimmy Tarbuck and I suggested that we go out to lunch together. He said, 'Oh, great, yes.' There was a smashing Italian place near by, and I said, 'I think we ought to have some Valpolicella,' which used to be Reggie's favourite. I think we had about three bottles of this, because our lunch seemed to go on and on. I can't bear being late and I never wear a watch, because of this complex I have: I thought, Oh, dear, I've been enjoying myself far too much and I expect I'm late for rehearsals, which I felt was disgraceful, so I said, 'I'll rush back, Jimmy, because I think I'm late.'

Freddie Carpenter was purple in the face. 'How dare you come back late from lunch – and look at you!' I said to him, 'Oh that's nothing; wait till you see Buttons – he's pissed!' Jimmy has a wonderful sense of the ridiculous, and he told this story himself on the Parkinson show.

In this pantomime Jack Tripp and I had a special version of the song 'Sisters'. Now Jack, though outstanding in other departments, isn't always perfect about words. After 'There were never such devoted sisters' we had different lines to sing, and he sang very loudly, 'Yes – Mama Mama Mardi Gras da, Fa da gee – ah' – absolute rubbish, and he didn't even sing it *quietly*. As the thing was live, we had to press on, and I said, 'Pardon?' then tried to think of what I had to sing next. It was a fiasco till we got to the dance part, when we're always all right.

I've had three Buttons in my life, Jack Buchanan, Jimmy Tarbuck, and, in the *Cinderella* record I made, Nicky

Henson. This came three years after the television version and the producer, Norman Newell wrote a variation on 'Sisters' for me and Barbara Windsor – and she *did* know the words.

For Norman I had recorded a four-sided LP of *Alice In Wonderland* with Dirk Bogarde doing the narration. It was staggeringly all-star. Dorothy Squires did the number with me, 'Speak Roughly to Your Little Boy', playing the Cook to my Duchess, which entailed the breaking of a good deal of crockery, and taking me back a few dozen years to a dressing-room at the Argyll, Birkenhead. I sang a number called 'Love Makes the World Go Round', which was so successful it came out as a single – lyrics by Norman Newell, of course. Karen Dotrice, then a little girl, played Alice, and I remember her saying, 'Oh gosh, Beryl, I expect I'll get a rocket for that!' when she'd made a tiny mistake. It was amazing that such a young child could work so professionally, but it was the way she'd been brought up. Harry H. Corbett, Peggy Mount, Charlie Drake, Frankie Howerd, Bruce Forsyth and Tommy Cooper were also on the record.

I was lucky to meet Ginger Rogers on the opening night of *Mame* at the Theatre Royal, Drury Lane. She's an amazing woman and looks no age at all. Her mother, Leila, was with her (the lady who dressed me in *Blithe Spirit*, incidentally, went on to look after Ginger Rogers' mother). She was her guiding light all through her life and stayed close to Ginger until Mrs Rogers' death only a few years ago.

Molly McPherson was an extraordinary person, but, like Mrs Malaprop, she did occasionally get things wrong. She said, 'Oh, Beryl, in the name of God, I opened this door this afternoon, and who should I see but Kenneth Horne.' I said, 'Molly, he's been dead for years.' She said, 'No, no, not him; I mean the one from the "Forsyte Sago".' She also said, 'My friend, you know, Beryl, is dressing at the Haymarket, in "The Hounslow Boy",' meaning, of course, *The Winslow Boy*. Naughtily, I used to send her to the lovely Italian pastry shop in Old Compton Street and give her the most obscure things to ask for, to see what she'd bring back. It was always all right, but it was a bit of wickedness on my part. In those days you didn't have to pay the dresser, the management did that, so you were able to give them quite a bit of money for themselves. Out of what I gave her, she bought herself some beautiful false teeth. She said, 'We have to keep wherselves nice, don't we, in this business!'

After meeting Ginger Rogers I recorded for Norman Newell's Major Minor label the score of *Mame*, playing the title part. I had previously recorded *Hello Dolly* for Norman, when he had Music For Pleasure, and I played the part Ginger Rogers did on Broadway. I had no idea that the score is so impressive. You tend to think that it has only one tune but it has hit after hit after hit, and beautiful melodies, and wonderful words, and I don't wonder that Barbra Streisand chose it as a film project. Norman Newell has produced almost all my discs, and he has a few words to say from the other side of the sound booth:

In *Alice*, Beryl's approach to the role of the Duchess was amazing: I remember this lady had difficulty pronouncing her 'Rs', and Beryl had invented this way of tackling the character from meeting several aristocratic ladies who had the same difficulty in real life. She made her Duchess 'live', and I shall always remember that when I needed some additional sound effects of animal noises, she got all the stars in the studio to imitate animals. It was probably the most costly collection of artists ever to record sound effects, and it was hilarious.

When she recorded the Ugly Sister with Barbara Windsor in *Cinderella* she took infinite care to have the script 'polished up' at her own expense, so the record would 'live' for its junior audience. She and Barbara were hysterically funny whilst they were recording, and how I wish I had the rehearsals on tape!

It is a tragedy that our plans for adapting Paul Gallico's marvellous book *Mrs 'Arris Goes to Paris* came to nothing. Beryl had got on fabulously with the author, and was his choice for the role. David Frost's production, which was all set for go, was cancelled because of a minor clause in Paul Gallico's contract that was unacceptable to the British management.

Beryl would have been great as Mrs Harris, the charlady setting off on the greatest adventure of her life.

One of the songs Roger Webb and I wrote for the show was 'Growing Older, Feeling Younger', which Beryl sang in her 1983 revue, 'A Little Bit on the Side'. She is perhaps our finest revue star today, but I think she would be sensational starring in a musical. Sadly, the only evidence of this to date is her recordings of shows.

Beryl once invited me to a nativity play at a home for spastic children, which she supports. One little two-year-old entered as a 'Wise man', with his body across what looked like a large cotton-reel – his only way of moving. Beryl turned to me and said, 'You can see he was born to travel,' which broke the emotional ice and made me feel, as she did, that they needed all the love and care it was possible to give.

On another occasion a lady came up to Beryl in the street when we were on holiday together. (She always has time for people, and so the public always has time for her.) This lady said, 'Ooh, I know you – you're off television.' 'Yes,' said Beryl, 'I *am* at the *moment*, but I hope they'll re-employ me one day!'

Norman has taken me to meet some quite riveting people, apart from Ginger Rogers. During the run of *Blithe Spirit* he arranged a dinner party after the show to introduce me to Marlene Dietrich, who really does live up to being a legend in her time. He warned me her mood could be unpredictable, but she was friendly – affable, even. 'My daughter tells me I am privileged to meet you,' she said, and during dinner she talked at length about her life and career. By the end of the evening I was left in no doubt as to *who* the privileged one was.

9

Mr Sloane and Creepy Time Gal

God's a funny fellow, and He had a big surprise in store for me. When I had left America, I firmly believed I was not going to be offered the film of *The Killing of Sister George*, which often happens. Julie Andrews was a sensational success in *My Fair Lady* on the stage, but she was replaced in the film by Audrey Hepburn, which to me seemed such a shame. I'd quite settled for not getting the part. I'd even relinquished the shoes and left them in New York. Then my agent said, 'Robert Aldrich wants to see you at the Connaught Hotel in London: he wants you to do *Sister George* as a film.' I nearly had a fit, and sent a telegram straight to New York: 'SEND ME THE SHOES STOP CAN'T DO IT WITHOUT THEM.' So dear Warren Crane sent the shoes by air – not by sea, because that takes such a long time. He couldn't believe my good luck in getting the film any more than I did.

Robert Aldrich was a really beautiful man, and his recent death is a sad loss: he made such gutsy films – *Whatever Happened to Baby Jane?*, *The Flight of the Phoenix* and *The Dirty Dozen*. But, Whatever Happened To Bette Davis? The press reports I'd read even went on to mention Olivia de Havilland and, I think, Stella Stevens for the parts of Mrs Mercy Croft and Childie, Alice McNaught, June Buckridge's girlfriend. Apparently Bette Davis had told Robert Aldrich, 'I'm not going to wear those terrible clothes that Beryl Reid wears.' He said, 'No you won't, because *she'll* be wearing them!'

Living in the Connaught is like staying in somebody's very grand house. The staff there behave as if they were working for you personally. When I was ushered up to Bob Aldrich's suite to discuss the script, there were a couple of things there that I didn't think were right. In the play Eileen Atkins and I had had no real physical contact. She once brushed the lapels of my rather tatty old gown and said, 'Oh, really, George, we must get you a new dressing-gown.' But that was the only time we ever touched. Well, Robert Aldrich, for reasons of his own – which proved to be right – thought that in the film there should be very sexy moments between George and Childie. I completely disagreed, and though I wanted to do this film more than anything else, I said, 'I'm terribly sorry, but I can't do that. I have no intention of making a sex film.'

He was astounded, and said, 'Well, in that case, I'd better go and see Coral Browne and Susannah York' (who were playing the parts that Lally Bowers and Eileen Atkins had done in the stage play) 'and I'll see what they have to say.' They both shared his view, and so Aldrich came back and asked me, 'How do I know that this isn't just the tip of an iceberg, and that you're not going to refuse to do all sorts of things?'

I said, 'No, I have to be honest with you. I don't want you to pay my fare to Hollywood and then start creating difficulties. Any worries I have, I want to make clear now, so that we understand each other from the very beginning.' There were two terrible days while all this went on, but finally he came back and said, 'All right, I agree. I've seen the play four times, and I want you to do the part.'

So off I set for Hollywood, a year after my first visit. It was extremely hard work: I was wearing tough old suits, and I took two grey wigs with me which Stanley Hall had made for me in London because, funnily enough, I didn't find the wigs in America as good as ours. I started to make the film, and I was up day after day after day at 5 o'clock in the morning. I had lots of friends in it, and I really enjoyed my work and the whole visit to Hollywood, because I was working 'civilians' hours', although

I rose so early: Robert Aldrich had given us a present of a picnic basket each, which had at first seemed a little bit strange.

He'd taken over a film studio owned by Mary Pickford which had last been used by her in 1913 to make independent films. Of course he'd had an enormous amount of work done on it, and it was a beautiful building, but there was no restaurant; so the picnic baskets were really a little softener to tell us that we couldn't get food anywhere. I left at a quarter to seven in the morning, but before I left I had to cook something which we could have cold at lunch time. When I say 'we', I mean 'we'. I finished with my caravan full of people: I seemed to be doing 'the loaves and the fishes' again; everybody had either forgotten to bring food, or didn't know they were meant to. They all sat where they could, and we had a fine meal.

I had a little caravan on the set, and again the language barrier cropped up. One day Bob Aldrich had said, 'Quiet – we're going for a take.' Then he said, 'No, there's a noise somewhere.' I said, 'Oh, I'm awfully sorry; I left my whizzer on in my Wendy-house.' He said *'What?'* I had to explain that I'd left an air conditioner on in my caravan.

We worked together, day in, day out, and if he'd said to me, 'I want you to fall over a cliff,' I'd have done it in one take. I was *devoted* to him. He was a marvellous director. As we walked around the set, he would explain what he wanted me to do and I completely understood him. He said to me one day, 'Do you want to give me a Christmas present?' 'Of course I do,' I said, 'but what?' He said, 'Well, after you've had the row with Childie' (Susannah York) 'and you've been over to the other girl's house' (he meant Patricia Medina, who was playing a sort of tart, because Lukas Heller's screenplay had replaced Madame Zinnia, the fortune-teller, as my confidante in the play): 'When you come back,' he said, 'I want you to go into Susannah's bedroom and kiss her.'

'Well,' I said, 'I'll have to think about it.'

I went back the next morning and said, 'I've thought about it.' 'And the answer's No?' he asked. I said, 'No, the answer's Yes – I'll do it for you.' When I'd kissed Susannah, Robert said, 'Well, you did it so gently you'll get about eight million conversions now: everybody will think it's wonderful to be kissed by another lady!' Then we came to the sex scene, and these two ladies shut themselves in their Wendy-houses for about four days and wouldn't come out. In the end the sex scene had to be done about six times: they did do it, of course, eventually – they gave it all they could. But I was so glad that I'd spoken the truth in the beginning and not had to let him down when it came to it.

Of course, this was his gimmick in the film, which was a tremendous success when it opened in London at the Prince Charles Theatre – they were waist-high in £5 notes, I remember, in the box office. When it went to the provinces Robert would say, 'If you go to Liverpool, you'll see the entire scene, but if you go to Birkenhead – or somewhere else fairly near – three-quarters of a minute will be cut out of it.' So, of course, people flew all over the place, and – apart from the fact that it was such a good film – that's partly why it did such wonderful business.

There were a few scenes towards the end when Robert Aldrich and the crew and I were quite alone in the studio. We had to do a lot of talking about these, to get them right. When he'd seen the play, he'd cried. But I wasn't able to make him cry during the shooting of the final scene. So I had several little goes at it, with nobody in the studio except the crew, until he was satisfied with the final result.

I was asked to fly to New York for the première, and that was when I surprised Harold, my lovely black butcher, and all my shop-friends in Columbus Avenue. I took a taxi and went back to see them all. It was a wonderful reunion.

The film opened and was successful, but it was an even bigger success in London when it opened in March 1969.

At the opening they had a surprise for me, and kept saying, 'Oh, guess where your party's going to be?' I told Norman Newell, 'I'm dying to go to the loo,' so he took me to the Savoy, and I thought, This is where the party's going to be. Not at all; he just let me waltz into the loo and waltz out again, and we got back into the car. In fact the party was at the Duke of York's Theatre, where I'd done that long run in the play, and there was a big banner outside, saying 'Welcome home, George!' By the time I got there, everybody was waiting to greet me. What a great big wonderful surprise!

I hate to be typecast, so I was delighted to accept the part of Kath in the film version of *Entertaining Mr Sloane*, even though I hadn't done the play. This was a part totally different from the 'collar-and-tie job' of Sister George: as Kath I was an ageing nymphomaniac, and I wore wonderful transparent dresses, stiletto heels, and very lush wavy red hair. Kath was a poor soul, really – she'd had very few compliments in her life, but someone must once have said, 'Cor, your legs don't half look smashing, Kath, in them shoes!' – so, whatever the style of clothes, she was going to continue (crippled, and eventually pregnant as she was) to stagger about in stilettos. She was a child at heart, though she was very crafty on her own side.

She frightened Mr Sloane to death by walking up the drive with a pram! Then she said, 'I've just been up the gnomes' hospital.' (This was for one of the stone gnomes in the garden.) 'You see, bad weather damaged his 'ickle hat, so I had to take him up the gnomes' hospital.' By this time Sloane thought that perhaps she had had that baby she'd been on at him about. He was, incidentally, a murderer: the Dadda was short-sighted and wore pebble-lensed glasses, but he recognized Sloane as the murderer of the photographer that he'd worked for. The play is full of marvellous quotes: when I introduced the two of them, I said, 'Come along, Dadda, speak to Mr Sloane. Give him the benefit of your experience.' Of course, looking at the Dadda, he clearly had *no* experience – he was a terribly rude old man, played, wonderfully, by Alan Webb. Harry Andrews played my brother Ed, and Peter McEnery was Mr Sloane, who was very handsome and, because he didn't want to be recognized, had obviously dyed blond hair. I picked him up in the cemetery, where I was listening to a burial service and sucking an ice lolly. I found him doing press-ups on a tombstone. 'I think I have just the accommodation you require,' I said. Kath went on about the elegant simplicity of her house, which, of course, was not elegant at all: all the slats of the ceiling were showing through the plaster and there were Mickey Mouse pictures on the wall. But she was determined to get him in, and get him in she did.

By that time the Dadda had attacked him and stuck a gardening fork in his bottom. Kath said, 'He's never been like that before, Mr Sloane, I don't know what's come over him. I do hope you won't think there is anything behind it if I asked you to take your trousers off: I had the upbringing a nun might envy.' She then did a very sexy bit of bandaging, saying, 'Ooo – what lovely smooth legs you've got, Mr Sloane. Some of them dancin' birds would be pleased to have legs as smooth as you!'

At one time she had some 'very urgent knitting to do', and she showed him her snaps, wearing a dressing-gown that you could see right through. She said, 'I blame the manufacturers for this sort of thing. I'm all in the rude underneath!' Standing under a standard lamp to put the light out, she said, 'My hair was always a feature, Mr Sloane.'

Of course, she'd had very few chances in life: she'd pinched one of her brother's boyfriends before, and had a baby, but I imagine the baby had been adopted, and of course Eddie watched her like a hawk, because he didn't want the same thing to happen again. He was going to throw Mr Sloane out, but Kath says, 'He's resting upstairs, Eddie; you mustn't disturb him.' Eddie says,

'Oh, got the trousers off him already, have you?' and he goes upstairs to see Sloane, who is lying in this darkened room because of his wound. Eddie hasn't really seen him, and he's saying, 'Brought up in an orphanage, was you? Well, I think you'd better get out, mate, as soon as you can.' Then he draws the curtains, and suddenly sees this beautiful young man lying in bed. He stops short, then goes on, 'Oh, it must've been a very hard life for you in an orphanage. Ever worn leather next to your skin, boy – anything like that? The outdoor life – does that appeal to you?' He's absolutely sold on him!

He had the most monstrous car – a terrible old American model which was sort of puce and of course every coloured person in the neighbourhood was after it. They all thought it was the smartest thing they'd ever seen in their lives. All this was done at Camberwell Cemetery, except for the interior shots, which were filmed at a very small studio we hired near Staples Corner.

There was one lady at the location who had come to lay some flowers on somebody's grave. She didn't realize we were making a film, and she saw me stepping over the tombstones in this transparent dress. 'You dirty bitch,' she said – 'get off!' I tried to explain, and she said, 'I don't want to talk to you!' We had a real vicar from Chelsea who was doing the burial service, so I explained to him what had happened, and said, 'I don't want her to be upset. Please go and talk to her.' He went up to her and said, 'I do want to explain to you, madam –' She said, 'You – a curse to the human race, you are. You're the downfall of Christianity – that's what's the matter with you!' It was far from uneventful at Camberwell Cemetery.

Incidentally, the boxer, Freddie Mills, who died in extraordinary and still unresolved circumstances in Soho, is buried in the cemetery, and there is a statue of him about seven feet tall, with his boxing gloves crossed at his feet – a riveting sight. Some of the tombstones are really extravagant. In the scene where Peter McEnery

chases me and is going to kill me amongst the tombstones, I must say I was terrified. We had not discussed
the scene at all, and his only determination was to have
me dead!

There had been an amazing coincidence just before we
started filming *Mr Sloane*. Patrick Cargill was planning to
write a television series for me in which I'd play a rather
plain secretary who'd sort out everyone's troubles –
nearly a detective. He wanted to call it 'Angel', because
that's what I'd turn out to be for everybody else. Patrick
invited me to his beautiful house near Uckfield, in
Sussex, with tennis courts, which was near a health farm
called Buxted Park. Patrick was so courteous and so
loving when I was staying at his house: he even got me
on to hot chocolate at night, which was brought to me in
bed. One day we were driving along the road in his open
Rolls-Royce, which was really rather grand, and I kept
saying, 'All I want is some watermelon,' because it was
very, very hot. He did find a shop that sold watermelon,
and we ate it as we drove along. We came to a sign that
said, 'No studs for 2½ miles.' I said, 'In that case,
Patrick, we'll just have to wait.' This was one of our great
big jokes – we've got dozens of them.

I was so impressed by Buxted Park that I went to stay
there. It was a very, very lovely house, situated in
marvellous surroundings with every care and attention
that you could imagine. You had two treatments a day
and you did exercises in the morning. I'd got fairly
desperate, as you do from time to time: I wanted
absolute gob-shut, no telephone calls and not to meet
anybody. I stepped into the entrance hall of Buxted Park
and ran smack into Harry Andrews and Douglas Hickox,
who were going to do *Entertaining Mr Sloane*. I nearly fell
over, as I was there for complete rest and also to lose
weight, because if you're photographed by any camera
you look seven pounds fatter than you are.

Douglas Hickox said, 'Good, we can rehearse.' I said,
'Oh no we won't!' So that was that. They were eating
normally, which of course you can do at a health farm,

but I had hot water with a slice of lemon in the morning, half an orange for my lunch and for dinner a tiny little pot of yoghurt and a little bit of honey. There was also something called mint tea, which I didn't like at all – there was China tea too, so I had that instead. I was on an absolute starvation diet, which is hard to take to begin with, and I soon got fairly desperate. (A lot of the ladies used to sneak into Uckfield and have beautiful cream teas – but you might just as well go out and throw your money down the drain.) Like Alice in Wonderland I found a great wall. I'd been having a walk, picking some flowers and trying to keep my mind off eating grass, when I suddenly saw this magical black door in the wall. I thought, I wonder if it's open – it was just like Alice – and when I opened the black door, there I was in a vegetable garden. I thought, I know you're allowed to pick flowers, but I can't pull up vegetables that are growing. Then I saw a greenhouse full of lettuce. So I broke through the window into the greenhouse, and I just stood and ate five young lettuce, dirt and all.

When you go to Buxted you have blood pressure and everything checked by a doctor, and one day my eyes got very swollen. Now, what I didn't realize was that when you go to a health farm, if you're on a starvation diet your brains fall out – you couldn't possibly learn anything, because if you're not having food not enough gets to your brain and you get a bit dotty and words elude you. The doctor said, 'Have your eyes ever swollen like this before?' I said, 'Only once, and that was when I was bitten by a goldfish!' What I really meant was 'stung by a jellyfish', but words don't mean anything when you're on this sort of diet. Once I went to Buxted with Terry Hacking. I said to her after a few days, 'I think I'd better practise driving the car, because I don't want to be a sort of ninny when I leave here.' Terry said, 'Yes, that's a very good idea,' and so we decided we would have a little run into Brighton. Suddenly she said, 'Oh, isn't there a lot of furniture on the road today?' The word 'traffic' had eluded her.

Buxted was my favourite place. You used to walk through the orangery to get into a heated outdoor swimming pool, which I bathed in every day. It's one of the most peaceful places I've ever been to, in beautiful grounds, with the deer running free. And every year, instead of saving up to go abroad, I saved up to go to Buxted Park. Unfortunately it is no longer a health farm – it's been bought by an Arab gentleman, who apparently only uses it for four weeks a year.

Though it wasn't an immediate success commercially, *Entertaining Mr Sloane* has become a cult film: everybody tries to get videos of it, which is quite surprising. It has always been my favourite film and certainly it was brilliantly adapted for the screen from Joe Orton's play by Clive Exton, with Douglas Hickox doing a marvellous job in what I believe was his first direction of a feature film.

I was given a beautiful little kitten there – a formal presentation by the grave-diggers, who pushed the spokesman to the front and said, 'You seem to be very fond of our little kitten, so we would like you to have her.' So, of course, she was called Kath. She'd crossed that enormous main road opposite Camberwell Cemetery quite safely so many times in her life, but it was here in the country, just when she was coming home for breakfast across the little lane, that she was killed. I call the place Kath's Leap, because she was just leaping across the road when she was hit by a car and smashed.

The opening of *Mr Sloane* was a grand affair at the Carlton Cinema in the Haymarket, in the presence of Princess Margaret and Lord Snowdon. They sat just in front of Reggie (in town for the occasion) and myself, and they kept looking round, and sort of digging us and carrying on. All my close friends came, and we had a wonderful evening.

There were a couple of funny incidents involving Alan Webb during the filming, which tied in remarkably with the graveyard humour of the whole thing, but which were never intended to find their way onto the screen. At the little studio there was a waiting-room, and Alan had

had a few glasses of port after his lunch. He was bright green, because rigor mortis was setting in – I mean in the film – and bloodstained, having been kicked to death by Mr Sloane. At the time Kath wouldn't believe it: she said, 'Don't be so silly, Mr Sloane – you're not that kind of young man. Do you want a boiled egg?' Alan had gone out to this waiting-room to get a breath of fresh air, had fallen sound asleep and was snoring, all green and bloodstained, while people kept coming in and applying for jobs. But when they saw this monster in the corner, they left hurriedly.

Later we had our revenge on him. It's very difficult not to breathe when you're playing dead, as all actors find during their lives. We'd all worked out a little plot with director Douglas Hickox and the crew. He said, 'Alan, I want perfect quiet and I want a shot of you not breathing.' Alan drew a breath and Douglas called 'Action!' We all crept out of the studio, cameramen, everybody, and we left Alan in there, laid out and 'not breathing'. Eventually he burst out, 'How long is this going on?', only to find the studio totally empty. He was furious at the time, but being tremendously good-natured, he did have a laugh with us afterwards.

The title of my next picture was going to be 'Young Man, I Think You're Dying'. It's a line from the folksong 'Barbara Allen' and would have made a wonderful title, but apparently somebody had written a book with the same name, so eventually, after dallying with 'Are You Dying, Young Man?', director James Kelly, who also wrote the screenplay, settled on the rather nasty title, *The Beast in the Cellar*. The filming was at Pinewood, just up the road apiece from me.

It was, I thought, a frightfully good story, and it was a joy to work with Flora Robson. We played sisters and I was Ellie, the timid one, while Flora as Joyce was the one who ruled the roost. Tessa Wyatt was in it, in what I think was her first film part, and there was dear old T. P. McKenna, looking as Irish and handsome and dashing as ever, with John Hamill as the handsome juvenile in army uniform.

This was a really difficult film to do, because we were on a limited budget and we had very long takes. I had to do an awful lot of talking. When you're getting ready for a take, you think madly of the first words you're going to say. They would say, 'Right – we'll go for a take' and Flora, dear soul, said to me, 'Do you know how to recognize the hall-marking on Georgian silver?' I said, 'No – I can't go for a take, I can't go for a take!' Everything had gone right out of my head, because I didn't believe anybody would ask me such a question at such a time. But that was just her way.

Flora and I were both disappointed that they'd slotted in some rather cheap effects afterwards – you have absolutely no control over this – which turned it into a much more bloodthirsty and horrible picture than either of us had imagined. We thought it was going to be just this rather splendid script that I'd taken to at once. Another great loss to our profession was Flora's sudden death in July 1984 when we were completing this book.

As far as movies were concerned, this was obviously my time for my silly season in the cinema, with ghoulies and ghosties and four-legged beasties and things that go bump in the night. I was then cast in another Horror, called *Psychomania*, but humour lurked just around the corner, to take the kiss of death off things. They really wanted a very tall, dark woman, but I was asked to do it with about three black wigs on, and enormously high-heeled shoes. I was in touch with the dead. There were some terribly funny moments in it, because my son, whose soul I'd sold to the Devil when he was a baby at some phoney graveyard they'd rigged up near Sunbury, was played by Nicky Henson, a vision in black leather as the leader of a motorcycle gang of young tearaways. Nicky and I had to keep waltzing together whenever we spoke to each other, and neither of us could waltz, so we were delivering this terrible dialogue while we kept going round all the time, giving each other bruised trodden-on toes to keep the talk going, and sort of falling over at the end of it. If we had been able to waltz I'm sure it would have been a great asset to the film.

Something that was a great asset to the picture, and to my life, was working with George Sanders in his last film. He was a wonderful man: so tall and so elegant. We were walking to the restaurant one day, and I couldn't keep up with him because I'm a little short thing, and he said, 'Of course, I'm not walking as quickly as I usually do, because I had one of those little strokey things, you know.' But he was absolutely on the ball, and there was one moment in the film when the director, Don Sharp, who was also responsible for the script, said, 'Now I want you to give her a rather strange look, doubting her sanity.' George said, 'Oh, you want me to look at her and think, Oh, I see, she's slipped her trolley and she's ready for the laughing academy! Yes, I understand, right-ho.' That was done very quickly, and in one take. He was playing my butler, actually the Devil's henchman and the contact between me, Mrs Latham (a medium), Old Nick himself and young Nick Henson, whose soul I'd offered him in exchange for eternal life. A very devious plot, you see.

George Sanders also told me that when he was married to Benita Hume and they were making a film in Jerusalem, they'd decided to spend Christmas in Bethlehem. An Arab who was working on the film had booked them into a hotel on the Dead Sea, which was rather a sinister beginning. It was Christmas Eve by the time they got there, and when they went into the lovely little square for midnight mass they were deafened by Bing Crosby's 'White Christmas', blaring out over every loudspeaker in the square. Next to the lovely little church there was the Holy City Stores, and on the other side was the Manger Cafe. They went into the church, determined in spite of all this to have a lovely midnight mass, but when he saw them the priest said, 'Oh, look, there's Baysil Raythbone!'

George was a great giggler, and would go off into gales

of laughter at the drop of a hat. Once the script made me say to Nicky Henson, 'Now, if you commit suicide, are you absolutely certain that you have the power to come back alive to this earth?' And when Nicky said, with the passionate conviction required by the script, 'Yes!', George Sanders said, 'Then you're very silly!'

The title underwent changes during the filming from The Frogs to The Living Dead, before settling on *Psychomania*. At the end I did turn into a frog for the first time in my life – and, I hope, the last.

A very short time after this George Sanders committed suicide, going to Spain, quite alone, to do so. It was an appalling shock, and the saddest loss to us all.

I first met Ronnie Corbett at Danny La Rue's nightclub, and then, having worked with him at Windsor, I was asked to do the film of *No Sex Please, We're British* with him, which was even then, in 1973, a long-running play. It is now the longest-running comedy in the West End. This was a Columbia–Warner production, directed by Cliff Owen, and another lovely experience, because we worked mainly in Windsor and, as I said to the Queen whenever I went with Peter Brough to entertain the staff party at Christmas, 'I only live up the road, you know!' The Queen Mother got onto that first, and never asked me where my home was.

In the film Arthur Lowe played a bank manager who was making a pass at me. Ian Ogilvy played my son, and the delightful Susan Penhaligan played his wife. That was the first time I worked with her. The inside shots were again at Pinewood, so the whole thing was really on home ground. I took lunch in every day, and Susan and I ate it in my dressing-room. We did ask Ian Ogilvy if he'd like to come and join us one day, and he said, 'Oh, no, I have to get to the restaurant, because I have to go rubber-necking.' He meant table-hopping, to discuss the next part, I suppose, but I thought, I shan't ask again!

Ronnie came to the set several times, and he invited me to his lovely hotel in Windsor, saying, 'Don't bother

Perfect peace at
Honeypot Cottage

Below: My lovely Footy

Right: The swan and I

Right: Little thing posing with brother Roy, kilted and four years bigger
Below: Little thing on a picnic (first left, front)

Roy and I, bigger and several years on. Note identical hands! Taken at a press showing of *The Killing of Sister George*

Below left: An early 'Gretchen' – Mother Goose's maid. *Below right:* 'Soubrette' – the card I sent to Brian Seymour. On the back it says, *Wanted. Engagement. Young Soubrette with lovely singing voice, beautiful juddler and head balancer, wardrobe mistress and turtle-oil demonstrator, in fact quite versatile. Wanted: young male stooge*

Above: The reception: Bill, myself, my mother, sister-in-law Pat and Roy

Right: Setting off after wedding to Bill Worsley

Above left: As Estelle in *Betty* – as Constance Bennett's hair got swept on top, so did mine. *Above right:* As Burlington Bertie in *The Good Old Days*

Monica takes aim

ne from the Midlands shows she has earrings to suit every occasion

Right: At the Watergate:
'I changed my sex a week ago today,
I don't know what my friend is going
to say'

Below: Aladdin at Coventry, with Sam
Newsome (centre), Pauline Grant,
Eve Boswell and others. Our
bouquets overshadowed almost
everything, except Eve's legs

Bottom: Peter Brough introduces
Archie Andrews to Marlene, Graham
Stark and Benny Hill

Above: 'Spanish Maid' by Paul Dehn, with Tony Selby on my left and Joanna Rigby (from *On the Avenue*)

Above: With Sheila Hancock in the Pinter sketch 'Black and White' from *One to Another. Right:* 'A middle-aged, middle-class barfly' – from a Watergate revue

Above left: 'Red Peppers' with Graham Payn, from Noel Coward's *Tonight at 8.30*

Above right: With Harry Secombe at the Palladium in *Rockin' the Town*

Rehearsing *The Merry Wives of Windsor* with Jimmy Edwards and Cedric Messina

Above: After the wedding to Derek Franklin: left to right: David Reid, Anne Shelton, Bunty Meadows, Derek, myself, John and Terry Hacking, Joan Turner

Below: With spastic children at a lovely Nativity play

Right: South African rhythms

Above: The Belles of St Trinian's.
Left to right: Mary Merrall,
Renée Houston, Hermione
Baddeley, Betty Ann Davies,
Arthur Howard, Alastair Sim,
Guy Middleton, Joyce Grenfell
and myself
Below: The Dock Brief with Richard
Attenborough

Above: The Beast in the Cellar with
Flora Robson

The Killing of Sister George

Above: The London cast enjoying ourselves outside St Martin's before our transfer to New York. Left to right: Eileen Atkins, myself and Lally Bowers

Below: A birthday celebration on the film set with Robert Aldrich

Above: Susannah York tops me up

Above: The graveyard scene in *Entertaining Mr Sloane* with Peter McEnery. *Below left:* With Reginald Vincent at the première *Below:* With Noel Coward at Simpson's of Piccadilly

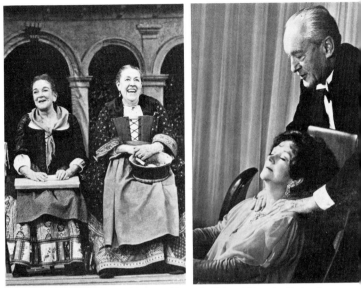

Above left: Making tagliatelle with Peggy Mount in *Il Campiello* at the National
Above right: George Sanders extends mystic influences in *Psychomania*
Below: 'Beryl Reid, This is Your Life!' – the moment of truth, with Eamonn Andrews and Richard O'Sullivan

Television work of many varieties

Right: 'Blankety Blank', Christman 1981, with left to right, Lenny Henry, Lisa Goddard, Terry Wogan, myself, Larry Grayson, Lorraine Chase and Jimmy Tarbuck

Below: 'Get Up and Go' with Mooncat (David Claridge) and Stephen Boxer

Bottom: As Mrs Knox with Lettuce as Balthazar in *The Irish RM*

Above, left to right: The Godchildren. Verity Stauffer ('the Boring Rotter'), Susan Reid, my niece, and Brian Holland. *Below:* The right shoes for the character. Fred is on my left

With Alec Guinness in *Tinker, Tailor, Soldier, Spy*

about dressing up, Beryl, just come in anything, I mean, just wear a beret and a mac.' I was very tempted to do exactly that, with nothing on underneath! When I told him this later he nearly had a fit!

We moved on to location at a farm in Langley, which is also very near here. In one of the barns there was a weeny little ginger kitten – a tiny little thing it was, about three or four weeks old, and dying of cat flu. There was a vet on location, because I was working with a pig, which had to be in the car and I had to say to it, 'I'm afraid you'll have to get out, because I'm a vegetarian!' So I said to the vet, 'I really can't leave that little thing here,' and he said, 'Well, it won't live, you know, Beryl. I'll give it a flu injection, and you can have nine pills for it, but just don't let it near your other cats.' I called this kitten Ronnie, after Ronnie Corbett, and today he is the most beautiful great big butch, goldeny-ginger tom cat. He looks as if he's wearing cowboy chaps; his knickers are rather thick at the back, and he's lovely! Of course, he had his nine pills and got better, and that was absolutely wonderful. Whenever I see Ronnie Corbett I always say, 'Your child's doing very well, thank you!'

In *No Sex Please, We're British* I was able, perhaps for the only time in my films, to wear really glamorous dresses, even though I was playing a fairly strait-laced mother-in-law. Evelyn Laye had played her on the stage, and no one would ever have thought of asking her to wear anything but elegant clothes, so I got the benefit. The only thing was that while she was called Eleanor in the play, which has kind of an elegant ring, they changed my name to Bertha. I never did figure that one out.

It really hurt, turfing that pig out of the car. You see, I have a great affinity with pigs, and years ago I even bred them. I had a field in Wraysbury with fruit trees in it – and, because I had more time then, I used to have a lovely time up a ladder pruning the seventy-five fruit trees and looking after the pigs. I had thoroughbreds: I had a Large White sow, a Saddleback and a black pig, and I also kept a Landrace boar called Fred Olympus and a Landrace sow. The Landraces are the long Danish pigs, and, because they're so highly bred they don't make very good mothers – they roll on their babies. The commoner pigs, like the Large White and the Saddleback, are wonderful mothers and never ever kill a baby by rolling on it. Pigs are very intelligent and they're as clean as the owners allow them to be. By nature they are very clean animals.

Animals play a great part in my life and I do a lot of work for them. The RSPCA, Animal Vigilance, any worthwhile animal charity you could name, I work for extremely hard. I'm *horrified* at all the cruel things that go on, such as the shipping of live cattle across the Channel, when they are not fed or given water. This is something I would fight to the death over. I want them to be shipped as carcasses and not as live cattle, because this is a cruelty that could so easily be prevented. There are cold stores on ships: there is absolutely no reason why they should be made to suffer in this way.

You should never take animals for granted. Like humans, they can be full of surprises, and they're extraordinarily intelligent. At another farm in Langley, there was a herd of Jersey cows, terribly pretty – they've got very pretty faces. Every night quite an ordinary black-and-white cat used to round up the herd of cows at milking time. It would nip their heels, this teeny little cat, and drive them in to be milked. He'd been doing it for years, but whether he's still alive and with us yet, as A. A. Milne said, 'unfortunately I forget'.

Having virtually started 'on the wireless', I have always loved it as a medium and still appear on it whenever possible. One programme that I was on a great deal at this time was 'Petticoat Line'. Anona Winn, one of the great names of early broadcasting, was the chairperson, and Renée Houston, a regular panellist, gave full scope to her outrageously dotty Scottish ad-libbing. Once Baroness Stott said, 'My children went to Lady Barne

House and they absolutely hated it. It wasn't fair, because Miss Jenkin-Jones liked *you* – but not them!' It was quite extraordinary to hear all this from so many years ago. I really enjoyed speaking off the top of my head again, without any sort of rehearsal, so different from plays and films where you have to stick to the script. On the panel you had to answer quite smartly, as you do these days on television in 'Blankety Blank', which also goes ahead without any real rehearsal.

'Petticoat Line' was great fun. The programmes came from the Playhouse on the Embankment, and the show was devised by Anona Winn and Ian Messiter. On different programmes I met Mary Whitehouse, and took to her immediately, and also the late Isobel Barnett, Sheila Van Damm the racing driver (whose father ran the Windmill Theatre), Rachel Heyhoe-Flint, the wonderful lady cricketer, Barbara Cartland, and my old school chum, Marghanita Laski. And of course no programme presenting 'the feminine viewpoint' would have been complete without Germaine Greer. It was, as you can see, rather a mixed bag.

I enjoyed telling stories for broadcasting, and this again is something I do to this day. Roald Dahl's book *Kiss Kiss* is full of brilliantly macabre short stories, and I was asked to read one on television, called 'The Landlady'. I didn't read it, I learnt it by heart, and it was very sinister indeed. It's about a young man getting a job in a bank, and he goes to Bath, where he's been recommended to a little hotel. He sees this lovely big fire in the fireplace, a dog sitting on the mat and a parrot in a cage, and there is a great feeling of warmth about the place. The landlady opens her door and says, 'Ah, there you are, dear, I've been waiting for you. . . .' But I won't tell you any more, because if you read *Kiss Kiss* it will spoil the end of the story.

I reviewed the book on Radio 4's 'Choice of Paperbacks' with Norman St John Stevas. Once before he had, I thought, been fairly rude to me, when he said, 'Who are you supposed to be married to now?' and that made me fairly ratty. I can't remember what I said, but I'm sure it wasn't all that polite. He had chosen, for his book, the work of St Teresa of Avila, and I, of course, had chosen *Kiss Kiss*. There were four books under review and we had to read them all – which was a great chore for me, because of the dyslexia. St John Stevas had criticized my choice, Roald Dahl's book, a book I had thought was absolutely great – extraordinary, but great – then I was asked what I thought of St Teresa.

I said, 'Well, I can't understand it at all. If she wanted to do so much good, she should have got out and done Meals on Wheels and mixed with a lot of people – not just shut herself away in a nunnery. In that way, surely you're only pandering to what you most want to do. I felt her work would have been so wonderful if, like Jesus, she had gone among the people and fed people and cared for them outside the nunnery.'

I had a fairly fierce argument about this, but I do feel that what you have to do in the world is help the people you are nearest to, or make yourself nearest to, and the people who are in need. I'm sure St Teresa was a wonderful person, I was just rather incensed by the fact that he was Joe Dogmatic about it. I will never have just one religion rammed down my throat. Actually I did read and memorize some of the things that she wrote, and they were marvellous, revealing and very, very compassionate. So I wasn't being totally obstinate. I did admire immensely the things that she wrote.

Harry Secombe and I were always getting up to larks, and shortly after this uplifting radio experience I played Anne of Cleves to his Henry VIII. I always dreaded him landing on that bed, because I thought he might go through it. He was not the slim Harry that we know now, but just as lovable.

Then I appeared with the Goodies. I *love* the Goodies – Bill Oddie, Tim Brooke-Taylor and Graeme Garden. They're all so clever in their own ways, and Bill Oddie is a great musician. I think I'm the only other person in the world who has been on that 'bicycle made for three'. It's an amazing thing; you mustn't ever turn your handlebars if you're not the front one, because these have to guide all the others. Of course I made several errors and we all landed in the ditch. I played Mary Whitehouse, disguised under the name 'Desirée Carthorse – anti-filth campaigner' – and I said to them, 'I don't think you should be too silly. I think we should really act this out in a fairly straight way.' They said, 'Oh, yes, yes, of course.' Have you ever seen them be straight? No.

I got off the bicycle, we laid it down, and I immediately fell down a hole. They said, 'Oh, I see: you're going to play it straight, are you?'

I appeared in a couple of shows with Val Doonican, who never sang a wrong note, and gave me a wonderful book of Irish fairy stories. I sang 'Walk Tall' with him, dropping my voice somewhere down to my boots, and I also had to sing 'She's a Great Big Healthy Lump of an Agricultural Irish Girl', which, of course, I found terribly difficult, but he found dead easy. The whole appeal of his singing is his ease and charm.

Ronnie Fraser is a very splendid actor, and was adored in Hollywood, when he came over with me to do *The Killing of Sister George*, because he is so very English. I was cast as a lady called Mrs Low Road Jones in his programme 'The Misfit', called *On Paperback Revolutionaries*. My greatest pleasure was to play opposite Freddie Jones, whom I admire so much as an actor. We used to exchange pleasantries on the pavement when he was in *The Dresser* at the Queen's Theatre and I was in *Born in the Gardens* at the Globe – the stage doors were our common meeting ground. In the play about paperback revolutionaries he was making high explosive bombs and I, as the Welsh Mrs Low Road, was determined to get him in the end. I always rode a bicycle, and showed black knickers with a bit of lace.

I remember I was standing in a barn shivering, because it was pelting with rain, and a young actor who was in the play said, 'Would you like a Fisherman's

Friend?' I said, 'Well, I'd have anything at this moment.' Of course what he meant was one of those lovely throat sweets, because, standing out in the wet and cold, my throat was getting worse and worse.

There was a fraught moment or two on the 'Edward Woodward Special', because, though our side of it was going quite well, they were badly behind with the musical part, and I was delighted to see my old bosom buddy William G. Stewart, with whom I worked several times on the Patrick Cargill show, 'Father Dear Father'. He'd popped in from the next set and whispered, 'How's it going?' I said, 'Like Pearl Harbor' – and nothing else needed to be said.

The next month I found myself in another TV play, called 'Will Amelia Quint Continue Writing "A Gnome Called Shorthouse"?', in which, believe it or not, I again played an author, the Amelia Quint of the title. This was a good play, written by Roy Clarke, produced by Jacqueline Davis and directed by James Gatward, whom I got to know terribly well. I think he's now the head of Southern Television. I was dallying with glamorous young men in an exotic foreign isle, instead of getting on with the business of writing children's books. The publisher had a deadline, and we all know what that means! It was a wonderful vehicle and hard to learn, as I remember. We used to rehearse in Kingston and you had to get there very early to get a parking place. I think Roy Clarke is a fine writer and I've always hoped that he would write another play for me, but that hasn't happened yet. I did enjoy being Amelia Quint, though, and the other pleasure at that time was that my friends Terry and John Hacking were still living in Kingston, and I used to have frequent meetings with Terry. Sadly Derek, my husband, who had brought us together in the first place, was no longer in my life. In fourteen years of marriage we had had some wonderful times and so many laughs, but a relationship can only take so many disappointments, and, to avoid being hurtful to either of us, let's just say our two ships finally did pass in the night, and leave it at that.

10

The National Theatre

With so much going on in my life, taking stock was a luxury I simply didn't seem to have time for. After *Sister George*, which occupied, in all, four whole years, the sixties soon passed into the seventies and every year was full to the brim. It reminds me of a great cockney character, the comedian Jimmy Wheeler, who had a line in his act which always made people laugh. He was talking about when he thought he was drowning: 'My whole life passed before me: I enjoyed looking at it, too!' But I didn't have time for looking – I just got on with it, and only now have I looked back. Like Jimmy Wheeler, I find I *have* enjoyed looking at it. Mostly.

Between the years of 1967 and 1969 I fell in love and had a wonderful love affair with someone who everybody told me was totally homosexual; I was on the wrong wicket, I was a hopeless case and I would never win. There was no question of winning: we loved each other very much and my whole life was very satisfactory at that time, physically and emotionally and in every way. But of course in the end I had to accept what people had told me: homosexuality did win. I was the loser, but I did have a very, very happy time and so many laughs with this lovely man.

Once he did say, 'If I ask you to marry me, promise me you'll say "No".' I think he felt he wasn't up to that, because he'd seen his mother quite badly treated by his father; it was very kind of him and it put me a little bit on my guard, but I was so vulnerable at that time I couldn't be very much on my guard.

171

This whole experience was absolutely wonderful, and the only sad thing is that I was left at the end with a heart that was knocked about a bit. But not, of course, for the first time. I mean, all through my life I've had knocks – who hasn't? – but that's all part of living, and it's all part of making your character up.

I was asked to go to the National Theatre by Bill Bryden, one of my favourite directors. He's very Scottish and terribly handsome, and looks exactly how I imagine Robert Burns looked. But he also has a great deal of common sense. He asked me to do a part in *Spring Awakening*, a classic play by Wedekind, who wrote it at the age of twenty-four. Cyril Cusack was in it, and Peter Firth, who'd had such a stunning success in his first part for the National in *Equus*, Jenny Agutter, Bryan Brown, who is now a top film star in his native Australia, and also Veronica Quilligan, the young Irish girl who played my daughter. I had never had the chance to play this sort of part before. It was totally straight with no funny lines at all. I played a German mother who never told her daughter about how babies happened. I completely failed her, and simply said, 'It's because people love each other.' Then she had a great romp in the hay with Peter Firth and became pregnant, because I had explained nothing.

It was an extraordinary play, and it had been banned for years, because there were some very risqué scenes in the borstal to which Peter Firth's mother (played by my friend Susan Engel with whom I dressed on tour) had her son consigned, because she was so bitterly jealous that he had actually been to bed with a girl. He had his head shaved and it was horrifying. I, in my turn, did an equally bad thing to my daughter, having thought I was a lovely mother: when she told me she was having a baby, I got hold of an abortionist, but said to my daughter, 'Things will get better, things will get better.' When this Frau Schmidt came round, I opened the door to her. I said, 'Oh, you're late, do come in,' and that was the end of the scene. The girl died.

It was very harrowing, but a wonderful play for me, and it was Bill's confidence that allowed me to do it. In the meantime he had the idea that I should play the Nurse in *Romeo and Juliet*. I said, 'I can't possibly do that, Bill: I'm doing "Those Good Old Days" on Sundays at Bournemouth.' I did two shows every Sunday, presented by Robert Luff, with Arthur Askey and Walter Landauer, from the end of June 1974 and all through the summer months.

I said, 'I can't be the Nurse, I can't be the Nurse – I can't learn it, and I can't do all those journeys.' But he really is a big event, Bill Bryden, he can talk you into anything. He said, 'Och, come on Beryl' and I said, 'No, no, no.' He'd sat in the pub where we went, next to the Old Vic, and he'd written me a long letter, saying, 'It'll break my heart if you don't play the Nurse in *Romeo and Juliet*.' So I had no option. I said, 'Well, I'll try, and if I can't manage to do it all, Bill, I'll just have to give it all up!'

He was quite satisfied with that. Only one thing worried him at the rehearsals: he kept saying to Peter Hall – 'Do you think she's ever going to know it?' Peter Hall said, 'Oh, I'm sure she will,' but they were both quaking in their shoes.

After we'd done a run at the Old Vic with *Spring Awakening* we went on tour and I stayed with my friends Alan Rook and Dennis Woodford. Denis and I would sit all day while he'd hear my lines in *Romeo and Juliet*. We had terrible clues: I could never remember things like 'By my troth', so we made 'Ma Troth' into a landlady, so I'd associate 'Ma Troth' with 'My troth', and it became quite easy. Of course, I had learnt the play by the time we opened, and nobody had to be shaking in their shoes.

I used to cook a chicken every Sunday morning before going to Bournemouth, where I had a hotel room booked for three hours – sounds rather tarty, but it wasn't, because the manager was very stagestruck and Margaret Bissett, Joan's daughter, used to be my minder and drive me back after the two shows. We had our lunch, and then I slept for an hour, watched some old television on Southern TV, woke up, got made up, packed up, went over to the Pavilion Theatre – and there we were, ready to do two shows. We drove back at eleven o'clock at night. It was really quite an experience.

I was actually doing three things: Frau Bergmann in *Spring Awakening*, Old Time Music Hall with Arthur Askey, and the Nurse in *Romeo and Juliet*, doing a gigantic what they called in those days 'Mobile' from the National. This meant you did one-night stands, and that wasn't easy at all. We did eventually have a little run in the National Theatre and that was much more comfortable.

I had a great feeling for the Nurse, because again I'd been helped and I'd done a lot of research. I didn't realize that the wet-nurses used to breast feed the children till they were seven, because all they had to put them on to afterwards was rotten meat, marinated in wine, and that's why the death rate of children – very young children – was so enormous: they had nothing, after the breast feeding, suitable to take its place. That's why the Nurse was so demented about Juliet, because she had had two children while she was feeding her, which Juliet's own mother never did. Because she hadn't got milk enough for Juliet and her own children, her own children had died.

To me it was a tragedy, really, though she was perfectly happy, and that's why she was so absolutely incensed and demented when she thought Juliet was dead. The one thing she didn't understand was love. She understood sex very well, because she was still in the market, and this is why she should never be played by somebody very, very old. She was still flirting with all the boys in the street. Of her husband she says, with great feeling, 'Oh, ah were a merry man!' and I can imagine her dragging him out of every pub that she passed. She tells of how he taught Juliet to walk, and how she stumbled and had this great lump on her head because she'd fallen forward, and he said, 'Oh, when you're old enough you'll fall backwards and lie on your back, my love.' She did not understand when Juliet said, 'I love Romeo,' a love expressed in some of the most beautiful words ever written.

> ... And when he dies, I will
> Take him and cut him out in little stars
> And he will make the face of heaven so fine
> That all the world will be in love with night.

But the Nurse couldn't understand why she wouldn't have any young chap that came along. She didn't understand the difference between love and sex and that was her only failing. But she loved Juliet very much.

I did wonder what prompted Bill Bryden to ask me to play parts so very dissimilar from anything I'd ever done before. He was busy rehearsing his new production of Clifford Odets' *Golden Boy* when Eric Braun went to see him, but he gave his time and help with the kindness and understanding that I've always found so endearing. This is what he said:

I'd just joined the National Theatre, and I was doïng Wedekind's *Spring Awakening* in a new version commissioned from Edward Bond. The play is mostly with children, it's a very young cast, with only two really major adult parts, Mrs Bergmann and the man at the end, who is the author. When I came to the National there were two people I wanted very much to work with. One was Beryl Reid, the other was Cyril Cusack, both of whom I managed to get into the play. I have a feeling that performance is performance. You can tell about certain performers like Beryl and to an extent, in recent years, like Dave Allen; you know that if they can do what they do themselves, they will be able to bring that performance sense to a role. They tend to be very good actors. I'd seen Beryl, of course, acting in *Sister George* on the stage and in the film: I'd seen her as a panellist, as a comedienne, as a revue artist, so I was a kind of a fan. I just – the way one does, one plays a hunch – I immediately thought of her to play this part.

I think it was the right time for both of us. We met, we liked each other very much and we became very friendly: there was nobody else in my mind for the part, and Beryl said, 'If you think I can do this I will do it.' I thought it was right for her to have the status of being at the National Theatre or the RSC, and I think it's right for people who have come out of the real show business, the real vaudeville, if you like, to be seen in these centres of excellence.

She was superb in the part. And then, thereafter, the same company (a very young company, as I've said) did a touring production of *Romeo and Juliet* and I asked her to play the Nurse. She was very fine. Yes, she did have her doubts at first, because my taking on *Romeo and Juliet* was in a sense a last-minute thing; John Dexter had been set to produce it, then he got a job at the Metropolitan Opera House in New York, and Peter Hall asked me to take over the *Romeo* production, which was for these young people and Peter Firth to play Romeo. It was a thing called a Mobile, which is a kind of barnstorming tour of university theatres and so on.

Well, it was a very tiring thing for her, because she was already committed to do her Sunday shows in Bournemouth, and the idea of travelling from Basildon to Bournemouth, then back to Hull or Stockport in what she called this 'ENSA Tour' understandably did not appeal to her. But finally she did it. It was important for her to use the time at the National playing a classical part; and of course since then she has done the Restoration plays and my feeling is she should do still more. With Beryl it's the question of finding the time to do one thing and then another; for example, I think it would be good to see her in revue again.

The hard thing in the National or the RSC is judging the length of engagement: there's no point in coming unless you're coming for a decent time, and yet there's no point in playing something like Mistress Quickly for ever. The thing is to find a range of parts – maybe a classical part and a new play: if that situation presented itself, I'm sure Beryl would rejoin the National or the RSC.

In assessing the new play she did for us, you have to turn back the clock to 1976. *Counting the Ways* was an extraordinary situation: we'd moved from the Vic to the National Theatre in the new building. We were playing *Tamburlaine*, a nine-hour show, and we had to have something to balance that. This play came in from Edward Albee, who wrote *Who's Afraid of Virginia Woolf?* and I found it absolutely marvellous. What attracted me was that the two characters, eventually played by Michael

Gough and Beryl, had to improvise, they just had to talk to the audience about anything. Of course, Beryl was extremely skilled at that – it was second nature to her.

The play itself is quite slight, and it was a very hard play to learn. Albee told me afterwards that in America – we did the world première here – they never got the improvisations as remarkably as Beryl and Michael did. Some nights they went on for ten minutes, and the play itself only lasted about half an hour, and sometimes the improvisation, when she just talked to the audience about whatever came into her head, was absolutely breath-taking. The remarkable thing was having a comic performance by a comedienne within the structure of a play. She came on playing a character, truthfully and honestly, and then the play let that character step out of the character and say, 'Hello, I'm really Beryl Reid and here's what I think.' Some nights she got onto a kind of vein which had the audiences in stitches, and this is what I remember most vividly about *Counting the Ways*: the performance structure rather than the play itself. It was a minor play which contained a very attractive technical breakthrough, where somebody could actually *be* the character, and then tell the audience, 'I'm not the character now, I'm myself.'

Beryl was inspired, and Michael never tried to compete with her. Because of Beryl's exquisite timing and her ability to have the audience just where she wanted them, the contrast was just wonderful. They were very friendly and still are: they were a lovely couple.

At this time the National Theatre was the first public building to open in London for many years, and I think the play got a more hostile reception for being a trifle than it would now. The pressure was enormous. It was a very tough time and a very exciting time, and Beryl was one of the pioneers in there, actually doing it. It was a big thing to open this building, and part of the experience was the mobile tour getting all around from El Alamein to Tobruk. Beryl's great triumph, for me, was in *Spring Awakening*, where there were no laughs. It wasn't 'Here is this great comedienne being funny' – I think there is no funnier woman in England – it was 'Here is this little woman from Germany whose child becomes pregnant.' That was her triumph: they weren't depending on her to be funny – she was depending on herself to be true.

Before *Counting the Ways* I directed Beryl in *Il Campiello*, which was chosen for the royal opening. Probably it was too slight a play for that. The previews were all going fine – though Beryl got ill during the previews – but in the event it was like a little string quartet in a circus ring – too slight a piece for all the panoply around it. But the scene which Beryl and Peggy Mount did was particularly funny, and very inventive and good. I think what killed *Campiello* was all this Royal Opening of the National Theatre: they should have opened with something far more solid, like *Hamlet. Campiello* would have worked much better in the Cottesloe, the smaller theatre round the corner, than in the Olivier. It was, though, like the runt of the litter: one had great affection for it, but it didn't seem as strong as some of the other children.

Beryl's next, for John Barton at the RSC, was *The Way of the World*. They must have had a good understanding as she went on to do *The School for Scandal* with him. I think her need for total rapport with her director goes back to the basic thing of the relationship with the audience. To be that successful with an audience you're very exposed, you're very vulnerable and you're seeking love: you've got to have love from the people you're working with. There's nothing more vulnerable than a comic talent. It's easy to imagine Beryl getting into a depression if she feels that somebody doesn't love her or trust her. The act of being funny is the hardest job in the world.

She has a natural perfectionism, as opposed to the fuss-potty kind of pretending to be perfectionist, that makes her surprised when other people don't live by that code – a kind of astonishment. That natural perfectionism, I'm sure, from time to time during her career has given her unhappiness.

Joan Bissett was a dear friend of mine, and really part of my house. She filled it; she was a wonderful person, who died before she was fifty, and though she came from somewhere near Reading she had never been to London before she met me, which I found quite extraordinary. She worked for me for twenty years, and gradually I got her into the way of thinking that she could go to London, in a car. She did actually come to a performance at the Television Centre of a show that Harry Secombe and I did for the Queen and Prince Philip.

Joan was rather unexpected about the Queen. She said, 'She's very softly spoken, isn't she, and there's not an ounce of fat on her.' Joan was a very down-to-earth person, and the only time she kind of cracked up was on her birthday, when I used to think of treats that she couldn't possibly expect, such as for her three daughters to be there, all invited separately. I pretended I was getting lunch ready for somebody else, saying, 'Oh, come on, Joan, polish those glasses,' and 'Have you laid the table?' Then, when I'd got this lovely meal ready that I thought she would like – Tournedos Rossini was her favourite – the three daughters arrived at the door, and I said, 'Joan Bissett, This Is Your Birthday!' We toasted her in champagne – 'Toff's Lemonade' or 'Charlie Goldtop', which she loved.

There was always some terrible new scheme to give her a special birthday, because she was an extra special person. Apart from the joy of her daughters she had very little of what I call real pleasure. She was tremendously loyal: she was really one of the best friends I've ever had. Since she has died, the house is still full of her: I say that not in an occult way, I mean exactly that. Although she used to approve or disapprove of friends who called, we were always friends: we never had a wrong word. She loved the cats; she was great with the animals when I was away. She was a quite remarkable, undemanding person and just relied on me for her health.

During the three days I was at the Harrogate Festival, playing the Nurse in *Romeo and Juliet* with the National company, she died. I just couldn't believe it. But, there we are. She will never go out of my mind or heart or head. We had a great lot of laughs together, a great deal of fun. We enjoyed ourselves something rotten all the time that she was here and I know that's the best way to think of her now. I feel she's quite close always: I can never feel really parted from her.

After Henry Fielding's *Tom Jones* had been the most tremendous success as a film, Tony Richardson, who directed it, asked me to be in his next film of a Fielding novel, *Joseph Andrews*. It was most exciting to make: it was a beautiful summer, warm and sunny, and we were a month in Bath where some were even allowed to go into the Royal Baths including Ann-Margret, Michael Hordern, Jim Dale and Peter Firth (who played the romantic footman the book is about). Usually nobody was allowed to go into that warm swimming pool, but they all were – I wasn't, because I was a servant. I had to jump in during the lunch hour, when all the cameramen and everybody swam, because it was really far too good to miss.

I played a character called Mrs Slipslop, faithful servant to Lady Booby (Ann-Margret). I really was an awful slut. One tiny scene was cut out, which was frightfully important to me: as Lady Booby left the room, I put some of her lipstick (actually it wasn't lipstick, but what passed for it in the seventeen hundreds) on my mouth – or rather half-way up my nose. So I always looked as if I was eating a raspberry tart or as if my nose was bleeding. It was the joke of Mrs Malaprop again – Mrs Slipslop got all the words wrong. When she wanted to say, 'They are brother and sister,' she said, 'They're fraternally intermangled, madam!'

Michael Hordern played a vicar, and we had a wonderful scene where I was pegging out the clothes and Joseph Andrews was going off with this little girl. At the end there was a rather sweaty scene in a fourposter bed, where the vicar is mistakenly pressing his attentions on me – a case of mistaken identity, you understand – and I was astounded when Michael Hordern took his trousers off as directed, and had absolutely nothing on underneath! That was one of my few body-blows in the film!

On location I stayed at Upper Slaughter in the Lords of the Manor Hotel, and this was the first time I'd seen Jacob's sheep: they are extraordinary, they look more like goats – something awfully funny must have gone on at some time to make them that shape. They have long legs and four or five horns and they're sort of spaniel colour – liver and cream. They were in the field opposite my bedroom, and absolutely fascinating.

The people at the Lords of the Manor were so kind to me: again, it was like living in somebody's beautiful house. We did two days' filming at Upper Slaughter, which was lovely because I could just run home or sit in the cottage allotted to me. When I got home in the evening they always had a brandy waiting for me. 'You must be so tired,' they'd say, 'you must have a brandy.' I would go up to my bedroom, and if I hadn't rung down for a meal within half an hour – when I have to get up so very early I find I have to go straight to bed – they'd be on the phone to me saying, 'Are you all right, and what would you like for your supper on a tray?' There was a cat called Lord of the Manor, a beautiful great big black cat, who became a close friend of mine.

The first scene we did was in a coach on the road, one of those terrible roads where all the dirt flew up. I learned at that time that when people shouted on the street, 'Buy my lovely white oysters, buy my lovely white cake,' white was not a colour to them – it meant clean, before all the dust from the streets had got on things. Nobody ever washed then except at Whitsuntide, when they got married. They'd throw their winter clothes away, burn them and have new ones for the wedding. They just got dirtier and dirtier together, so they didn't really notice. I think this is why Whit weddings are very frequent still. Also at the time mothers had very young children's teeth taken out, so practically everyone was toothless. They sold the teeth to elderly gentlemen and said, 'If you hold it onto your gum it will grow a root, and become an established tooth.' This, of course, was not true, but they tried, anything, really to make money, because they were all so desperately poor. This was a century I became very involved in.

Eleanor Fazan did the choreography for the film, and I ended up by having a wonderful time with Tony Richardson. I rather dreaded him to begin with. My first day of shooting I was in this carriage and Tony said, 'Do something funny!' I said, 'No – you're the director, tell me what to do that's funny.' There we sat, staring at each other. But soon after he got me into the coach, he knew it was going to be funny anyway, because I'd established Mrs Slipslop. Then he'd get silly. He'd say, 'I think what we'll do, darling, is put a few pigs and hens in there with you, and a cockatoo . . .' So I'd say, 'Tony, you're being silly, and if you get silly like that, you'll just have to go home!'

When we were in Bath Tony created what would then be described as a traffic jam. There was a flock of sheep: because I was a servant, I had to sit on the very top of a four-in-hand coach. The aristocracy were inside and I was sitting with the luggage. The coach-driver said, 'You know, Beryl, if one of those sheep goes under the horses, we've had it!' – which of course I could understand, because the horses would bolt, and, as there were four of them, and they weren't all the same temperament, this would be the natural thing to do. He also had sedan chairs, every sort of possible vehicle, and some bullocks charging about in the middle.

This was his great big inside joke: he made his way across this little square, which was crammed with every sort of thing in the world, came up to my coach and said, 'Darling, just in case you think I'm enjoying this, I want you to know – I am!'

Ann-Margret was rather shy to begin with, but then we kind of fell in together, which you do, because making a film or doing television or rehearsing a play is like a crash course of living with somebody. She and I got on like a house on fire, and, though I think she's Swedish, she has a totally English sense of humour, and we had a million laughs on this picture. Unfortunately I haven't been in touch with her recently, but that happens in our world. It's like a piece of woven material, really, the threads keep crossing occasionally, and it's so lovely when they do.

Now, in this extraordinary order of my life, I was asked to do the stage play of *Entertaining Mr Sloane*, which was quite turn-about-Charlie, really. I was delighted, because I'd had time to think even more about Kath. Malcolm McDowell was to play Sloane, Ronnie Fraser was to be my brother and James Ottaway to play the Dadda. We opened as part of a Joe Orton Festival at the Royal Court Theatre and didn't know whether it would be successful or not, and by that time Malcolm – poor little thing, he didn't mean to do it – but he had broken my foot. I went to James Cyriacs, and he said, 'Well, all these bones leading up from your toes are broken and I have to put it in plaster.' I said, 'Oh, you can't, because I have to wear stiletto heels, and I'm opening tomorrow. I'll get you some tickets for the play and then you'll understand why I have to wear stiletto heels!'

Of course I did walk on that broken foot and work with it: Malcolm also broke my hand later on, but again he never meant to. As a film actor he was a kind of one-take fellow, but when you did it every night everything about you became absolutely smashed! But he was marvellous to work with: I can't remember when I was happier. He kind of moved into my dressing-room, he used to use my make-up and – I always have smelling-salts in the dressing-room – he used to come in and say, 'Have you had your first fix?' Then he took them too, which nearly killed him. He was great fun and made me feel exactly the same age as him – my tights were tied in a knot, there was a notice on my car from the police in Dorset . . . he just did anything to make me laugh. I had a very, very happy time.

And we did have a success, indeed Eddie Kulukundis said that it was the first play which had made money for him at the Royal Court. He transferred it to the Duke of York's Theatre, which was lovely, like old home week for me. We also had real success there. Harry H. Corbett, from 'Steptoe And Son', eventually took over from Ronnie Fraser as my brother, and, when Malcolm had to do a film, Kenneth Cranham stepped in – he'd also been in *Joseph Andrews*.

We had a pact in that show, which was rather good. In the interval before Act III, I said, 'You must all come to my room and have a glass of whatever you want, and if anybody's done anything that annoys anybody, we must all talk about it — nothing must be allowed to fester, because I do realize that sometimes, if things are not brought into the open, they're allowed to grow into something that's quite out of proportion and much too big.' So, at the interval, everybody used to come and have a drink with me. If they had anything to say about my performance, or I'd walked in front of them, or spoilt a laugh or whatever, they'd say, and if they'd done it to me *I* could say it: we could all say exactly what we wanted, and nobody was offended. That was an absolutely satisfactory way of dealing with any situation because, as I say, things do fester, people don't speak out and, with a company of four people, it can become very, very difficult indeed.

Although I had never met Joe Orton, his brother and sister came round to see me at the Royal Court. They come from Leicester: people think Orton's plays are written in the cockney idiom, but they're not, they're written in exactly the way people speak in Leicester. When his brother and sister came round, they said, 'Did you ever meet our Joe?' I said, 'Oh, no, I *wish* I had.' They said, 'You know, when you had that mauve dressing-gown on with the bit of maribou and the high heels — ooh, you were just like our Mam!' I wondered then what 'our Mam' had been like and I wondered why Joe Orton so obviously hated women, because there are some very cruel lines about women in the play. I don't think it could have been because of 'our Mam', because they seemed to be very fond of her.

One night at the Duke of York's, a couple decided to have it off in the stage box, which is in very clear view from the stage. Malcolm was whispering, 'Look at them!' but, as usual, I was so busy on stage I couldn't really see: besides, I had my back to them! The couple were obviously so engrossed in what they were doing they didn't know or didn't care that they were also visible to a large part of the audience. When someone made a complaint, the manager tapped at the door of the box and asked them to 'desist'. 'Oh,' they said, 'That's all right, we've finished' – and left! The ghost of Joe Orton might have appreciated the situation. I had a phone call from Malcolm in California not so long ago. He said, 'Have you got a room for me? My name's Sloane!' The fool!

Betty Milne dressed me then; she was what would now be called my minder, and she is the most fantastic dresser. She now automatically comes with me wherever I go in London, and we have a great relationship, because she knows everything that goes on in the theatre; she knows when to speak, and when not to speak. She's a wonderful woman.

She came to me after dressing Dandy Nichols at the Savoy in *The Clandestine Marriage*: she will only work in London because, as she says, she 'can't live in a suitcase' because she 'loves the comforts of home'. She has a beautiful flat, and I know just how she feels. She did say, though, that if there was an occasion when I needed her desperately, then she'd 'tour'. She only does commercial managements, too, because places like the National have their own dressers.

Everything was marvellous about *Mr Sloane* [she writes], Beryl always had hordes of admirers and visitors backstage. Her dressing-room is never dull. I remember one occasion we were leaving rather late on a Saturday night, and we got out into the front of the theatre. There's a regular busker in St Martin's Lane, and it was summertime and Beryl was looking very glamorous in a white suit and a white turban hat – with her rollers underneath, I think. The busker started to do a little tap-dance and a song, and Beryl joined him. It was wonderful: within seconds we had a crowd all round as they did their little session, then Beryl said goodnight to him, and we went home. Of course people knew who she was: Beryl only has to say 'Hello' and they know.

Born in the Gardens at the Globe was also very interesting – and very successful. Our little Saturday night jaunts to the garage to get Beryl installed in her car were also crowded with incident. Soho was very hectic then, about four years ago, and we used to have little happenings on the way to the garage, like getting involved in conversations with drunken lads, which were very entertaining. Boss-cat was a Soho cat: he was an alley cat and he was barred from the Globe, but every chance he got he was into the Globe and in Beryl's dressing-room, and of course the stage doorman recognized him by his smell. He was a real alley-cat, a dirty cat, and he used to do naughty things. Then Brendan would be on the warpath looking for him. He came from the market, and, of course, Beryl can't pass a cat, so she spoke to him, and he probably watched where she was going and that was it. He was stagestruck!

The theatre cat was Beerbohm, and he also roamed the dressing-rooms and made his mark. He was a dear little cat, rather strange at times, and very temperamental, which is understandable. Beryl used to entice him into the dressing-room, and he'd come in when he felt like it. Otherwise he'd sit outside the door. We had great fun about that: we did everything to get him into the dressing-room, but if he didn't want to come in, nothing on earth would make him. And there was a beautiful cat who lived in the little hut with the car park attendant: Beryl would send meals over for him, and I know she wanted him – everybody did, but he was eventually adopted by one of the council people from the little flats nearby. He still visits the car park, but he has a comfortable home to go to. I think his name is Tiger.

Beryl's home at Honeypot is just like fairyland to me. The cats are beautiful, the river's lovely and it's all very Beryl. Hardly ever does anyone find somewhere that's just right for them, but it is perfect for Beryl. I can't imagine anyone else in the Honeypot – only Beryl.

She does everything from the heart: she gives so much, people don't realize that she never stops and it's all for the benefit of people to make them happy and their lives brighter. Cats, too, of course, but it's not only cats, she really cares for people. Some time ago we went to the St Martin's crypt when she went to open something. All the homeless people were there – all the strays of London and it was for their benefit. We went down into the crypt and there were all these people, very shabby, very weather-worn and some sort of people that I personally wouldn't like to get too close to. When Beryl opened the function they had stars in their eyes, these old layabouts, when they were watching her. And when she got off the platform one man went up to shake her hand and she kissed him, which was so moving. I said, 'Beryl, how could you?' He looked so dirty, as if he'd been lying in the gutter. She said, 'That's nothing. We're all the same.' It was a real lesson in humility: she has that gift, and she uses it.

I think – and I must say this – that Beryl ought to be Dame Beryl. In my opinion she's given everything to this country, she doesn't work for people abroad, she works for people generally. She loves this country, and she's a true blue and I would be happy to go to my Maker if Beryl was given this recognition.

Betty's right about my love of country. Nowadays, like old wine I don't travel well, and I'm very happy in the British Isles. I don't believe in living abroad to dodge taxes; if you're taking from the land, you should also be prepared to put back. When I look at my home I think, You've been very, very lucky.

For sheer beauty and romantic associations I can't think of anywhere more appealing than Glencoe. But then, when I first went there I was in the *Half-Past Eight Show*, and had fallen madly in love with a man called Conway Stuart. I seem to have so much love that it gets distributed from time to time! Though we were so hard worked we went to Loch Lomond many times, because I had a car and there was a wonderful family there that they called 'the mad Colquhouns of Luss'. I did actually swim in Loch Lomond. It was then that I discovered that there's a great difference between lochs and lakes. A loch has an inlet and an outlet – this is part of my useless knowledge I'm passing on to you! – and a lake is still water. Of course the lochs are always ice-cold and don't get any warmer, because of the water coming in and out.

We visited Loch Katrine and then we went to where my ancestors fell: Glencoe. We drove there on Sunday morning and came back at 5 a.m. the next day. At Glencoe the Campbells attacked the McDonalds, which is my mother's clan. It's the most riveting place, very narrow, like a pass would be in mountains. There were beautiful, beautiful pink-coloured rocks, and it was really frightfully romantic driving into Glencoe. I realized that here was an ideal place for the Campbells to jump on the McDonalds, who were going through the pass all unsuspecting. They massacred all the McDonalds who were on that mission. In the middle of the loch there is an island which is called the McDonalds' grave, and, of course, they just chucked them all on there and that was the end of that.

Leaving at 5 o'clock in the morning, we saw stags in the middle of the road, in the mist: it was really an unbelievable setting. I'm just sorry that my ancestors fell there. But when my aunts used to say, 'There was never a good Campbell, Beryl,' they had never even been to Glencoe, so they knew none of the atmosphere that I discovered.

Conway Stuart, incidentally, married the ballerina Rosa Apollinari, who was in the show at that time. She was an Italian–Scottish girl, one of the great contingent of Italian families in Glasgow, and a lovely dancer. So he obviously wasn't as much in love with me as I was with him. But that was just part of it all.

Bill Bryden has told you about the play *Il Campiello* from his viewpoint. On my side I was looking forward eagerly to acting at the new National Theatre: I hadn't been there, and it was fascinating to be in a play which Bill had translated from the Italian as well as being about to direct. I think he'd seen it in a very small theatre in Italy and fallen in love with it, but it obviously wasn't the right play to put in that great big theatre for a royal opening. The Olivier wasn't an easy theatre in those days: there were no real signposts and none of us could find our way about. I cracked it eventually – I got from the stage door to where we were rehearsing, which was a great achievement – but I made more friends than I ever did in my whole life, just asking them the way to get there, or, do you know where I am, do you know what I'm doing?

We had a sort of mock set, because there was so much climbing up stairs, as we were supposed to be living in a tenement in Italy. The families were always having rows and interfering with each other's lives and it was a great deal of work running up and down those stairs and just going to one window to shout 'Hey!' or something equally riveting. We went on rehearsing and then I thought, I'm going to be terribly brave and not go to the canteen for my lunch, but, instead, I'll bring my own lunch to my dressing-room and have a quiet three-quarters of an hour looking at the words and thinking about what I'm doing.

I hadn't realized I didn't know my way back from my dressing-room to the rehearsal room, but I knew we were working in a batten of light, so that was what I was looking for. I walked along all those corridors, demented, and then suddenly I saw a lot of light. Oh, good, I thought, that's where we're working, and I walked straight onto a stage, like the one we'd got set up. Oh, God! There was a play in progress! Not *Il Campiello* but *Tamburlaine the Great*!

I looked a mess! I was dressed in terrible old black trousers and a black sweater, and I had my shopping basket with me. I had that dirty-face-and-hands feeling that you get when you're rehearsing. On the other side of the stage there were a lot of people in gold, and I didn't recognize any of them. Albert Finney was there, acting his socks down, and then I looked and saw the audience. I thought, This is the worst thing that could ever happen to anybody – the great thing is, don't panic, and walk off slowly. So I did so. Perhaps the audience thought that it was some marvellous message in the play that they were being given and they didn't quite understand.

Albert Finney didn't realize I'd been on, and it was only when we met months afterwards at some great reunion that I told him that I'd had a walk-on part in *Tamburlaine*: 'That was the only performance at the National that I haven't been paid for!'

We had a buffet supper with the Queen and Prince Philip after the *Il Campiello* opening and they chatted to us a great deal and it was all a wonderful experience, but I felt there'd been an awful lot of running up and down stairs with very little result. The scene with Peggy Mount, mentioned earlier on by Bill Bryden, turned out to be successful in my mind because we actually made tagliatelle; we cut the pastry into these very thin strips, which is how you do it, and hung them over the backs of the chairs while we gossiped about what was going on with the other people in the apartment.

Counting the Ways was a quote from Elizabeth Barrett Browning's poem 'How do I love thee? Let me count the ways'. The play was set in Boston, where the author Edward Albee was brought up and, of course, was a two-hander – just Michael Gough and myself on that enormous stage. It lasted a very strange length of time, not long enough to make a full programme, so we got a bit pushed about when we did get on, because we were either before a show, like a curtain raiser, or after one.

Michael lives in Windsor, and we used to drive backwards and forwards rehearsing the play. One terrible night I was so glad he was with me. My car had been stolen and my whole house ransacked from top to bottom, and everything of value taken. This has happened to me three times, so really now I have nothing of value left to take. It's no use bothering to do a robbery here, because there's nothing left. I think perhaps that's the best way: one shouldn't hang on so closely to possessions, though I was very upset at the time, because all the jewellery my mother left me and grandmother had given her had been taken: that's totally irreplaceable. She would have said, I know, 'Well what does that matter, Beryl? You're all right. You're alive.' That's the only way you can look at these things. But that evening I was totally stripped of everything. Broken double glazing – awful – a terrible mess they'd left. Michael said, 'Now, what I'll do is make you a cup of tea.' I said, 'Oh no, you won't – you'll get me a brandy!' because I can't bear tea, it's one of my pet aversions.

The most challenging part of the play came when a neon sign lit up behind us on stage saying, 'Identify Yourselves'. Michael said, 'You go first,' and I said,

'No, you go first.' This bit was all scripted. Then we had
to get up and do five or ten minutes or whatever – it was
like the Quakers, they speak when the spirit moves them
– but we had to get moving pretty quickly. We had to get
sharply onto our hind legs and say, 'My name is Beryl
Reid,' 'My name is Michael Gough,' and then get on
with it. I made a list during rehearsals of all the things I
could possibly talk about, so when I was getting made-
up, I used to cross them off one by one and think, Oh,
that's what I'll talk about tonight. I had sixty or seventy
stories, but the terrible thing about the National is you
get every message that comes to the stage door and every
call for every theatre on the speaker, so it is frightfully
hard to concentrate. I didn't wonder that one or two of
the loudspeakers in the dressing-room had been ripped
out by actors who had practically gone off their chump
listening to all these messages – and very gentle actors,
too, I can tell you.

I found it very easy, because of my early beginning in
variety, just to say, 'Good evening, ladies and gentlemen,' and simply chat to the audiences. I got a lot of
laughs just telling them things that had happened to me,
but that was my natural way, my upbringing in the
theatre. Michael used to say the most extraordinary
things, sometimes, like, 'I'm sixty years old and I'm
looking down the barrel of a gun!' and, 'When I went
home, so distressed with tears streaming down my face,
and went into my little daughter's room, she said "Never
mind, Mickey Gough – it'll all be all right!"' The
audience were really upset by the end of what he had to
say, although it was marvellously clever and terribly
revealing – really soul-baring time.

I had to do a very funny but very long speech about a
girl going to a prom, and she was allergic to the smell of –
it was written in the script – camellias. I said to Edward
Albee, 'Camellias don't smell.' He said, 'Oh, don't they?
I didn't know that.' I said, 'No, gardenias have this very
strong smell.' The first beau called to take her to the
prom, and he pinned a gardenia on the right-hand side of

her dress, so she spent a lot of time with her face turning to the left. Then a second beau arrived unexpectedly, and he too was carrying a gardenia, which he pinned on the left-hand side of her dress. She said, 'There I was, listening to this music, with no direction to turn my head!'

There was also a great thing about my husband in the play, Michael Gough, who was used to having crème brûlée every day. I said, 'Today there is no crème brûlée.' 'No crème brûlée – what do you mean? No crème brûlée?' I said, 'Well, when you're making crème brûlée and you have it under the broiler – that's the grill to us – you have to remember that this is no time to gaze into space, to think of nothing, to let your mind wander – because otherwise it gets *burnt*!' Which is why he hadn't had crème brûlée. There was a long explanation about how to cook it, which thank goodness I knew before I joined the play, because it might not have been right. I would have had to make the correction, like the camellias.

It was a very adventurous play, a splendid play to be in, and though it couldn't be described as a total success it's something I wouldn't have missed for the world. And it was a joy to meet Edward Albee: a very shy, retiring, softly spoken gentleman from Boston, who, I think, was adopted by the people who brought him up. It's a very rich family and he was always covered with gold, which I didn't envy, but it was very nice to see. I got on well with him and liked him so very much.

11

This Is My Life

My passion for cars goes right back to childhood. I've always driven myself to work, sometimes hundreds of miles at a time, so much so that some of my friends have thought occasionally I was being silly. When I was taken to the Motor Show and could afford it, I bought a Lancia Fulvia Zigato, which was very 'goey', except it was really useless for driving into London every day, because it has twin carburettors which have to be tuned – so you spend all the time at the garage with an expert carburettor tuner, who is something like a piano tuner! I then went to a BMW, so when Teddington Television asked me if I would go and do a programme called 'Drive-In', I felt I had really quite a lot to say on the subject.

I prepared a little programme, including some of the improvements I believed should be made, like windscreen wipers on the side mirrors. I also thought there should be windscreen wipers on the headlamps, because when you're on the motorway in dirty weather, everything gets gunged up so you haven't got clear vision or good lights – you haven't got anything that's good – and you get the spray from all the other cars.

I was quite prepared to go and do this programme about cars, but when the day dawned I had Olivia and Terry staying with me in the flat I had then in London, and I said to them, 'I don't want to do this at all – I feel awful.' Then Joan Bisett's daughter, Margaret, who was helping me in the house at that time, said, 'Why don't you have your hair done?' I was supposed to be going out to dinner, and she obviously thought this would cheer me

193

up. I said, 'Not likely, I'm not going to bother to have my hair done to go out to dinner!' Margaret said, 'Oh, it would be nice if you had your hair done' – everybody tried to get me to make the best of myself.

Terry Ward, Olivia's husband, took me to the car and I said, 'I don't feel a bit like going, Terry: the back of my nose is all raw and I feel as if I'm going to have a cold, and I feel thirsty. . . .' He said, 'Oh, well, you'll feel better when you get there.' I said, 'What I'd really like to be doing is staying at the flat with you and just watching the television and having a bit of a gas, you know, a gossip.' But I got into the car and drove to Teddington Studios, and they interviewed me, and I thought it rather strange that at that time in the afternoon – it was about half-past three or four o'clock – the bar was open. There was this one lady, whom I knew well because I've been going there for years and she said, 'Now, would you like a drink, Beryl?' She expected me to say 'a Courvoisier brandy', but I said, 'No, actually, I feel as if I'm going to have a cold; I'd like a glass of soda water with a piece of lemon in it, you know, nice and cold – a long thirsty drink.' She said, 'Oh' – and was really quite disappointed, but she said, 'Well, that's fine.'

I thought this was a little bit strange, but obviously they knew I was doing a programme and thought I might be thirsty. I said, 'Will I be able to get into the car park?' That is an impossibility at Teddington, unless you've had your name down for three weeks, but they said, 'Oh yes,' and there was the car I drove in, I think it was a BMW, and a lot of other cars assembled there, all of which I drove round the car park. The one I liked very much was a Scirocco, which is a Volkswagen, and so I said, 'Oh this is a smashing car – I'd love one of these,' and, in fact, I've had nothing else since – I've had three of them, because if I keep them for two years I get the maximum amount of service out of them, without them having to be sold for nothing.

I did try an enormous car, which cost something like £46,000, and was hand built, but it had an automatic gear-change and I've no time for those. I like *driving*, I like actually changing gear and being in charge of the car. I said, 'Oh, no, I wouldn't have one of those: I'm sure it's beautiful, but I certainly wouldn't have automatic gears,' so that was that car written off in one.

They said, 'Are you ready to start filming?' I'd got this rather nice little suit on, which is something I would have worn outside and I asked if I should put some make-up on. They said, 'Yes, just an ordinary sort of television make-up,' which I do myself anyway. I always say to the make-up artists, 'I'll do it, and you make all the improvements!' and then nobody's offended.

I started talking, about my invented windscreen wipers and how fabulous I thought cats' eyes were in the road and that they were one of the best inventions of the century; then I saw this big car pull round and Richard O'Sullivan was driving it. Eamonn Andrews got out and I thought, 'Whyever has he got make-up on – how ridiculous!' Still nothing – I mean, I must be very thick – but nothing entered my head. He came over to me and said, 'Beryl Reid, This Is Your Life!'

I said, 'I'm very sorry – I'm very busy with a programme called "Drive-In", Eamonn. Get off' and sort of pushed him back. He said, 'No, no, this is your life.' I said, 'No, no – "Drive-In".' This was the opening of the programme, of course, and eventually it dawned upon me that it *was* my life. I was in a total state of shock and he said, 'Just leave your car there.' I said, 'Who's going to collect it?' He said, 'That's all arranged,' and we were on the way, driving to London and I said, 'Nobody'll be there, Eamonn – everybody I know is dead! What am I going to wear – I've no clothes with me,' and so on. He said, 'No, all that's been seen to; Margaret's bringing your dress.' I said, 'How's she going to know what dress I want to wear?' And, of course, she did bring exactly what I would have chosen to wear.

I had no idea what was going to happen. I was put in this very nice dressing-room with a lot of little presents around it, and flowers. Knowing me, they had this security man standing outside, because they knew I'd try to get out to see who was going to be on the programme. I was really quite well behaved and didn't try to escape. Little did I know what was in store.

My brother Roy was there and his wife, Pat, my niece Susan, my nephew Peter and his wife: Andrew Gardner was there, Richard O'Sullivan, of course, whom I'd done a television series with at Teddington, called 'Alcock and Gander', Jack Tripp, Reggie Vincent and Pat Kirkwood – lots and lots of people – and Warren Crane, my dearest, dearest friend from New York was flown over as my big treat after they'd located him in some motel in California. Mind you, I don't know what he was doing there, but as he's Californian-born he was probably doing something quite all right! It was the most over-exciting evening in the world: in a way, I don't think they should do it to people. Unless you've got a very strong heart you could drop dead with excitement.

I was so excited I couldn't possibly go to sleep for two nights after seeing all these people, having not really realized at all that it was going to happen to me. I hadn't had a clue; Olivia and Terry knew, Margaret knew – that's why she tried to get me to have my hair done – everybody but me knew. My brother and his wife had had to register in a hotel under her born name, which is Hall, so they were Mr and Mrs Hall, not Mr and Mrs Reid – they and Reggie and Jack Tripp and all the people who were going to be on the programme had stayed at the same hotel, had all had breakfast, lunch and dinner together for the last three days and been driven about in a great white Rolls-Royce all over London, peeping round corners in case they saw me.

You can imagine it is one of the biggest possible surprises in your life. The marvellous thing is I have photographs of my brother, who has died quite recently – I am very fond of him and miss him dreadfully – I have his voice on record, and that is something I would never have had, unless this had happened to me, because he was very shy altogether. It was only occasionally, when he'd been here a little while and had a couple of Pimms, he would perhaps juggle with three oranges and say, 'This is the life, you know, Beryl,' and that sort of thing. We were so totally opposite, yet we were such great friends.

One of my dearest friends, William Chappell, who has always piloted me through my own shows, often called just by my own name, usually has to be billed as the 'Artistic Director', because he doesn't work for the BBC. We have done several, which have been a combination of tried and true sketches that have always worked for me, and new material as and when it presents itself. Robin Nash has produced most of the programmes, but Billy Chappell put all of the words into our hands, into our mouths – everything. In one of the 'Beryl Reid' TV shows Malcolm McDowell came in and we did an extract from *Entertaining Mr Sloane*, while John Standing and I did a rather jolly Noel Coward number where we wore tail coats. We made rather a mess of it at rehearsals and Billy gets terribly angry if I do it wrong or if I forget the steps and don't concentrate. This time we had Derek Fowlds, who I'm also rather crazy about – he's a built-in giggler and has a face creased from laughing – old friend and dressing-room mate Susan Engel (the other mother in *Spring Awakening*) and Avril Elgar, who I think is one of the best younger straight dramatic actresses we have in this time. I liken her to Eileen Atkins – they're not alike at all, but that's just me.

Bill produced or staged or was artistic director of the two all-star TV variety shows at the time of the Silver Jubilee, 1977. The first, at the Palladium before the Queen Mother, was one of Harry Secombe's annual *Fall In the Stars*, and I'd been a bit what they call in Scotland 'peely wally', which means really not at all well, with a bright white face, and I had to go home immediately after I'd done the number 'Big Spender' with Harry – 'So good-looking, so refined'. I was a very seedy, very tatty waitress and he was an absolute lout, who'd come into the café. But after the dance we did at the end of it, I just had to go home. The Queen Mother did say, 'Why isn't she here?' and Harry told her, 'She's not been at all well and she's had to go home.' That was indeed my loss.

Night of 100 Stars was at the Olivier Theatre in the new National: Robert Nesbitt was producing the whole shoot, and Billy Chappell was doing the music hall section. It seemed to me that the others' songs sounded so good, and I was lumbered with 'Burlington Bertie'. I heard Barbara Windsor, Dora Bryan – even Penelope Keith – sounding off with lovely numbers, and I said, 'Oh, Billy, why have you given me this awful song? Why have I got the worst song? Because you don't care about me!' Billy and I have terrible shouting matches; in a way we use each other in this terrible way. When we've nothing else to say, we say it to each other. But he had, very cleverly, given me an extraordinary step to do. He said, 'Do it whenever you can.' I answered, 'Oh, all right, then' – I was terribly ungracious to him, in spite of my great love for him.

It was done as a sort of cabaret, the music hall thing – and all the stars were on the stage. The rest of the show had been all the big musicals from the past, from *Floradora* on, and everybody had been in them. I thought, Right, Billy, you've given me this terrible step and I'm going to let the audience know it's extremely difficult to do. There I was, dressed as a tramp, doing 'I'm Burlington Bertie, I rise at ten-thirty', and I did this step whenever I possibly could, and, to my total amazement this number stopped the show. I'd done it many times before and it had never been such a success – all the people on the stage stood up and applauded; I had a standing ovation from that audience, and I really don't know why. I dread doing it again, because I doubt that I could ever recreate what happened on that night. Something extraordinary happened, and there it was.

I was so over-excited when I left, that in the National Theatre car park I backed my car straight into one of those stone pillars that confront you there. I've swanked about being a good driver, having passed the advanced test, but I was so sort of drunk with power and overcome by the success of it that I didn't care. So I'd bashed my bumper in – what was that compared with the triumph of that evening! It's something I really will never forget.

I'm sorry to keep saying 'my dear friend', but I have so many dear friends, and John LeMesurier, who died recently, was one of the dearest. He played an elderly vicar who had been married to Dandy Nichols in David Mercer's play *Flint* on television. As she didn't want to go to bed with him, I was given to him as a sort of wedding present, being a younger sister. It was a very strange and, I thought, splendid play, perhaps because I so enjoyed acting in it. I loved meeting Dandy and of course being with John. Besides, Julie Covington was in it. In the part I was a bit batty: the vicar kept being drummed out of every church he went into, because they all seemed to be set fire to, and they thought he was doing it – but really it was Dandy Nichols who was doing it all. I pushed her wheelchair and collected the petrol, and she set fire to the churches. In the end I murdered her – there was a great knife in her back which we eventually saw – but I had a wonderful speech climbing up a ladder in the conservatory saying, 'Oh, d'you know I had a most wonderful dream last night: Jesus was in a white suit and a beautiful blue velvet cap, and he was batting for England!'

I was, of course, totally dotty. I remember the director Peter Wood said, 'When you sort of collapse after explaining to John LeMesurier why you did it, we're going to keep the camera on you for quite a long time, while you're sitting under this ladder. We might get a lot of things out of your face then, that would tell us all the meaning of it.' So I sucked my thumb and I cried, and I did all the things that I imagined people who had had temporary mental lapses would do. It was, again, a great time of learning.

I also worked with John in a television film called *An*

Honourable Retirement. I was his landlady and I was absolutely besotted by him. He never really paid any rent, because he used to go out fishing. He'd bring back fish for me, and I'd say, 'I think that's £7 off the bill, at least,' and so on. Donald Churchill wrote the script that I thought was full of meaning. John, poor John, got mixed up in a spy plot which he had absolutely nothing to do with: he'd been a perfectly ordinary civil servant, and suddenly they mistook him for some spy or other. They saw him going up to London – I gave him sandwiches and so forth; I was a very cosy landlady, because I was so enamoured of him – and when he got to London he was surrounded by people who were catching spies.

We did most of the filming in Swanage. One day our driver, a frightfully dishy young man called Tony, accepted my invitation to dinner with John and his wife Joan, to repay some of the lovely meals I'd had. We ate in a beautiful restaurant in Lulworth Cove on a superb day – just like today, when I'm writing this. We sat out on the veranda, and had fresh crab to start with, then fresh lobster, and white wine – we were all so barmy about seafood. Tony had arrived in an immaculate suit, just right for the occasion, as my guest, and it seemed to me to be an idyllic day. We got into his car to go back to Swanage, and my only thought was bed, I was so tired and happy.

Then a very strange thing happened. Tony got out this little pipe. It was a very beautiful pearl pipe, and it was handed round. I thought, I can't be left out of this, I don't know what it is, but I'll have some. I can't inhale, you see; that was the trick about smoking five cigars a performance in *Sister George*. I don't inhale, though I do admit that I looked forward to tasting them, and that became a habit – but I've never smoked one since. This exquisite little pipe was full of something that everybody appeared to know about; it seemed something very exciting that I ought to join in, and, of course, it turned out to be pot.

I had smelt pot, when I was in Hollywood – I could smell it as I went past the rooms – but I'd no idea of what it was like to smoke. I was like a stupid child, really. The others all took great drags, and I, because I couldn't inhale, said, 'Oh, how lovely, thank you' and blew the smoke straight out (even if I try to smoke a cigarette now, that's what I do). I watched them all get so relaxed and contented, and then they all told me, 'You'll sleep like a baby when you get home.'

It was absolutely wasted on me. But, of course, because I'd done this, when I got back on location, the crew used to say, 'Would you like a cigarette?' I said, 'Well, I don't smoke.' And they said, 'We know you don't smoke. But you *smoke*.' And it became a very sinister thing: of course, I would put them out as soon as I wasn't being watched. It was, for me, terribly disillusioning, this pot smoking. I've never done it since, and I'd never done it before. I wouldn't consider it, because I think it's rather an expensive habit, and really a bit dangerous. Anything where you lose control, to me, is dangerous. But this was something that John and Joan, as Joan has written in the *Mail on Sunday*, both enjoyed. This was my first and last experience of it: I suppose, as Mae West sang in a movie when she was eighty-five coming on a hundred, 'You Gotta Taste All the Fruits'.

That was, though, an absolutely wonderful day at Lulworth Cove, though I didn't sleep like a baby when I got back, just kind of tried to suss out what I was trying to do. But the whole experience of that film with John was memorable. His wife Joan is very dear to me: when she came to Honeypot, she said, 'You see, this is Shangri-La. You must get older when you leave this house.' I said, 'That's just what happens to me, Joan.' So she really understood how much I love it.

John played a part which required him to be terribly brave. He got into this grist mill, where they grind the corn, and he did about eight takes, where he was absolutely squashed and suffocated by the corn falling at great speed through this iron contraption set up by the villains of the piece. (Of course, in the film he had nothing to do with being a spy; he had been mistaken for somebody else.) But for him and me it was a very, very happy experience, that was the last really big thing I did with him.

John Betjeman was the last person who brought John LeMesurier and myself together professionally. Writing one's life story seems all too often a case of recording goodbyes to people you've known or loved or admired. I had met the late Poet Laureate many years before, when my husband Derek was playing in a cricket match at Pusey House, a very beautiful house in Oxford, the sort of place with a great lily pool on the terrace – the most gracious sort of home. They introduced me as 'Beryl Grey', which wasn't a very good start. But, never mind, I recovered from that, and spent most of the afternoon with John Betjeman.

It was confession time for him, because he said, 'You know, the people I most admire are the music hall stars. My great hero is Eddie Gray, who was in the Crazy Gang. I can't believe that there's anybody funnier in the world than Eddie Gray.' We had a marvellous afternoon together, and his daughter came up and said, 'Oh, you know, Daddy's quite dotty, I mean, I ask friends round and I feel so ashamed, because he sits a lot of teddy bears on chairs round the table, and I have to explain to my friends that he's quite batty. He talks to all these teddy bears during the time that we're having tea, and you know how ashamed you are of grown-ups.' I was a grown-up, but this was the sort of effect I've always had on children: they don't ever think of me as a grown-up person. So this was her sort of confession about him.

He did come to see me in *Born in the Gardens*: I was terribly pleased, but he was rather ill at the time and couldn't walk downstairs to my dressing-room, so I walked up the stairs to the stage door entrance. I was dressing below ground.

During the day it was always, 'Hello, carbon monoxide', because the cars from the mini-cab business opposite used to asphyxiate me below ground level with their fumes. Also all the guys I knew who were almost vagrants used to spill their meths down my wall when they fell asleep against my window, and I used to try and open it to get a little bit of air. I must say the smell of burning methylated spirits is something I don't want ever to experience again – unlike the smell of oil lamps, which takes me back to my very early childhood in Dunure, where we had oil lamps. That and tar, and matches that have just been struck, are wonderful smells – very nostalgic smells to me, because they all belong to my childhood.

Anyway, a man called Charles Wallace asked me if I would appear in a thing for the big screen called *Late Flowering Love*, based on some of John Betjeman's poems. I was to be in one of the stories, called 'Feed The Fowls', playing alongside Susannah York, John Alderton and Eric Morecambe. Also, this was a time that I was going to meet John LeMesurier again, though we didn't actually have scenes together in the film, which was planned as a very special kind of short.

We ran out of money, and the last shot I did of it, sort of for nothing, was done in pelting rain and freezing cold in a field in Wraysbury. I couldn't go on into the evening, as I had to get back for the show at the Globe Theatre. The first scenes were done in a lovely country house, but miles from where I was appearing, so I always had to leave in time to get back for the performance of *Born in the Gardens*.

The Wraysbury set-up was a totally different atmosphere – not at all glamorous picnics or anything like that. When I went back to the house on my own, hot noodles were handed round. When Charles Wallace said to me, 'Can't you run any faster?' I said, 'Well, actually, I wasn't engaged for the running. I was engaged more for the acting.' I realized in the end that they had totally run out of cash, and I was just there for good will, to finish off what I hadn't finished when we were filming on this beautiful location.

Charles Dickens' *Nicholas Nickleby*, turned into *Smike!*, a rock musical by Paul Ciani, the producer, and John Morley, didn't please everyone, but it was great to play the part of the appalling Mrs Squeers, the headmaster's wife, and there were some good lyrics and music by Simon May and Roger Holman. Leonard Whiting, the Romeo of Zeffirelli's film, turned out to have a smashing singing voice, and in particular I liked young Ian Sharrock who played Smike as a boy. Again, it was a case of instant friendship with a bright and talented youth; we had so many laughs and exchanged so many confidences together. Andrew Keir, who played my husband, is, of course, a true Scot and, again, the feeling of sympathy was mutual.

My only Bernard Shaw play to date – and I hope I'm asked to appear in another – was brought my way by Cedric Messina, who adapted and produced *The Apple Cart*. Nigel Davenport was the King in Shaw's political comedy, set in the year 2000, and I was Amanda, the Postmistress General. It was a very difficult play to do, because we were actually supposed to be seated in the parliament of that time and you had to be frightfully careful not to nod off during the spaces between the speeches, which could last anything up to fifteen minutes. You had to be sure to be looking intelligent when they came back to you. But we did have very comfortable chairs.

For the very first time I flew in a helicopter – it was wonderful. In fact, Shaw gave them their name although helicopters had not even been invented at that time, when the Queen said, 'Oh look, here come the helicopters from Downing Street,' as we were flying over Blenheim Palace at Woodstock. It was a great experience to fly in one sitting in the front, with a breath-taking view through that unbreakable false glass beneath you. I couldn't believe it: I was very, very excited! I remember I had green fingernails, because we were trying to imagine what it would be like in the year 2000. At that time I had just leant to fly in a Cherokee, and I was given lovely things by the helicopter pilots because they thought it was rather smashing that I should have learnt to pilot a plane.

In the same play Shaw said, 'Great wealth will be brought from the North Sea.' Nobody at the time had any idea about the oil: that was just another of his remarkable prophecies.

I have two favourite quotes of his: the one I've already mentioned, 'Be sure you like what you get or you'll get to like what you've got.' This is something I try to remember whenever I start doing a play and I get obsessed by the people in it, and fall in love with all of them. You may have had doubts about the play when you start to do it, then, because you are mad about rehearsing and the people in it, you forget that this is a danger – this is *really* a danger in the theatre. He was the one person to point it out.

He also went to a very grand dinner party one evening, and said to a lady sitting next to him, 'Would you sleep with me for a thousand pounds?' In those days, of course, a thousand pounds was a tremendous amount of money. She fluttered and said, 'Oh well, I don't know, it's rather silly, but I suppose I would – yes.' He said, 'Well, would you sleep with me for five shillings?' She said, 'How dare you? What do you think I am?' He said, 'We've already established that – we're now haggling over the price!'

J. B. Priestley's *When We Are Married* is now also established as a classic. I played Maria: Thora Hird, Eric Porter, Richard Pearson and Patricia Routledge were also in it. Ronnie Barker played the photographer, which is really quite an exceptional part, which so many great comics have tackled.

I always enjoy doing things like this – but you can't help feeling that the comedy is dated. These things don't really, in my humble opinion, stand up today, unless you regard them purely as classics of their time. We were very well matched all of us, very happy to do it; we had a lovely time, no doubt about that, the director, David

Giles, was great and the end product was all right. To be married for twenty-five years and then discover that you're not married at all was a horrible shock to everybody in that period. And that is, really, the great joke of the play. The husbands walk out in high dudgeon and so do the wives, and nobody's speaking to anybody.

I've followed Hywel Bennett's career very closely from the time he was a very young actor, playing juvenile parts, and I think he's now one of the best young actors that we've got. Having played his way through a series in which he was a murderer and did away with his wife in the Victorian era (he was totally convincing) I don't ever want to miss him in 'Shelley'. He's so outrageous, never wanting to go to work, but he's actually put his finger on the button, because so many people now don't want to do a good day's work for a good day's pay and that's why we're slipping down a bit. But he's made it into a very funny situation, and I admire him with all my heart. I met him in a repertory company some years ago and he's a very nice person, but, above all, a marvellous actor.

I first really got to know Judi Dench when she played Millamant in William Congreve's Restoration comedy, *The Way of the World*, presented by the Royal Shakespeare Company at the Aldwych Theatre, for which Judi has a specially soft spot because she'd met her husband Michael Williams there. I was cast to play Lady Wishfort, and the most awful thing happened.

It was reported in one of the gossip columns that Judi and I had delayed rehearsals because we rowed all the time. Now we have never had a row in all our long friendship. I feel nothing but pleasure in knowing her and being fond of her. The goodness just shines out of her. Together we rang this press office, and the company manager was with us. I said how dreadful it must be to be a third-rate citizen if you had to make up lies about people to earn a living. I was appalled by it, and Judi also spoke to him, though not quite as harshly as I did. The excuse was, 'There's somebody in the company who tells us these things.' I said, 'Then tell us: here's the company manager. He'll deal with whoever it is. Is it a male or a female?' He said, 'Oh, it's a man.'

I'm sure it was a lot of nonsense, and when I went to the greengrocer's by Covent Garden Station they said, 'You been duffin' up Judi again?' I said, 'No, no.' He said, 'There you are, I told you she wouldn't do anything like that!' But, you see, people do read these things, and believe them, when nine times out of ten they're absolute rubbish and invention.

In this RSC company, I watched people work really closely as a team, because they would never let anybody be in a hole. Roger Rees was one of them, and he's done marvellously well since in *Nicholas Nickleby* and everything else. We used to give each other presents of Lemsip, because we all had colds the whole time and were in such close contact we couldn't help re-infecting one another.

They were all lovely to me. I had just been accepted to play Lady Wishfort because they hadn't anybody in the company to do it, but they made me feel like one of them. They worked together like pages in a book: they never would let anybody dry (forget their words) on the stage: somebody would always step in. I got the message then about how wonderful it was to be in a really bonded-together company, something I'd never fully experienced before.

Discussing Lady Wishfort with the director John Barton, a brilliantly gifted man and an academic, I found he had read her as something of a grand lady. But I saw her as someone who had pulled herself up from the gutter and married well. When she talks to her maid, it's in terms that she understands. Lady Wishfort must have experienced life in the lower orders. She really has no illusions – glancing in her mirror she describes herself as an 'old peeled wall' – but she's going to do everything she can to paint over the cracks and present herself as desirable to young gentleman callers. That was the way I played her, and I believe John was quite happy with the result: the notices for everybody were very approving indeed.

I did repeat part of it on television in one of the 'Beryl Reid Shows' for William Chappell, 'artistic director' – Billy, who is my Svengali when it comes to revue, because he makes me do things I don't believe I can do. It was the scene from *The Way of the World* which I had rather invented myself, when Lady Wishfort is expecting this gentleman to call. She's going to practise all her moves: she's practising dangling her foot off a little from the chaise-longue where she's reposing. I got into a terrible physical mess, and the end of the speech is, 'There's nothing so alluring as a levée from a couch.' By this time I'd got my heel caught in the back of my very long dress with a train on, and I was flat on my face. This was just a little thing of invention with Congreve's words going through it, and nobody could knock him.

Or, indeed, Richard Brinsley Sheridan. Having done Mrs Malaprop on television it was doubly exciting to be asked to play the part at the Old Vic, and opposite Anthony Quayle, who's a great man, a lovely man; he's Dorothy Dickson's son-in-law and married to Dorothy Hyson, star of so many British movies until she left the acting profession to help him run the Shakespeare Memorial Theatre at Stratford-upon-Avon.

Sir John Clements was originally directing it, but we didn't seem to get on very well. I don't quite know why, but I think he just had very set ideas about it. If people have set ideas, they say, 'This is how we *did* it': that is really absolutely hopeless for somebody like me. When I'm given a part, I never stop. Each night I try to create something and add to it. Eventually Anthony Quayle took over the direction.

But, at that moment, you know, God wasn't on my side. I was sitting at home, and somebody had come round to hear me do the words – of course I have to have a lot of hearers because I'm not very good at learning, as you know – and I was talking on the telephone. I've got a rather long lead on it. I had three dresses over my arm, and I didn't know that the telephone cord was wound round my ankle. I stepped over the bed with the three dresses on my arm (I always step over it, I never walk round it) – but I was trapped by the wire, fell flat onto the floor, and broke my arm in three places.

Yvonne Dalpra, who was hearing me, said, 'Are you all right?' I said, 'Oh, yes, I just hurt my arm, Yvonne.' She said, 'Your face has gone very white.' I said, 'Actually, I won't do the words immediately, if you don't mind – I'll just lie down for a little while.' She said, 'I'll give you the number where my husband and I are and if you want us, ring us up.' It was a Sunday, which made it all doubly difficult.

I didn't know how badly hurt I was. I always try to ignore it all, but you can't ignore your arm being broken in three places, and within an hour I was crying on the telephone, saying, 'Please help me, take me to an emergency person or a hospital, or anything.' They were marvellous, Yvonne and her husband Terry O'Connell – Dalpra is her stage name – and they rang their doctor and said, 'Could you please come to our house in Datchet and we'll get Beryl Reid there – help her, because something terrible has happened to her arm.'

Dr Smith-Walker, who has been my doctor ever since, is wonderful and was actually there before them. He rang up all over Windsor, all over everywhere, and eventually he found a specialist. I had an X-ray on a kitchen table and they found out about my arm. These days they don't choose to set them; my arm was just bound to my body, and Dr Smith-Walker used to come every morning at 8.30 (because I went on with the rehearsals) to rebind it. Terry, Yvonne's husband, then had a garage in the East End, and he drove me to the rehearsals at the Old Vic every day.

I even had my clothes designed by Jean Hunnisett so that my hand could appear sort of out of the middle of my bosom, and I had lovely little butterflies all round it and things like that, but, in spite of everybody's good will and good wishes – and Anthony Quayle and the whole cast were wonderful to me – I just couldn't make it. So I never did *The Rivals* on the stage. I was so sure I could do it that I went on rehearsing until we were almost due to open. But sometimes I don't win, however determined I am. Margaret Courtenay, who had played Madame Zinnia in the London run of *Sister George*, took over from me at very short notice. My mother used to tell me that when I was in my cot I used to cling to the end of the rail and push my knees back and stand there and defy her. I suppose that is part of the determination, which hasn't turned out to be a bad thing. But, as I say, I don't always win.

I really had to sit back then and let my arm get better, but it wasn't all relaxation. I had to work like stink to get the arm moving again, because when something's been broken, the muscles all go. I had a pulley attached to the ceiling, and I used to pull my arm up. It's very strong now, but only because I worked so very hard. It's awfully easy just to let injured limbs hang about spare, and not really get them into use again. But otherwise during this time, for almost three months, I was just lazing.

The next lovely thing I was able to do was recorded for radio at the Redgrave Theatre, Farnham, and put out on both Christmas Eve *and* Christmas Day, 1978. It was called 'Beryl Reid's Christmas Collection', with Billy Chappell again doing the 'artistic direction', while Brian Patten was in charge of the overall production. Spike Milligan contributed two marvellous items: one was his poem called 'Christmas Day' – a very short poem, which goes:

> A little girl called Emily Jotte
> Said 'Oh, what a lot of presents I've got!'
> A little girl in Biafra said
> 'Oh, what a beautiful slice of bread!'

Spike does write the most amazing things. The other thing of his which I did was called 'The Singing Foot', one of the funniest things he's ever written. It's about his uncle who works in a laundry and is fifty-two years old.

He's terribly happy going home on the bus, when his foot suddenly bursts into song, and unfortunately he doesn't know the words of it, he can't even mime to it, so he has to get off. As he walks home, it sings 'God Rest Ye Merry, Gentlemen', which he *is* able to mime. He does, however, have trouble during the night, and has to sleep with this singing foot in a bucket of sand, because it will do selections from *The Desert Song* at about 3 a.m. In the end he has to shoot the singing foot. Now fifty-three, he still works in the laundry, but walks with a slight limp.

We had things that Paul Dehn had written for me, bits of *Alice in Wonderland*, A. A. Milne – everything that we could possibly think of, and I did enjoy it. I didn't think I would, because of the reading, but, again, I had practically learnt it all, so that wasn't so difficult. Yvonne Dalpra was with me and we sang a song by Arthur Macrae which I later did on television, 'The Pretty Miss Brown and the Other One'. I was 'the Other One'.

Still on the mend, I almost immediately flew up to Scotland again – to Glasgow to do the Hogmanay programme, 'Out With the Old, In With the New' – this was mainly girls. I met Janet Brown again and Aimi Macdonald, Rikki Fulton (great in drag or any old way), Lulu and Molly Weir, whom I hadn't seen for years. This was New Year's Eve, a time I don't really like working, but it was a very orderly sort of audience. We didn't do it at midnight, when people in Scotland go mad and do all their first-footing with bits of coal and salt that they take round to the houses, and, of course, it's got to be a dark person who comes to first-foot you. It was done early in the evening, before the rot had set in! I found it very exciting to be with all these Scottish people again, and to hear the bagpipes and to do all the dancing and things that I love. I did a number called 'Technique', which was written by Robert Gould and I'd kept from the Watergate days. It was just short enough, and just long enough to register.

I enjoyed doing 'Blankety Blank' from the very first one,

but didn't realize that it was going to stick to me for years. I had met Terry Wogan on television once before, and I instantly got a great feeling of being at home with him. I *love* doing the show. You really don't rehearse it at all, you do some almost silly questions with the people on the panel that you're *not* going to meet and they record two shows at once, so you meet the people on the second show's panel, as it were, and not any of those in your own, to influence them. So you just try and answer the questions and play the game.

Terry Wogan and I have a great feeling of safety when he gets to where I'm sitting. There's a fairly established pattern: there are two layers of people, and I always sit in the middle at the top. There's the bird who's knocking on a bit, which is me, with a comic on one side, and somebody perhaps like Patrick Moore at the other side, and when Lorraine Chase is in it she's down in my left-hand corner. There's an outrageous comic in the middle, then there's some lovely girl on the end seat.

The whole point of the game is to get points for the contestant: if the contestants play properly and don't try to be smart alecs and give outrageous answers to the questions they're asked, we can match them up. You just have to get on the same wavelength as the people. If they're nervous or showing off, then you can't get points for them. It's a game that has really become part of my life, I'm afraid. I know lots of people don't like it or think it's rather infra dig: I don't. It's done me nothing but good, and to Marcus Plantin, who asks me to do it, and Terry Wogan, who's lovely, I really give thanks for having given me such a great opportunity on television just to be myself. I play so many parts that it's wonderful to be given this kind of chance for a minute and be totally abandoned. You know it can all be cut out if you say quite the wrong thing.

The great thing is the head-to-head at the end, and usually if I am on the programme I am asked to do that. I remember once I could have kicked myself because I got one wrong. It was 'Semi – Blank', and I just hadn't looked at this man carefully enough. I'm sure it would have sprung to everybody's mind, like it did to mine, 'Semi-Detached'. If I'd studied him a bit more carefully – and there's very little time to do this – I might have guessed that his answer would be 'Semi-Final'. He was a football fan, and I hadn't studied that carefully enough in the few seconds I was given.

'Blankety Blank' was, of course, absolutely slated by the press: we were ridiculed for even appearing in it, which, looking back now, is extraordinary. I've just kept on and on and on doing it.

Panel programmes, serious and funny, educational and silly, go back to the early days of 'the wireless' and received a new lease of life when television became popular. I do have my favourites, as the last few paragraphs may suggest. Intellectuals may grumble and confine their viewing to 'Mastermind' and so on, but the panel and the quiz is here to stay, so there's nothing to be done but sit back and relax, or turn off. For me, if the personality of the host, chairman or whatever, appeals, and if he or she is good at the job, then I love being on them. At the same time as 'Blankety Blank', at the end of the seventies, I was constantly in 'Celebrity Squares' with Bob Monkhouse. He's a very sensitive man, not at all as self-possessed as he appears. He worries all the time about people not liking him, and yet he's got one of the fastest, smartest, wittiest brains that I have ever come across; he's never at a loss for words.

Bob was the chairman, and I was on 'Celebrity Squares' so often I met or re-met almost anybody you care to name in the show. Spike Milligan, for instance, can be either a wonderful or a dreadful experience, because you never know what he's going to do. He's totally unpredictable. Willy Rushton I didn't get to know well then, but when I met him again later I got very fond of him, when I did the television version of the classic radio show 'Does the Team Think?' with Jimmy Edwards and Tim Brooke-Taylor.

When I did do 'Celebrity Squares' we couldn't talk as

much as we would have liked, because we were all divided by squares. Magnus Pike hardly had room to wave his hands. When I appeared with him on 'Any Questions?' for David Jacobs I discovered during the dinner beforehand that he never waved his arms once – we even had drinks, and they all stayed in his glass – but as soon as he got on he did a great deal of waving; so I think it might be called his 'gimmick'.

I had seen very little of Dick Emery since 'Educating Archie', when he joined us the last year of the four that I was in that programme. He asked me to be a guest on his 'Comedy Hour' on television, and that was another bit of the weaving of the tapestry that goes on through all our lives in the profession. He was very, very creative in his humour; he had a lovely voice, too: there was really nothing much he couldn't do. Eric Merriman, who has done me several favours in the way of writing, did a sketch for us which, I think, turned out to be quite funny. That was just another job I enjoyed: you see, the whole thing is, I *do* love it! This is what it's all about.

I have made several appearances on 'Give Us A Clue', but I really don't feel I'm very good at it. You have to read those postcards very quickly, and I'm frightened that I'm going to make a mistake. Once I did misread one of the postcards (I don't mean me, Miss Reid, but mis-read!). In my frenzy about the reading I read 'Friend' and I kept sort of linking arms with somebody and walking round. In fact, the word was 'Fiend'. I had got it totally wrong.

Michael Aspel said, during the break, 'Do you want to do another take?' I said, 'No; I think people ought to know that you can get it wrong, that you can misread and not be right.' Of course, I was really telling myself what I knew about myself in that programme, although I loved being with Lionel Blair ('Come back soon!' he said at the Watergate, and I keep doing just that) and Una Stubbs, whom I've known for years. She actually gives me credit for something, because she was going to play Aunt Sally in 'Wurzel Gummidge' and she said, 'I have to be really beastly!' I said, 'Well, Una, if you've to be a baddie, you have to be a real proper baddie, and never play for sympathy or try to win the audience. You've got to be really rotten!' And, of course, it's as foreign to her nature as it is to mine. She was a great success in 'Wurzel Gummidge' and she always thanks me for being the one who forced her to be really frightfully bad.

You can go off people, you know; but I keep finding you can be wrong about them, or rather, about their assessment of you personally. I always enjoy doing 'Looks Familiar', but originally I thought that Denis Norden didn't like me very much. But he's been so very gracious and affectionate towards me since, that it proves that I was absolutely wrong. It's a lovely show to do, because you can look back, you can wallow in the past, and I can look at all the people I worked with, like Jimmy James, Revnell and West, and Wilson, Keppel and Betty, who were absolutely riveting. I believe there were about seventeen Bettys altogether: I knew a great number of them, including the mother and the daughter. But the men were very interesting, because they were very industrious in the dressing-room. They had lathes – things that you make shoes on – and they used to cobble shoes, or do woodwork between the acts. When you were a turn in variety there was nothing to do while you were waiting to go on, unless you had industry in the dressing-room, or unless you were watching practically all the time, like I did in the beginning.

Once I had got to know the acts, I didn't watch all the time: in fact, I made myself cami-knickers, stitched with French seaming, 'the like of which a nun might envy,' and I did it all by hand, always in the dressing-room. Of course, my eyesight was very much better then than it is now, and all my underwear – nightdresses, everything – were made by hand. This was because we had time to spare.

There was a magazine then, called *Lilliput*, and in it was something that appealed wildly to my imagination, called 'Sillistrations'. Wilson, Keppel and Betty and I

215

had endless fun with these. There were always little captions under these drawings – for 'She tore up the stairs!', there would be a lady tearing a lot of stairs. One was 'Striking a happy medium', showing a man with a mallet behind a very jolly-looking lady gazing into a crystal – he's obviously going to hit her on the head! There was also 'Make the table shipshape', with somebody putting a mast up the middle of it, and sails. I had – and still have – the most ridiculous sense of humour, but Betty and I used to think up our own Sillistrations, like a 'Pretty kettle of fish', which had to be a very pretty kettle with fish in it. We thought of dozens, but they're not easy to come by, and always when we met we used to say, 'Have you thought of any more Sillistrations?'

When I do things like 'Looks Familiar' I have a chance to see those people again, and I'm very happy at that. Apart from Denis Norden, whose little asides are marvellous – I can't remember any of them, but viewers will fill in the blanks; they're all totally quotable, but not by me, because, like The Boring Rotter, my brains have fallen out – one person I did totally enjoy being with on that programme was Roy Hudd. He's such an Old Time Music Hall buff. He really knows everything about everybody: he's a great Max Miller fan and has such tremendous knowledge of the very early theatre. From time to time he sends me a selection of old numbers that he thinks I might find useful if I ever do Old Time Music Hall again – and no doubt I will. I was so glad he was able to put on in the West End that show about Flanagan and Allen, *Underneath the Arches*. It was obviously something he knew and loved and got great pleasure from. He's very clever: I think his 'News Huddlines' programme on radio is brilliant – I don't know how anybody does it, really. I certainly couldn't.

Finally, prompted by all this parade of 'Looks Familiar' people I worked with – a backward glance to the most unlikely stripper of all time, Phyllis Dixey. She was married to a very low comedian called 'Snuffy' Jack Tracy, whom I referred to as 'Snuffy the Cab-man'. She had such dignity and looked as if butter wouldn't melt in her mouth. She had blonde hair with a bun at the back, and she took every stitch off. She did what were called 'artistic poses'. I remember one time I worked with Phyllis Dixey, and Steffani's Silver Songsters were on the bill – Ronnie Ronalde was one of them, and they were quite grown-up boys who wore shorts and shaved their legs and tried to be twelve, but weren't. They weren't allowed on the side of the stage while Phyllis was performing, and 'performing' is the word.

But, of course, the 'flies' (where the backcloths and things are pulled up by rope to a little platform) were crammed with Steffani's Silver Songsters, all hanging over the side and watching Phyllis Dixey take off the last stitch for her Artistic Pose.

12

Awards, Green Cats and Pom-poms

I think Peter Nichols is one of our finest playwrights. The gardens in his wonderful play *Born in the Gardens* were the zoological gardens in Bristol. Alfred, their celebrated gorilla, was on show there: the play is about being captive in a cage, really. I had a difficult part in it as the mother of three children whose husband had just died. I was called Maud, and my 'children' were Barry Foster, Peter Bowles and Jennie Linden.

On the first day of rehearsals I found that Peter Nichols can be biting at times. We were at Bristol and he took us all on a boat and said, 'You must all have a drink for my birthday lunch.' We were meeting each other for the first time as a cast. Although I had worked with Peter Bowles before, and with Jennie Linden in the TV *Rivals*, I hadn't met Barry Foster and I really didn't know Peter Nichols at all, so I knew only two out of the five. They were all talking about which drama schools they'd been to, and I said, 'Well, I've never been to a drama school.' Peter Nichols said, 'There's still time, you know!' I thought, Oooh! I might come up against something here.

I never came up against anything. At that time he was directing the play and he was wonderfully encouraging to me. In the story, one of my sons, played by Barry Foster, had an overwhelming desire to play the drums. I was playing someone terrified of anything to do with electricity, and when he told me that if I touched the television it would blow up, of course I believed him. When my daughter, Jennie Linden, came from 'Californial', it became clear that he'd only turned the sound down.

218

The Bristolians, for those who don't know about it, put an 'l' on the end of any word that ends with a vowel: that's why it's called Bristol. It was originally called Bristo when it was a sea-port town, but as all the locals called it Bristol it had to be renamed, so that people knew where they were going. It's a beautiful city and I'm most fond of it. The theatres are lovely.

While we were rehearsing, my brother Roy suddenly became very ill indeed. He'd had another massive heart attack, and was going into a heart clinic. His poor old heart was so misshapen that there wasn't enough blood going round it to serve all the rest of the organs in his body. While I was learning the play I was on the phone all the time to see how he was. He died on the day that we opened in Bristol. This was terrible. I had to start the play with a coffin on the stage. I grieved for him so much – I still do – because we were so very close to each other, and I can't believe that he isn't alive any more. I so wanted to go to the funeral, but if I had, the play couldn't have continued: there simply wasn't time to get understudies ready. I knew my brother wouldn't have wanted me to close the play, so, of course, I didn't go to the funeral. But my grief for him was tremendous: it was like my mother's death. There is so much grief in losing people, but you don't really lose them: if you think about them, they don't actually leave your life. But the initial blow is terrible.

At that time I met some dear people who had an off licence just across the road from me. Nita and Dasher are husband and wife, and there are about eleven in the family. Now Dasher doesn't move very quickly, and it makes me laugh to think that he's called Dasher. I love them all so much. When I first went into the shop, they said, 'Oh – look who's there!' They sort of turned me round, and said, 'Oh, isn't she a little thing? I thought she was a great big fat woman. I'd no idea she was a little thing like that. You must come in the back and have a drink.' It was an instant friendship. When Roy died, I just went in one morning and said, 'My brother has died.' Nita said, 'Oh, my dear, that is awful for you. You do come in the back now and just sit down and we'll have a little drink, and we won't speak about it if you don't. And if you want to talk about it, my dear, then you do that.' Our absolutely lovely relationship began just then, when I was totally desolate, and has continued ever since. Another friend, a very young drama student called Paul Strike, was very helpful to me at this sad time. Paul was with me really all through the rehearsals of the play, and when Roy died he would bring food every night and say, 'Now this is what we're going to have tonight, and you've got to cook it. We'll do the words first, then you cook the food, then we'll do the words again.'

In fact, he made me eat. I did lose two stone in weight, purely from grief, but that's not to be dwelt upon at all. It's a very simple thing to do, if somebody steps out of your life. It's of no concern, really, to anybody much, except the immediate family and the people who are directly concerned. But this very young man seemed to understand.

Well, we opened at the Bristol Old Vic, the Theatre Royal, where *Sister George* had first opened her eyes to a hostile world, and it was a sell-out for the entire run. I think I had learnt to do the Bristol dialect quite well. Jennie Linden was not, I believe, entirely at one with her part and wanted to give it up: when we started re-rehearsing for the London opening, Jan Waters took over, and since then she has become a great friend of mine.

In London we rehearsed in the Synagogue in Dean Street, and I always parked my car in the Dean Street car park: I've known all those car park chaps all the time I've been working in theatres in that area. They've taught me how to run a car park. If I'm broke, I can always do that. It's not easy, but I could manage. It's funny, people are very nervous at being in Soho, but I always feel extremely safe there. I know so many people who live or work there that nothing bad would ever befall me. Betty Milne has described some of our little 'happenings' on the way to and from the theatre and talked about some of the friends, two-legged and four-legged, that we made there.

The people who ran the Synagogue had been very clever, because they had a Christian coloured guy as caretaker who didn't have holidays at the same time as they did. He kept working and let us in.

In London Clifford Williams took over as director. Our opening at the Globe was again a great success, but I worried because Isobel Baillie wasn't there. She was eighty-four, and when she eventually turned up to see me and I said, 'Thank goodness; I've been so worried about you,' she said, 'Well, I've had a little stroke, you know. I've not been able to have my hair done or anything. If you see Nancy' (and the possibility of that was very remote, because Nancy lived in California) 'don't let on to her that I dye my hair, will you!' She looked beautiful: she wore a maroon mohair coat and a beautiful black hat with a black osprey. She said, 'I'm working this Sunday in Birmingham.' I said, 'Oh, do you think you ought to, Moona, what are you going to do?' She said, 'I thought I'd do something easy, like the *Messiah*!'

Betty was dressing me again at the Globe, and I think she really rather liked those Maud clothes. Maud wore very fussy things and had a pink what she called 'aphrodisiac' wig. We had a marvellous season, with a long run, during which I did the John Betjeman film, a TV film for Eric Sykes called 'Rhubarb, Rhubarb!', a Peter Cook Special and an episode of the Maureen Lipman comedy series, 'Agony'. In undertaking all this I was, I know now, being fairly silly. But in 'Rhubarb Rhubarb!' I had only those words to say, as did all of us, including Jimmy Edwards, Bill Fraser, Charlie Drake, Roy Kinnear and Hattie Jacques. It was the last time I ever worked with her. I always managed to get back to London in good time for the play, but that was also a very hard show to do, so I was, like Jake Thackray says on one of his super records, 'narkered'.

I was doing what I said I would never do, which is

serve two masters – in fact I served more! But so many exciting things turned up: In 'Arrivals and Departures', one episode of Maureen Lipman's series, I played a terribly silly Scottish woman giving pre-natal instruction, for which she was no more fitted than my left foot. I rehearsed well for director John Reardon, but by the time it came to the recording, I had totally run out of steam. It is one of the things I feel a bit ashamed of. It turned out all right on the screen, but all the guts I'd had at rehearsals had gone out of the performance. I did the part and the audience seemed to laugh, and, of course, Maureen Lipman was absolutely first class: the way it was 'cut' I appeared to be in fairly good acting shape, but really it was another time my brains had fallen out. This is what happens if you try to do too much. God's a funny fellow: that's the time to pack up.

In their reactions to *Born in the Gardens* people were shocked that my daughter from California had had an incestuous relationship with her father, who was then dead. As she'd been eight, she couldn't forget it or forgive him. I, as Maud, knew absolutely nothing about this, because I was very busy with American officers at the time! Maud only had good things to say about her husband when he was dead and in his coffin, which of course does apply to a great number of people, I'm afraid: they only say nice things about husbands or wives when they're no longer in existence.

We had some wonderfully comic lines. Barry Foster said to me, 'You enjoyed your haddock, didn't you, with that crème de menthe?' We always had the most terrible drinks, but the Barry Foster character liked Maud to enjoy herself, because he didn't want her to get rid of their big old house, where he could follow his own lifestyle with his drums, old gramophone records and occasional stranger diversions. Maud's politician son (Peter Bowles) and Americanized daughter (Jan Waters), both for reasons of their own, wanted her to sell up and move out, but Barry Foster won.

I was given the SWET (Society of West End Theatre

Managers) Award for the Best Comedy Performance for *Born in the Gardens*. It's strange – I knew it was funny, but I thought of it more as acting, because I was so touched and moved by some of the things that Maud did and imagined. But I'd been incredibly moved by one of the most riveting performances I've ever seen in the theatre, and could only applaud when Frances de la Tour got the Best Actress Award for her inspired interpretation of the part of the great musician suffering from multiple sclerosis in *Duet for One*.

My very beautiful statue lives happily in Honeypot, but I don't know why they're always so heavy: you're already in a state of shock when you hear you've got one, and then they hand you something which weighs about two tons, so of course you almost fall over. There should be an urgent recap about the making of Awards, because they are far too heavy for nervous people to carry!

While I was in Bristol I became very attached to a little tortoiseshell cat belonging to a lady German radiologist who had married a Sikh. Their three children, I felt, weren't quite all they should be to the cat, which was very, very nervous and terrified of people. I asked her the cat's name and she said, 'Aah – Puzzy.' I thought it must have been very difficult to think of that. She told me, 'She's so dirty – she's always makin' a mess in front of my friends, and she is ruinin' the carpet.' I know cats: they are so clean, they're so much easier to train than dogs. If you just put a kitten's paws in a litter tray and scrape the paws, they will never go anywhere else. Even when they're playing in the garden, mine have been known to rush for a quick little go at the loo on the litter tray. Anyway, by the time I was on chatting terms with her I said, 'I would love to have your cat: I live in the country, not on a main road.' I showed her photos of my house and the lovely garden. She said, 'Oh, your cats are so big.' 'Yes,' I said, 'they're all very happy and very well fed. I'm sure if you let me have this little thing, she too would be happy.' I had, of course, christened her Elsie, because we had this cat called Elsie in the play, which we never saw. Barry Foster never openly complained about the food that Maud gave him, he always said, 'It's just that Elsie's been grumbling.'

Eventually she agreed and I went to collect Elsie. In their house there was no carpet, just bare boards. There was an enormous fridge freezer, a gigantic colour television and a sort of slashed settee. I sat on a tea chest, and about twelve layers of paper, which were being scraped off the wall. We got 'Puzzy' into the basket and Anne, the sister of my friends Nita and Dasher at the off licence, looked after her during the day while I did my two shows.

But I had the most terrible journey back with her, as you can imagine. She was a hell-cat. I put her in the spare room – the bedroom where all the cats go when they first come here – and she flew at me. My legs were lacerated, and this went on for weeks and weeks, until I really began to lose patience. I got so desperate I said to her one day, 'Elsie, how do you fancy a one-way trip to the vet?' And d'you know, she changed completely. It was almost as if she understood my threat. I would never have done anything terrible to her, but I thought, If I speak to her in such a way she might change. And she did. She is now the most lovable cat, very affectionate, and we have great cuddles. She's an absolute push-over now – she sits on the vet's knee when he comes. She does hiss at the present kittens, but that's neither here nor there. She's always going to hiss, one way or another, her whole life through.

My cats' lifestyles are always so different. Take Lulu, who one day decided she wanted to live outside the house. I went up the ladder to feed her four times a day on the roof, which people around used to think was a bit eccentric. I didn't think it was eccentric at all, and when it was snowing I was so glad she had the chimney to sleep against. Then the people in the next house had their pine trees cut down, which I was delighted about. But I hadn't realized that Lulu used to shin up the pine trees to the roof. She had no access to the roof, and she disappeared again. I immediately got on to a chap I know, who works for the Forestry Commission, and he cut a willow branch off and we built this little run up to the roof for her, with little slats sort of plugged into the side. But by that time, because of her state of mind, she had forgotten about living on the roof. So I had to build a bridge – the bridge over the River Kwai – by going all the way up the stream at the side of my house and collecting enormous concrete blocks for a base. I got very long planks, which the thatchers who'd just repaired my roof had left, and now she has a bridge across the stream, should it flood. She comes across for her meals, and now she's very affectionate. I can cuddle her, and I feed her there every day. We have a great deal of loving talk together. That is, of course, if Elsie hasn't seen her first, because Elsie chases her and Dimly chases her: they're the only two naughty cat people I have in the house, for the moment. They just do it for sheer devilment, and she's silly enough to run, if she's not eating her food. If she is eating, she stays put at the Honeypot end of the bridge over the River Kwai.

I have taught my two new kittens to 'sit and stay', which Barbara Woodhouse didn't think I could do. Their names are Billy and Clive. I also taught the litter of three that I had from the RSPCA on my birthday – they'll be three years old by the time this book is out. I taught them to 'sit and stay', on the end of the bed. It was really very sweet, the three of them waiting there till I walked out of the room: they wouldn't move. They are Dimly, who should have been called Brightly, Muriel and Sir Harry, named, of course, after Secombe. When Dimly got his back leg caught, presumably in a trap, it was torn through to the bone. He had to have eleven stitches and went to get better into the spare room, where he remembered everything he'd learnt there as a kitten. He did all the things he did as a tiny baby, and he must have been eighteen months old. He is, as I've said, rather bright, and we have a naughty bit of bacofoil that I roll into a ball that he runs after. But he does bring it back and drop it at my feet: I've taught him to 'retrieve'.

Let me tell you how I met Barbara Woodhouse. It's rather an involved story. They asked me to be a panellist on the television version of Jimmy Edwards's original radio show, 'Does The Team Think?', on which I had appeared as a guest. (You didn't stand an earthly on the radio show, because there were those snappy talkers like Ted Ray, Tommy Trinder, Jimmy Wheeler, Big Jim – all the very smart getting-the-jokes-in boys.) Anyway, when it came back in its new form, there I was on the panel with Jimmy, Tim Brooke-Taylor as the chairman, William Rushton and Frankie Howerd. We had some terribly interesting guests, including Steve Davis, that lovely young snooker champion with the red hair. He was absolutely enchanting. He's like a little tiny boy, with nothing written on his face. Somebody said, 'He's a millionaire' and I said, 'Well, if he is, he certainly doesn't tell anybody he is.'

One day the special guest was Barbara Woodhouse, and when we got talking, I remembered that I had met her when I'd gone to judge a dog show at Chobham. I had even, all unknowingly, chosen one of her dogs as a winner in the pet section. At Chobham there is a sanctuary for lost dogs, dogs that need rehousing and so on, and I had rescued a little dog here called Sunday, and the RSPCA inspector had been round. He's a splendid man named John, and he had said straight out to the people, who had this tiny puppy with a broken leg shut in a shed, 'Do you want this dog?' They said, 'Well, actually, no, we don't.' You know how the novelty wears off with some people, and they do dreadful things like throwing dogs and cats out on the motorway. I think people are sometimes terrible to animals – it's something I can't bear, and find totally unforgivable.

Anyway, Sunday was taken by the inspector to Chobham and rehoused, and, instead of this tiny shivering little puppy I was presented with this beautiful, bouncy little dog, who was so happy. Barbara's dog, which wasn't a thoroughbred, was a tall slender beautiful creature. It could have been a Newfoundland – I don't remember exactly. It was a definite winner, and I didn't know her at all then. Of course, I had to choose Sunday as well, because she'd grown into such a pretty, lovable little dog.

It was so good to meet Barbara Woodhouse again. She has an absolutely inspired way of dealing with animals. However, she did doubt that I could get my cats to obey orders in the way that dogs do. Well, I did, which takes us back to Dimly, Muriel and Sir Harry, who is quite a different personality. Harry Secombe won't have a word said against him. He was really the runt of the litter, and I didn't know how they were going to turn out. Muriel looks like a sheep at the moment: she's a long-haired Old English tortoiseshell and has the most beautiful colours, but she's so enormous – a great big eater.

I said to Harry – it was like Letty in Africa – 'I'm a little bit disappointed because your friend Sir Harry keeps falling asleep and going missing.' He said, 'Oh – I was just like that!' Sir Harry has turned into the most beautiful, enormous tabby cat: he does have this tendency to shack up with a group who live at the big house up the road and he also loves children. He loves a lot of noise, and if there's a child in a house nearby he moves in there and I have to go looking for him every day. I broke my ribs one day doing that, but it doesn't matter, because he's so lovely: I was flashing a torch in the bushes where I thought he might be hiding and not looking where I was walking. We have those 'sleeping policemen' in the road, and, of course, I fell over one and broke all my ribs.

That's just one of the hazards: you have to go out in snow and in all weathers, if you have ten cats. I feel rather like Marjorie Main, who played Ma Kettle in the movies: she called the children One, Two, Three, Four, Five and Six – she had so many children she clearly didn't know what to do. There were hens on the draining board, cattle in the kitchen – all manner of things. In the morning when I'm doing something like filming and getting up terribly early – 5 a.m. – I find it frightfully difficult to remember their names and what they eat, because they all eat different things. They look at me as if I am so stupid, which, of course, I am: it's just that I'm forcing my brain to work at a very early hour. And I certainly have a good laugh at them.

People say cats are totally independent: mine are not. They rush out when they hear the car: they all meet me when I come back and they're all waiting to have head-rubs, or tummy-rubs, or whatever. Though sometimes they are a lot of trouble. You can't have holidays away from them. But they afford me enormous pleasure. When I had to spend so much time in America, first with the play, then the film, of *Sister George*, they showed their extreme displeasure by refusing to come into the house for quite a long time. It took a good deal of work and patience and just being there, before one by one they returned to hearth and home. During that time I was most definitely in, if not the dog-house, the cat-house.

At present count there is Elsie, from Bristol, the two kittens, Billy and Clive, Lulu, the bridge dweller, Dimly, Sir Harry and Muriel; there's Ronnie, Emma (who lives a very happy life after a successful operation to remove an injured eye) and there's Georgie Girl, who's a wonderful twenty and does her best not to leave my side. She exercises her right of seniority to be dogmatic (sorry – catmatic?), and all the time I've been recording this story, she raises her voice in protest if ever I raise mine, as if for dramatic emphasis!

Some of them have tinned meat, but I must never give them the same tins two days running, because that's fatal. Some of them have fresh meat. We put out seven boxes of minced offal, mainly hearts – not liver, because that's inclined to give them diarrhoea – and kidneys, which they like best. They won't eat lights, which cats used to like: my mother used to feed Jumbo and Hamish on boiled lights. The butcher's bill for them is quite immense every week. Some of them like red meat, some of them like tinned meat: none of them like fish, which isn't as curious as you might imagine. If you think of it, they belong to the Big Cat family – lions, tigers, panthers, pumas, and all of those are meat eaters. They'll have fish on sufferance, but it's very bad to feed a cat entirely on fish, because you'll find they will have eczema if they have too much, because there is not enough in it of what they need to get by.

I'm afraid the two kittens, Billy and Clive, have rather taken to the red meat: I dread it, because it's so expensive to buy. The three-year-olds won't eat meat at all, but Emma, Ronnie and Georgie Girl like red meat. They also love cooked rabbit, and if I can get to Berwick Street market for a proper rabbit, or some fresh legs of rabbit, I give it to them and put what is left over on the lawn for the foxes at night. Happily, the foxes get on very well with the cats, and I see them sitting in circles. This is such a countrified place, and an interesting thing is that, when it's very cold, I buy those very fatty cheap breasts of lamb and cook them in the oven and put them on a great big dish or a tray outside, and there is a truce between all the animals when food is short. I've seen water rats, seagulls, my cats, ordinary little birds, voles, mice, all eating together. There is no fighting: that, to me, is like having my own game reserve.

When cats don't like their food, they just 'wall' it, push it out of the way and then ignore it. 'Walling' goes back to when my friend Bobby Bishop and I got rid of the food by simply throwing it out of the window for whichever animals in my private 'game reserve' happened to be around. The window turned out to be closed, so we had a cascade of mutton and vegetables running down the wall. Very messy!

I really enjoyed reviewing two books on cats on television. One was purely to do with breeding pedigree animals, Rex cats, Abyssinians: if I had a thoroughbred cat I would have an Abyssinian because they're lion-coloured and they've got beautiful natures and they don't make any of the extraordinary noises that Siamese make – they sound almost like a baby crying, and I can't bear that. Of the two books, the RSPCA one came up trumps, because it had very practical advice.

Finally, about cats – though there's nothing really final about cats – they are acknowledged to be great relievers of tension: the act of stroking or caressing a cat brings down the blood pressure and lessens the likelihood of heart attacks or nervous breakdowns. I firmly believe that to be true.

When I was asked by the BBC to be in *Tinker, Tailor, Soldier, Spy*, from the book by John le Carré and starring Alec Guinness, I thought, this is really something totally beyond me: I tend to think things are beyond me but then when I get to grips with them I find that if I really work hard enough, they're not. The director, John Irvin, was absolutely fabulous. I was to play Connie Sachs and I was asked to go to Oxford: I don't think we rehearsed at all for that. It was completely up to me to do the learning before I went. We went into the house of some people who had been missionaries in China for years. They were a very beautiful elderly couple with most wonderful faces, and they were both dressed in the Chinese style. It was like going into another world.

It was snowing heavily and they couldn't get the doors shut. I thought, Oh, dear, I'm going to make an awful mess of this. It was a tiny little room, very claustrophobic. Because Connie Sachs was very arthritic, I'd practised how arthritic people walk and move. At the beginning I had to open the door and there, as bold as anything, would be Alec Guinness, standing smiling. So I opened the door, saw Alec Guinness standing and smiling, and said, 'Oh – knickers – I can't remember your name!' His name was George, and he was George Smiley. If I'd had any sense about me I would have known he was George Smiley. He broke up entirely, and screamed with laughter, and that was a very good first mistake to make, having walked successfully in an arthritic manner to the door.

We then continued in this very claustrophobic atmosphere – you can imagine a whole immense camera crew
and a director, kneeling at your feet, practically, to stay
out of shot, and a little dog called Heidi who was, I think,
a Scottish terrier and very old, on whom my voice had a
terrible effect, like it does, as I've told you, on Georgie
Girl. She went 'Yowl, yowl, yowl!' every time I opened
my mouth, and she had to sit with me on the settee
throughout the scene. She was a terribly sweet dog, and
this poor little thing had to be given a tranquillizer. This
upsets me always in pictures, because it is against how I
feel about the treatment of animals. When animals are in
a picture, I always give it a big question mark, because
I'm never sure how they are treated. But Heidi was well
treated, and eventually was very quiet.

John Irvin was a splendid director, and he used to
whisper things to me all the time, and tell me what he
thought was right, and how to do it and all that sort of
thing. It was freezing cold; the doors, of course, had to be
kept open because all the cables connected to the
cameras have to come through, and we were absolutely
frozen in the house. But at the end of this session, after
two days, everybody was delighted, giving me great
kisses and cuddles and saying, 'Great! Great! Great!' I'd
been home for two days and thrown the script in the
dustbin – I was so glad to be rid of all those Russian
names, a great worry to me all the time I was doing it –
and the telephone rang. It was John Irvin and he said,
'I'm terribly sorry, darling, but the focus finder on the
camera didn't focus, and, in fact, we have none of that
scene that we can show. You'll have to come back and do
it again!'

I said, 'I don't think I can, John: I gave so much to it
that I don't think there's anything more in me that I can
give.' He said, 'Oh, yes there is. I tell you what: I don't
think you were harsh enough with George Smiley – you
see, this is a totally different angle that I've thought of' –
he was so cunning, so clever – 'this is a totally different
angle that I've thought of since you left: you could be

much more bitter about your love for him, and his absolute desertion of you.'

Of course, as I'd chucked the script away I had to rush to the village and buy a children's exercise book and write the part out while I remembered it, because I was clearly going to have to do it again.

I discovered just two days later, when I got to do it, that Alec Guinness writes all his words out in longhand, in very small writing. That makes the part belong to him. So in fact I was – not quite following in his footsteps, because I didn't know – but I was doing something, obviously, that was quite sensible. So I wrote the whole part out again in my children's exercise book. I went back to Oxford, and with these new, very good directions, I recreated Connie Sachs, and the poor little dog was brought back again. When you've done something, it's terribly hard, if you've poured your heart into it, to recapture the moment. You think, Lovely, that's that. At the end of a film you destroy it almost instantly, because it's not something that you want kicking about.

Heidi was much more used to me this time, but she still had to have her little tranquillizer, because there was still something in my voice that has this weird effect on some animals: I do understand how Heidi felt. I did the two days in Oxford, the focus finder was obviously finding the focus, and that was that. Away I went, and thought, Well, that was another job and I don't feel I've done badly at that. When it came to the BAFTA awards I found myself nominated. I knew I wouldn't get the award – everybody said, 'Oh, don't be silly,' but I knew this time I wouldn't get the award. I always have strange feelings about things, and I just knew that it wasn't my turn.

There were so many people who were up for so many things – more than one thing, in fact – and I was just up for a little cameo part. I was appearing in *Born in the Gardens* at the time, so I couldn't go to the award ceremony, and I didn't get one. That was perfectly understandable and simple.

When I saw that they were going to do *Smiley's People*, the sequel to *Tinker Tailor*, I wrote to the BBC saying, 'Please can I play Connie Sachs again?' I had a letter back saying, 'Well, we really wouldn't have anybody else.' But, you see, I always feel totally insecure about whether I'm going to be offered a job or not. I have no security at all. I had enjoyed the first one so much that I really couldn't resist another go at Connie Sachs.

I was all set to go, and they wrote to me to say, 'It has been put off. Another director is going to do it.' Simon Langton directed us this time, and when we finally began shooting, we went to a very strange house in Maidenhead. I was driven by Tony Van Heck, who drives me constantly. We've sort of grown together, as people do when they sit in cars for hour upon hour together.

As Connie was dying, they started making me up with a very pale green colour. I looked so very, very ill, and made it my business never to look at myself in the mirror during the day. (This isn't difficult for me, because I don't very often look in the mirror. I sketch in a quick· face from memory in the morning, and that's got to do me.) Of course, I'm the make-up person's joy: the make-up never moves. I've got the sort of skin that it stays on all day. I even draw in a mouth from memory, when necessary.

Poor old Connie had a very poor mouth: she was then on her way out. She was walking on a frame, and it's still very hard for me to convince people that I am not dying of arthritis. However, when they see me leaping about the village they know I'm not. We had two days' rehearsal in St Mary's Church Hall in Kensington, where they have a lovely cat, and I know them all well – lovely people too.

Unlike Alec Guinness I don't normally write all my part out, unless forced by circumstances to do so, but I do spend a great deal of time learning it. And, of course, none of it, with those Russian names, was very easy to learn; in fact, it was very, very difficult. But I realized, when I was mastering it in my head, that it was an absolutely marvellous part.

I've mentioned the very strange house near Maidenhead where we did it: I think the chap who owned the house had been arrested for hitting somebody on the head with a chopper, or something like that. They had an outside loo, which we weren't allowed to use. The lady said, 'Oh, it's lovely, sitting in there in the summer, watching life pass by.' That's not really something that I'd want to do – but it takes all sorts.

Again it was a frightfully claustrophobic house, but because of the absolute genius of the set designer the little room we worked in was filled with tins of dog food and so on – in the serial we took in pets, you see. The girl who was living in the house with me was played by Norma West. I can't believe that anything had ever happened between us, but Connie had found somebody who was fairly dotty, but would be very fond of her. Norma was a lovely girl and excellent in the part.

Alec Guinness is as wonderful when he's not on camera as when he is: he's acting solely for your close-up and he does really look into your eyes and drag the words out of you. We had to give a quarter of an hour's notice of going to the loo, when we had to be driven over mud flats to where our portable loo was stationed. I had a snap of Alec Guinness and me standing outside this construction, pointing to the sign which said 'Honey-Wagon'.

Well, I did *Smiley's People* to the best of my ability. It upset me a great deal at the time. Afterwards you have to get it out of your head, or you would get rather silly, dwelling on things. This is what you mustn't do in the theatre. And so I put it out of my head, and when, a year later, I went to see it, I looked at it in amazement and thought, Oh, where did all that come from? I had no idea what I had done.

The whole thing was absolutely riveting. The director was very clever. The first time, John Irvin, whom I admire very much indeed, had let Smiley pass off as a fairly nice chap. Now we saw him being an absolute bastard, which I'm sure George Smiley was. He came to me, knowing I was dying, knowing it was the last time he would see me, only to get some information; to use my brain, which had been so invaluable to them when I was in what they called the Circus, in the Secret Service. When I said, 'Do you love me, George, just like you used to?' he didn't even answer me, and that was terribly sad. Simon Langton had absolutely captured his character, in my opinion. He got to the root of us all, really quite quickly; a charming young man who whispered just the right things up my nose at the right moment.

When I went to the BAFTA awards, I told everyone at the table, 'I'm not going to get it, you know, so don't be disappointed. The opposition's too strong.' I didn't get it for *Tinker, Tailor* and I certainly didn't expect to get it for this. It was again a cameo part. There was Maureen Lipman, and umpteen people up for umpteen things. Julie Walters was up against me again for *Boys from the Blackstuff*, as in the theatre award when she'd done *Educating Rita* at the time I got the award for *Born in the Gardens*. Although we're great friends, I think she must have got a bit tired of me, though since then she's had almost every accolade possible – and very well deserved.

I repeat, I don't know why the award's so heavy. It's a bad enough shock to have got it, which leaves you with your knees shaking as you fall up the stairs in a long frock, and then the excitement of the beautiful Anthony Andrews giving it to me – the award, I mean – and hearing him say, 'Aren't you going to give me a kiss, Beryl?' It was all too much. I said, 'Oh, yes, of course I am,' and I sort of fell on him and said, 'I can't really say anything – I'm getting a bit silly, and I think I'd better go home!' That was my speech. Actually, watching this year's BAFTA awards I think a lot of people have taken a leaf out of that book, because the speeches were much shorter and less boring.

I had a letter from John LeMesurier. He said, 'Darling, I was so delighted to see you get the prize at

that show called "An Evening With Richard Attenborough".' Attenborough had, of course, got every
award for *Gandhi* and had a speech for every occasion.

I had been asked by Isobel Baillie's daughter, Nancy,
whom I'd been to school with, to do the address after her
mother's death, at the age of eighty-eight. She had been a
great feature of my life. I had never spoken from the
pulpit before: I just spoke as my heart directed. I said all
the things I knew about Isobel Baillie and what a lovely
person she was and how wonderful she'd been to me all
her life, and I was very moved by the occasion.

I then went back to the rehearsals for *The School for
Scandal* at Kennington Oval, drove home here to Honeypot Cottage and the garden was full of people I didn't
know. Then a man came up to me and said, 'Now then,
Beryl; John LeMesurier's dead, and we want you to do a
quick thing for the newsreel for tonight.' How anybody
could be so cruel, I don't know. I didn't even know my
dear friend John was ill. I was just pushed into the house,
all the cameras, all the crew, everybody came in and I
was compelled to talk about John, really in a state of
shock.

John had written me the most lovely letter, so
revealing of his sweet nature and his constant concern for
Hattie and Joan. It's also very funny, and a moving
memorial to him in my mind.

June 21

My dear Beryl

It was your birthday (as *you* may know) last Friday. I couldn't
find your number as Joan has it in her 'book' and she is at the
moment in Spain: Never Mind, it is quite chic to have a note
about the important happening a week later! We Both send
our love to you and all your feline creatures who may be
lurking about or sulking on roof tops.

I am trying to get this book done. I have talked of you *and*
"Whisky and Water and Gin and French" all those years ago.
I often think of those times. But try not to dwell on them too
much. I miss Hattie very much and I loved her. I now love
Joan very much and am happy about this.

I love you come to think of it.

As always

John

When I went to bed after learning about John and trying to get my thoughts together to make some sort of sense about him on the newsreel, I was left with the memory of another indefatigable person, a lady whose energy at ninety-one has to be an inspiration when those of us left behind feel sometimes a little bit like being sorry for ourselves. Eva Turner – Dame Eva Turner – was at the Isobel Baillie Memorial Service and she said, 'D'you know, I wanted to applaud when you'd finished, because it was so good. I only come when you're on, you see, because I can hear you. What's going to happen in twenty years' time when there's no projection? Nobody ever uses their lungs – nobody ever learns how to speak out, or sing out. I try to teach people, but they don't seem to have the energy.'

She's a person who's got all the energy and *loves* life. She's in such love with life, and goes to all the award ceremonies and other occasions, putting her best hat on, and being so chatty. She has something fantastic. I wish, with all my heart, that it could be passed on to younger people, who don't think it is necessary to speak up – who because of their misfortune in being brought up on either films or television, don't know about projection, or how to use their lungs and breathing power and everything that makes the sound come out.

I was very fortunate, because everybody can always hear me. That was really due to my mother. When I was born she went totally deaf in one ear. Things weren't very advanced at that stage, as you can imagine. When I got old enough, we took her to places to get hearing aids, but the trouble with a hearing aid is that it simply magnifies everything – not just the things you want to hear, but all the other sounds as well. She could only bear what she called 'Channel 9' for perhaps two hours at a time, because her nerves were all jangly. The noises that we, as hearing people, can take for granted, she couldn't. She'd never heard the clock tick until I got her to have this hearing aid. And so, not wanting her always to be saying, 'I can't hear you, Beryl,' I did learn to speak properly. I found it was the beginning and end of words that matter most. When you go to classic stables like the Old Vic and the Royal Shakespeare they have elocution people there all the time, saying, 'Please pronounce the end of your words, because you can't be heard!'

Another marvellous thing my mother said to me at one time in her life: 'Just remember, Beryl, everybody celebrates success. You must learn to celebrate the failures!' Ever since then I realize that, if I have a total disaster, I must celebrate it. She really was very wise indeed, and I don't know what I would have done, or what sort of person I would have been, if I hadn't had a mother like her.

The ability to cope with most likely – or unlikely – situations is another thing I learned from her. I think people know that I am no longer married and live almost alone, so I do get a number of what might be called obscene phone calls. I find these terribly funny: I never give them the right treatment when there's all this heavy breathing going on. I had one the other day. This man (a courtesy title, in his case) said, 'How would you like me to come round and lick your pussy?' I said, 'Well, which one, I've got ten!' That was him cut off in his prime. Another one said, 'I want to come round and do the most wonderful things with you in bed.' I said, 'Oh, Norman, what a lovely idea – I didn't know you were back from America!' He said, 'My name is not Norman – it's Bert!' If only you have the courage to do this, they are so futile when they're at this lark that you can knock them down in one. They are, in fact, highly vulnerable, alone in a telephone box, doing goodness knows what.

Courage of a very different sort helped me to get over the terrible fears of flying from which I'd always suffered. When I was flying to Africa I was so nervous that I saw the whole of the dawn over the Sahara Desert, which is the most beautiful thing you could ever possibly imagine, with the whole spectrum of the rainbow – every colour – there in the dawn. Being terrified, I hadn't been able to sleep at all. Also, flying to California, to Hollywood or New York – all of these were petrifying experiences to me. I used to grab hold of people I'd never met in my life – I was really a nuisance in an aeroplane, and I hate being a nuisance or stupid.

Whatever I am afraid of I have to turn round and face. That is the only cure for me. And so that made me absolutely determined to learn how to *fly* an aeroplane. I used to go to Fairoaks, near Ottershaw, day after day after day – I'd turn right when I saw a pub called the Otter, and there I was at Fairoaks. I used to take off in a field – there was no runway – and I learned to bank and 'fly on my false horizon'. The instruments are fascinating: there's an enormous great panel of them that confronts you. The 'false horizon' is in a little round-shaped thing like you'd have on your car on the dashboard – it's on the dashboard of the aeroplane – and you can tell if you're flying in mist or through a cloud, because there is a line across the middle of the disc and a mercury line that moves up and down, and you can tell if you're losing height or gaining height, or if you're flying absolutely straight – that's what's called the 'false horizon'.

I was obsessed by flying: I thought it was wonderful. I couldn't get a pilot's licence because I didn't have time to study aviation law, but I could do everything else: I could land and do all the technical things like twiddle my little rudder on the roof. I knew all the things that made it go. The instructor used to say, 'You are now in control' – this was the sort of jargon you used – so I'd say, 'Right; I'm just going to take you over Frensham Ponds, then we'll fly over Farnborough.' I mean, I was filled with adventure!

This was about seven years ago. I didn't have to become a pilot. I know that in an emergency I could fly an aeroplane, and this has stood me in good stead, because I now have absolutely no fear of flying. My instructions were to approach the aircraft and look at it, like I do at my car every day (and when I was living in London I used to look under it every day as well in case a bomb had been planted there). My instructor said, 'Just stand in front of the plane and look and see if it looks as if it's worth flying.' I would stand on my tip-toes, because the petrol was in the wings. We had nine gallons in each wing: I used to unscrew the petrol caps – there was no proper petrol gauge, you just had to take a kind of dip-stick thing out of the wing and see how much petrol was in. I would look at the tyres and all that sort of thing, then very happily take off, and land. It totally cured me of any fear of flying.

Little did I know there was a great deal of flying coming to me, like doing eighty-two programmes of 'Get Up And Go' for the children, in Leeds. I always flew there and back – not personally, there was a gentleman in charge of the aeroplane, you understand. Also I did fifty flights to Ireland to do 'The Irish RM', and there was also a gentleman in charge there, but I was often invited up to the cabin. I was there with the then Prime Minister of Ireland, and we were both marvelling at it all, but I had never before landed, actually crammed behind the pilot's seat. That was terribly exciting, because they land at such a pace. This is why when you land, when they've done the perfect three-point landing, hopefully, there's a terrible jolt in the aeroplane, as they bang the gears into reverse. They're travelling at such speed it is impossible to stop without this. It taught me that planes are meant to fly, unless something extraordinary happens. Then you could be in a plane that collapsed, but that's very, very unusual. And that's what gave me all the confidence in the world.

Lord Snowdon, who came to photograph me doing my flying, was very naughty: he said, 'Oh, go up higher into that blue bit!' and the instructor nearly had a fit, because the 'blue bit' was where all the big boys were. But it made me feel that, in a tiny way, I was following in the wake of my in-built childhood heroine, Amy Johnson, who made that incredible achievement of flying the Atlantic, with only a school atlas to guide her. I have total recall of it. 'Amy, wonderful Amy, how can you blame me, For loving you; You have filled my heart with admiration,' and so on. But that's another story.

Flying to Ireland for 'The Irish RM' was my first experience of 'Dublin's Fair City', of which I'd always kept a picture in my mind. The terrible situation in Northern Ireland, where for what seems an eternity religion has been made an excuse for waging war upon totally harmless people – is to me a great sadness. But I was going to work with some super people and play the most marvellous part. *The Irish RM* is the sort of book that Southern Irish people keep beside their bed – they all know the stories inside out and back to front. Mrs Knox – my part – was a magistrate and Peter Bowles was the man who came from England to be a magistrate – a Resident Magistrate.

Mrs Knox was an extraordinary character: the description in the script says, 'She resembles a scarecrow who is covered in diamonds.' I drew back in my mind to get the character right, and I thought of Dr Roydon in Yarmouth, and his wife, who always wore a hat. I suspected Mrs Knox had very little hair, so she always wore a purple bonnet, wherever she was. She was on nodding terms with all the petty Irish crooks of the time, as she was a magistrate. She was very, very outspoken and said, 'Come along, Fibber, tell the truth, or you'll be accused of something much worse.' When she thought she was whispering to Peter Bowles, the Irish RM, in the court house she could be heard for miles around. It was impossible for her to whisper. She did the Irish jig with her grandson, Flurry Knox, whom she adored (he was played by Bryan Murray, a beautiful and talented young actor). All in all the part was an amazingly good chance to be given at this stage of my career. I just couldn't believe my luck.

We went on location all over Southern Ireland, a day at a time, but I had a wonderful driver called Tony (so many of the drivers in my life are called Tony). I said, 'You don't mind me mentioning that the lights were red, do you, Tony, as you drove through them,' and he said, 'Oh, I don't bother with those, Beryl, not until after 8 o'clock in the morning.' They've only had to past the test in Ireland for the past four years, and I must say the standard of driving is absolutely abysmal. There *is* no standard, let's face it.

During my fifty flights to and from Dublin to get just two episodes in the can, I met so many people and made more friends than I've had hot dinners. There were some who were being rather quiet and so I chatted them up: they turned out to be, I'm sure, one of the richest families in Ireland. Their house, with 2000 acres, was absolutely unbelievable, and they apologized for only having one butler that day, because it was a Sunday. There is great wealth there, and tremendous poverty: it's a very strange mixture.

My little dog, called Balthasar in the script, was actually a girl called Lettuce. She had recently had a litter, so I had to keep my hand over her anatomy while we were acting together to hide the fact that she was rather full of milk. She was owned by friends of mine and was what we would call a Jack Russell terrier, but they call a hunting terrier, because they said that Jack Russell was just a man who rode about on a bicycle with a lot of dogs running behind him, so they won't give his name to any of that breed.

But it's a breed I'm familiar with, going back to Jimmy Edwards because he brought two of them to Honeypot with him. He let them out of the car and I said, 'Jimmy, you shouldn't do that, because I've got two cats' – Footy and Fred. They immediately saw Footy and chased her and I said, 'I'll never see her again, Jimmy.' But, of course, I was totally wrong: they came back in reverse order: it was Footy chasing the two dogs! That was rather a happy ending to what could have been a sad story.

Tony the driver and I became great friends, because

on a film you spend a great deal of time with the driver, and he always used to see me into the hotel, which was very nice of him. I said one day, 'I was awfully upset about that phone call, Tony, from my home. I rang back immediately, and the thing that's worrying me is that the thatchers are coming tomorrow. They can't come tomorrow because I'm having my drive tarmacked again, and, you see, when they do come, it's going to cost £4100.' There was a stunned silence from Tony: when he was able to speak again I found out that he'd thought I meant that Margaret and Denis Thatcher were coming tomorrow and it would cost that much to entertain them. I meant that people were coming to thatch my roof.

The thatchers were from Wokingham: there was a lady master thatcher, and a man who ran the business, who was, I think, seventy-eight, and who had a van dating back to 1939, painted red, white and blue. He was a master thatcher and they had an apprentice aged eighteen. What with Anne, the lady thatcher, George, the older man, and their young apprentice, I really had a great deal of enjoyment and, occasionally, frustration at them being on the premises. I said, 'It's been a lovely day today, George' – the cats were having a ball, because the house was surrounded for practically six months with scaffolding, and this was a lovely playground – and he said, 'Yes, it's been a beautiful day today.' I said, 'Isn't that lovely, because you'll be coming tomorrow.' He said, 'No, we won't, because we'll be planting the straw for the thatching next year!' I'd been on a year's waiting list to get this done.

They never wanted to come inside. They had all their meals from a Calor gas cooker on their van, and they would never come into the house unless I especially asked them to. They did the work beautifully, and wired the thatch in, to keep out the squirrels. Before they finished up, he said, 'I think that you should have a little pom-pom on the top of each circle.' I said, 'That's entirely up to you, George,' and indeed now I have got a little pom-pom on the top of all my circles!

Mrs Candour, in Sheridan's *The School for Scandal*, has been a great feature of my life for over two years (with several months in between) starting in Leeds at the end of 1982 and going on until just before I started to write this book in May 1984. There were highly successful seasons at the Theatre Royal, Haymarket, when I shared the dressing-room with their gentle ghost, and the Duke of York's, back on my own home ground. The casts changed slightly from production to production, but the nucleus remained: Donald Sinden, with whom I first worked on television in a hilarious episode of his series with Elaine Stritch, 'Two's Company', Michael Denison, Dulcie Gray and Bill Fraser, my old friend, who happily crops up in my life just about all the time.

Duncan Weldon, who keeps so many people gainfully employed in the theatre all year round and who is never afraid to take a chance on a production that other managements might consider too risky, has, I hope, found his faith in Restoration comedy financially rewarding: I was amazed when he told me, the first time I worked for him, that he had been one of the backstage staff years and years ago at the Garrick Theatre, Southport, when I was there in variety. He was stage-struck then, and put his enthusiasm to good use as he gradually made his name in theatrical circles. I hope he won't think it sounds patronizing if I say I'm resoundingly proud of him!

Anyway, when I first made the acquaintance of Mrs Candour, I thought her very unrewarding – a gossip with one funny line, on her entrance, 'My dear Lady Sneerwell, how have you been this century?' I discussed her with John Barton, again directing me in Restoration comedy, and eventually hit upon the key to her character: she did an awful lot of walking, from house to house. Distances in those days between the grand houses could be very great and over cobblestones. Also she had to hurry a great deal, to catch up with the coachmen, who rode in their carriages and would go into the most intimate details of their friends' lives within earshot of the men who were driving them.

So, Mrs Candour, who firmly believed that her tale-bearing was all done from the highest possible motives, was only tolerated by the likes of Lady Sneerwell as an endless source of tittle-tattle – she was not, like her ladyship, high-born, or fundamentally evil; she had worked her way into society by her wits. All the running about made her very rocky on her feet, so she was bent almost double by her exertions in keeping up with the scandal. Once again, the shoes and the walk helped me to find the character: I always start with the feet, and on this occasion I finished with the enormous beauty-spot on Mrs Candour's bust!

When Andrew Gardner stands up, you just can't believe it. He's about 6ft 4in. When I started recording children's cassettes for him, of course I fluffed an awful lot, which means not saying the proper words. Because of the dyslexia, however much I studied the stories I made an awful lot of mistakes. He said on 'This Is Your Life' that he'd recorded seventy-nine exclamations of 'Oh, knickers!' from me. The idea came to him when he was driving across France with his four children, and they were all so bored that he thought how marvellous it could be if he had something to play for them whilst they were doing this long dreary drive. It is a great idea because children say, 'Can I just have that one, Mummy, before I go to sleep?' – and of course they go to sleep while 'that one' is on.

I read several fairy stories adapted by Helen Cresswell, who is a remarkable children's writer. Reading is really neat hell for me, but as it was Andrew Gardner and he's very lovable I did do my best to do them well, and they still bring in a little income.

Lunch with a lovely girl from Yorkshire Television, Lesley Rogers, at one of my favourite restaurants, Bianchi's in Frith Street, was to be the beginning of something very big in my life. I think that was the first restaurant I had ever been to in London, and Eleanor, working there, was marvellous to me when I had very little money. They used to flog me nylons when everything was very cheap. There was a wonderful waiter there called Tony (not a driver this time!) who used to cry down the hatch 'Minestrone, spaghetti!' as if he was breaking his heart at ordering all the things for other people that he was going to eat after they'd left. He did die later in Florence – I think he burst. At Bianchi's then they had no decor at all; only little white tablecloths. The food was wonderful, but it was like eating at a café in a station. Eleanor moved on to grand heights at L'Escargot, but those were the great days for me in Bianchi's. There was an elderly gentleman who took the orders; I didn't know, but he was frightfully deaf, and whatever you ordered he brought something entirely different of his own choice, which made eating there a constant adventure.

By the time I had lunch there with Lesley Rogers, things, and prices, had changed more than somewhat. Lesley had a programme in mind which involved children, and, as she had heard all the cassettes I'd done for Andrew Gardner's company for children, she was keen on getting me to do a show in Yorkshire – and she was very persuasive.

We had umpteen working titles, but eventually we hit on the title 'Get Up And Go!' It was aimed at an absolutely new audience for me – the under fives. I have Mooncat (a green cat who comes from the moon) who is played by a puppeteer called David Claridge. Children avidly ask me why Mooncat isn't with me, or, 'Are you going to buy some green tins, Beryl?' as I go round the supermarket. Everything has to be green, because that's Mooncat's favourite colour. Coming from the moon, his room is a sort of space room, where you bang buttons and get into things you normally would never get into, and a great deal of magical things happen in the show, which is done on what's called Chromakey. They give me a cross on the floor if Mooncat is sitting at my feet, but in fact he's sitting at the other side of the studio dressed in his green suit, however much they want to show of it, and it has to be up against royal blue, because royal blue is the colour that fades out in some magical way and they can transfer him to be a cat at my feet. It needs a lot of imagination, because I have to address him during the stories I tell and I must say I've learned a great number of technicalities during this.

I've done eighty-two shows and I have begun to think that perhaps that is enough for the public. The times of the programmes also haven't always coincided with what time I had available. Very sadly, I think that eighty-two is all I'm going to do for the meantime, but I may, of course, go back to it. David Claridge is also Roland Rat, and he has had such a great success as that character that he might send a stand-in to be Mooncat. He is terribly clever and creative. So, indeed, is Stephen Boxer, who sings and writes those lovely songs for the show.

In my opinion, the standard of the show is extremely high as children's programmes go. Of course, the great trick is never to talk down to children, because they're much cleverer than any of us, and they're more outspoken. That's why I get on so well with them, because we just state our case when we meet.

During the second series we learned that Lesley Rogers had cancer. She was aged thirty-seven. Lesley's great friend was Maria Price, a designer who looked after me in Leeds. I said to her, 'Now, do go and see Lesley. It would be awful if anything happened to her and you hadn't been to stay with her.' She did stay with Lesley, and they worked out a wonderful meal. 'We'll have Beryl and Stephen and David Claridge,' said Lesley, 'and we'll ask them all to come to supper after the show. We'll do red cabbage, salad, sweetcorn and all these different sorts of meats.' And during that night she died.

It was an awful shock for Maria, but I was so glad that she'd gone to see Lesley. She did what she'd always done – lain on the bed, holding Lesley's hand, while they talked about it. Lesley left two little children, two sons: she was separated from her husband, who has since remarried and his wife has had a baby. Happily the children have always been in touch with their father. They all love each other. The wife has got the two boys now, so that was a happy ending for them, though it was a tragedy for us to lose such a wonderful, uncomplaining good-natured person as Lesley: she was so creative.

The show was put in the hands of Len Lurcock, whom I had known as a cameraman with Rediffusion. This was the first time I had met him as a director; you are then on a completely different footing. We got on very well together, and he has done wonders for the show. We were just feeling our way in the beginning: he has done all the magic things, all the trick camerawork and so on to make it work really marvellously.

Shirley Isherwood wrote beautiful stories for the show, full of lovely characters like the friendly elephant with the Margaret Rutherford personality, Mrs Pinkerton-Trunks. I told a different story every week. Rick Vanes, who does the scripts, is very funny – he's terribly north country: I love tripe (and I hope you do, if you're reading this!). Rick had given me a parcel, gift-wrapped, to go to the airport at Leeds, and I had no idea what was in it. When I opened the envelope, it said, 'In Oldham we're poorer, we spurn Interflora; we put all our love into tripe!' And, of course, when the girl said to me at the airport, 'What's that?' I said, 'Tripe.' She said, 'Oh, don't be silly, Beryl.' I said, 'Well, it is, and if you open it you'll have to wrap it up again,' because tripe's very difficult to wrap, as it has all this liquid flowing out of it. So I did fly back with two pounds of very good tripe from Rick, who'd spurned Interflora.

When I opened a cat show in Birmingham, and sat for three hours signing autographs, I could not believe that people of every age were standing in front of me. My very first fan *ever*, Phyllis Hart, was there, and that was lovely. But then there were children of two, children of five, people of eighty, people of every age group, including teenagers, and I thought, Oh, aren't you lucky: there isn't an age that you haven't performed for. Whether you've pleased them or not is another story, but there they were, all lined up. It continued for three hours.

I was only in charge of judging the domestic pets, because I'm not qualified to judge thoroughbreds, and I understand domestic pets. The man who actually won the prize was found with tears running down his face in the gents' loo, because he was so excited! From the first sight of this cat I was determined that it was going to be the winner: it appealed to me totally, and I think the feeling was mutual. I have always had cuttings from these people from the cat show, letting me know the progress of their cats. I hope they don't show them too often. I don't really like cats and dogs being 'shown', because I think it's rather cruel. They get left in those little cages for so long.

Living in a village and also liking to be quiet, I'm most fortunate that my nearest neighbours are Sylvia and Les Lee, who are frightfully quiet too: they don't interfere with my life and I don't interfere with theirs, and we're delighted to meet to have a chat. They are ideal near-neighbours, always there, in case I might need someone. They even came to the theatre, to see a matinée, and I said, 'Oh, Sylvia, why didn't you come to see me?' They'd never been into a dressing-room. She said, 'Well, we didn't like to, dear, we thought you'd be tired, and you'd like to have a rest.' They were quite right, I did like to have a rest, but I would have been delighted to see them and for them to see what it's like when I'm working: they have no idea of that. They're an ideal couple to live so near to.

My other great friends in Wraysbury are Lord and Lady Craigton, who live such a short way from me that if I had a boat I could whizz there in a minute. They try to understand why they don't see me for such long intervals, but it is because I just work, work, work.

Christine Piggott, who helps me in the house, is a great

girl and she's so wonderful with the cats. Her husband, John, has the local garage at the end of the lane. She has three children and one now is working: as you get a bit older, time goes by so quickly you can hardly notice it. Chris is a great friend, and really a great comfort to me. She doesn't live here – she lives a little way from me. But for two women to share a kitchen without a word of disagreement is a great achievement. She's smashing, I really love her. One of the remarkable things about Chris is that she loves the cats so much: when she came to me she had two dogs and didn't believe that cats could be interesting. She'd never seen them relaxing and unwinding and doing all the things that we wish we could do, if we could unwind far enough. They are the most relaxing creatures to live with, and each one is totally different. She has now got two dogs, and, I think, five cats. So, you see, she's kind of grown into it, really.

We have a frog beside the fireplace, named Fergus, after Fergus Montgomery, the Member of Parliament. Fergus is also a money-box, and whenever I have any spare money it goes into him. If my purse is rather heavy, I say to Chris, 'I think Fergus is rather hungry today.' Her three children come every Christmas, and they empty Fergus, and that's their little Christmas present, for whatever it's worth. Sometimes he's very full and I do my best to see that he is, because money doesn't seem to go anywhere now, and children also have really no idea of money.

I think money has very little value now. You go into a greengrocer's and buy a few pounds of potatoes and some other things, and there's all your money gone. I'm one of those people who never have any of the 'readies', as they say, because I'm always paid by cheque, which goes straight to my agent, then on to Commander Innes Hamilton, who looks after my money; I was going to say 'finances', but I suddenly heard my mother say, 'Don't be silly, Beryl – the word is "money".'

Innes is a remarkable man. He is a great worker for animals; he has a very beautiful garden at Virginia

Water, which he tends practically alone, quite amazingly, because, apart from doing all the work for so many theatre people, he writes books and takes an active interest in politics; he manages to do more than almost anybody I know. How fortunate I was to find him.

Another lovely friend of mine is Yvonne Renaut, who comes from Belgium. She lives at Datchet, which is really the best shopping village near me. She rang me one night, and said, 'But *when* am I going to see you?' This is the desperate state I get to. She said, 'I don't think I'll even know you when I see you.' I said, 'Well, I'll wear a carnation so you'll be able to tell me in the crowd.' This is what happens with friends. They must feel very much neglected, but they're not. I think about them so much.

Two boys I met at Huddersfield, John Addy and Anthony Porter, also feature in my life. They're wonderful, because they want to 'get away from it all', and so, sometimes, they do come and see me when I'm 'on the road'. They came to see my most recent revue, *A Little Bit on the Side*, in Bournemouth, one of its best weeks, though the very expensive hotel I stayed in was nothing short of catastrophic – a five-star 'Fawlty Towers'. So I was excessively glad to see them during the tour.

It was quite by accident that I met them originally. Of course, everything in your life seems quite by accident, but I'm sure it's all written out somewhere. I was asked to go by John Addy when I was doing 'Get Up And Go' and speak at a dinner, which is something I don't do. He said, 'The people have asked me to ring you up and see if you'd come.' I said, 'I suppose so, but I'm not really an after-dinner speaker, you know.'

It turned out to be a kind of gay community, although there were normal husbands and wives, all manner of people there, but it was mainly gay. 'Well, what if I am?' John said, 'I hope you don't mind.' I said, 'Of course I don't mind; I love it all!' and what was supposed to be a five-minute speech turned out to be two hours long. People kept asking me questions, and I find that's the only way I can talk. John and Anthony have become very close friends; they run what is called a flea market, which is selling antiques from stalls: they are extremely astute and successful, and dear, dear friends – I could fill a book with their exploits. But that's another story.

Gwen Pipe is a great chum. She has a dress shop in Windsor, and she buys with me in mind. I have very few things made for me. I spoke at a dinner for her on her last evening as Chairman of the Soroptimists. They gave me a cheque for my favourite charity, which went to the RSPCA. Muriel Carey, another great friend of mine in the village, runs a rehousing unit extremely efficiently, and takes in every little animal who's lost, strayed, hurt or unwanted. She does a completely remarkable job. She and her husband John, who comes here to fish, are really good to me and if Chris can't come here to cat-sit, she will step in.

Duncan Weldon put on *A Little Bit on the Side*, again showing his willingness to put his money where other people put their mouths, and his talented and absolutely enchanting wife, Jan Mahoney, was one of the great assets of the show. There was also Jan Waters, my dear friend from *Born in the Gardens*, and she is a great performer. She's got the most lovely voice: she and Jan Mahoney were both superlative. Harry Secombe's son Andrew was also in it: they were absolutely wonderful people, and there was never a wrong word. Nobody ever got grumpy, or argued. We were all terribly happy, but the material wasn't quite right and, in some places, the talent wasn't quite right. It was a terribly hard-working time for me – I mean physically hard-working – because I had something like fifteen quick changes every night and a lot of touring, which I don't take to very well, because it is hard work going from town to town and living in all these different places, and I worked excessively hard: I danced, I sang, I did the Spanish Maid, I did everything. Monica came back, written by Ronnie Wolfe, and that was a little send-up of the West End success *Daisy Pulls It Off* which was called *Daisy Doesn't* with Jan Mahoney as Daisy. It was directed beautifully by Billy Chappell. But the chemistry wasn't quite right, and however much we loved it, we didn't bring it to London. Maybe I'll do it again. I don't know. We'll see what the next challenge is going to be.

I don't think I could possibly manage without my own kind of religion. It doesn't belong to anything, really. My mother used to make me go to church, and it was the Scots Presbyterian Church, which I didn't much care for. She made me go to Sunday School, and every Sunday when we were at Dunure we used to go to the mission hall. There were wonderful ministers there. I remember one saying, 'Dear God, send us wind; no rantin', tauntin', tearin' wind, like you did last week, but an ochin', suchin', wooin' wind to help the crops!' There was no messing about: he knew exactly what he wanted.

That's how I think of what I call the Management, as I point to the sky – that wonderful man in an old tweed suit, saying, 'Oh, not you again: what have you done now?' He's really rather bored with me, but without Him I could do terribly little. It's a hand for me to hold, and I would be very poor without that faith and feeling of strength with me all the time. It's in the work, it's in everything. I feel He's a person I can totally rely on, and a friend. I've even been known to say 'The Lord is my shepherd, I shall not want,' when I've been looking for a place to park my car! I don't think He minds that a bit: I think He just takes me for what I am. I would feel very bereft without that hand and arm at my side that can get me through almost everything.

Robert Luff, of course, on the other side of the management, has been my agent for I can't remember how long – almost for ever. In the very beginning there was a man called Nat Day, and in my excitement I remember saying to my mother, 'Do you think I'll have to do a Natdition for Auday?' But Robert Luff is a tower of strength. He's a very quiet, very strong-in-business, most reliable, very kind friend.

His partner, Beryl Evetts, was originally Champion

Charleston Dancer of the World. She taught the late Prince of Wales, and people like the Tate and Lyle families, who paid £500 a lesson, I believe. She was a quite remarkable lady: everybody called her 'Auntie Beryl', which was rather nice, and she died quite recently. I think Robert Luff, who is a very reserved sort of man, must miss her tremendously, because they worked together for so many years, and when he went away in the war and became a Major in the Gordon Highlanders, Beryl Evetts kept the whole shoot going while he was away. She'd got umpteen people and the agency was really swinging and a lot of money had been made – the Squadronaires, one of the leading bands of the time, were on the books – so Robert Luff came back to a very flourishing concern.

I think his years in the Gordon Highlanders must have been one of the best times of his life, really, because he's got a great sense of humour but he is kind of serious. He is so true and so truly faithful to Beryl in his mind and in every way. He bought a hotel in Scarborough, the beautiful Royal Hotel, which had been owned by Tommy Laughton, Charles Laughton's brother. It was full of fabulous pictures, but was not really in very good repair when Bob took it over. Now it's a magnificent place and he's doing things to it all the time. When he asked me for a weekend there, I had the Gordon Highlanders Suite. I asked, could my friends Olivia and Terry come? They were put into the Beryl Evetts Suite, dominated by a wonderful picture of Auntie Beryl.

His right arm is a girl called Gillian Lindo. I first met Gillian when I was doing *One to Another*, because she worked for Baxter Somerville. She then went to Robert Luff's agency, and since Auntie Beryl died Gillian has been made a director of the firm, and quite rightly so. She is so efficient and clever with accountants and with my friend Innes. I have great regard for Gillie, who looks after everything for me, apart from really big decisions, in which case Robert Luff takes over. He's really quite a tough Luff, when it comes to business deals. I'm very glad about that, because I could no more say how much I was worth than roller-skate. James Sharkey, my other agent, looks after the film and straight theatre side of my career, and argues my worth. I sort of laugh. How do you *know* what you're worth? I don't.

I don't know anything much, really. When I worked with Peter Graves – Lord Graves, as the stage door keeper of the Strand Theatre would call him, to his embarrassment – in the days when Jimmy Sharkey and I were shaking a leg or two together in revue – I rang Peter and said, 'Do you know I've been living in a sort of Fools' Paradise? I thought nobody could see the elastic band which keeps my hair together at the back. In fact, everybody can see it.' He said, 'I have been meaning to talk to you about your hair – I think you really should have it restyled.' He recommended I should go to Mr Teasy-Weasy.

So I went. This man obviously had never heard of me: I'd heard of him, and he was doing my hair himself. After I'd had my hair shampooed by some underling, he then said, 'Now your hair is terrible. If you ever want to be well known at all you should have it platinum blonde, like Diana Dors. Now shall we do that today?' I said, 'No, we won't!' and I walked into Bond Street with my hair wringing wet. I went to lunch with Peter Graves with these strings of hair hanging down, and I said, 'You see what happens, Peter, when I go to have my hair "restyled"? Look at it; look at it!' He didn't want to laugh, but, of course, he had to. He said, 'Never mind, Bee. Don't forget, if you ever want a tall bald fool to assist you, I'm your man!'

Peter's sense of humour never fails him, and he certainly needed it that day. I have one or two theories about comedy, but it's impossible really to define. What I do feel very strongly is that audiences must love the people before they can laugh at them. There has to be a great deal of affection going between the audience and the performers, whatever you're saying and however witty or clever you're being. I think the great thing about women is that they should never really lose their femininity. I can't laugh at grotesque women, and I think lots of men can't. They do in America, but they don't here. Humour is so entirely personal: I think somebody's funny – somebody else doesn't think they're funny. But the audience must feel affection for the person who is aiming to make them laugh.

My mother's humour was great, but almost entirely unconscious. There were family phrases which now strike one as funny, but always because they conjured up a true picture of what she was aiming to express. If she was fed up with me, she would say, 'You can just hang as you grow, Beryl!' and I've always said, 'I just hang as I grow.' I suppose it means unattended for the moment. I was terribly untidy: I have had to make myself tidy: my dressing-room has to be tidy, my make-up has to be all in order – everything has to be tidy in the theatre. It's quite difficult to keep a house tidy with ten cats, because there have to be naughty paper bags to play in and things like that, but when I was young I was frightfully untidy and I just used to drop my clothes as I took them off. My mother used to look at me and say, 'Beryl, you're just a hashmagundy!' which, of course, meant, in her own language, an absolute slop-can.

I am, of course, a bit set in my ways, so it was very hard to do 'Desert Island Discs' twice. My tastes don't seem to change much in the way of records, but Roy Plomley's great for making you talk. He's a very, very fine interviewer, and has done so much homework before you get there that whatever happens, he's going to bring you out. It was because of doing 'Desert Island Discs' the second time around that I was eventually persuaded, after fighting against writing a book for fifteen years, that I had so much to say on that programme that the deal was clinched. I was taken out to lunch, a very good lunch too, so I said, 'All right.' I gave in, and this is the result of me giving in.

When Roy Plomley said, 'What would you say is your favourite thing?' I said, 'Oh, living at Honeypot Cottage.' So that is what he filmed for his television programme, 'Favourite Things'. Apart from its sheer beauty, it keeps me what I hope is totally sane, because when you are working on plays, all you have to do is get onto the M4, drive along a few miles and there you are, in complete peace and with beautiful water to look at. The water changes every day. Sometimes it looks as if it's going the wrong way, that's when the wind's blowing on it. Sometimes, first thing in the morning, it's totally still and there's the most perfect reflection. Opposite me is a great bank of chestnut trees: first of all you have the joy of their flowering in the spring, then, when the flowers fall, there is a carpet of pink and white under the trees. When they're reflected in the water, I think, I'm just the luckiest person in the world, a) to be able to see and b) to be able to enjoy what I do see, and get so much pleasure out of it.

We had two days with Roy Plomley filming, cooking and all the things I like doing, including playing with the cats, who get a bit temperamental when a camera crew is around until curiosity gets the better of them, when their natural love of being in on the action takes over. They don't like a lot of people and they don't like a lot of noise, and I think I'm the same.

Having given in to becoming an 'authoress' it was just a question of finding the time to get down to the book, and I was almost set to go when an offer came to appear in one of my favourite television programmes. So once again I gave in, because I couldn't resist doing a 'Minder'. I even played an authoress, called Ruby, who talks into a tape recorder. The episode is called 'The Second Time Around'.

I had never met Dennis Waterman before. He's really lovely to work with, full of energy and life, while George Cole, whom I've known for years, is very quiet. But they must get on very well together, because they share a caravan. They work extremely hard: George Cole leaves his home, which is further away from the studio than mine, every morning at a quarter past six, and he must have been doing that for a long time, when you think of how many programmes he's done.

Anthony Cornish is a wonderful director with whom I've had two absolutely lovely opportunities of working. He now works for Capital Radio, and the Duke of York's is owned by Capital so we could talk on the phone whenever we liked. We didn't see each other very often, because our times conflicted: my curtain didn't ring up till half-past seven, and by that time his working day, though he works very long hours, was practically over. The first play we did together was Arnold Bennett's *Riceyman Steps*, adapted quite superbly for radio, and the second, *Miss Lambert's Last Dance*, written with a touch of genius by Jennifer Phillips. Her powers of description are so remarkable. This woman is going on the bus in evening dress to play at a dancing school, and they think they're going to pension her off. She stands at the bus stop with nylon gloves on, and a long evening dress and a very tatty fur coat, telling her friend of the glory awaiting her, and in the end she gets quite beyond herself through drink and decides not to retire at all.

We rehearsed for four days and I think recorded for two, and Anthony Cornish sat with me all the time. He directs you as thoroughly as if you're doing a stage play. When you're on radio, having done a lot of stage plays and television, you have to realize that your voice is all you can use. You're solely dependent on this one thing – your voice, which you must play as a sort of emotional musical instrument.

Another challenge was to appear in 'Dr Who' as Captain Briggs. I was a very tough lady in this – all in leather – and I spoke in a very harsh voice, saying things like, 'Look, here, Mister!' to people. We did four episodes in two days, a heavy schedule although we had rehearsed them the week before. I worked quite hard at it, but I couldn't really take it seriously. I sat at this enormous machine like a Mighty Wurlitzer, and I really didn't know what it was all about. I had lines like, 'I'm going into Warp Drive.' 'Is that just off the Earl's Court Road?'

I said, but of course nobody laughed: nobody thought *any* of those things were funny – they were all so deadly serious about it.

I hadn't realized that nothing must be made fun of; it is a cult. I get magazines sent to me from America about it and all that sort of thing: it's very serious to a great number of people. I must say, it could never be to me. It was in an enormous studio, and we had these gigantic people – tall, tall, tall, who had come back into the story: they were the baddies, and as all sci-fi buffs will know, they are the Cybermen. The lady floor manager was at the other end, and there was supposed to be a bang from a gun, which, of course, we didn't hear, because it was recorded afterwards, and she said, 'Fall down – you're dead! Come along, now, fall down: don't delay; hurry up – fall down – you're all dead!'

That was something I was, in a way, glad I did, because children thought it was OK. Yet, in another way I'm sorry, because it is, perhaps, the only thing in my career that I've never felt really sincerely about. During this period James Warwick (with whose brother, Philip York, who calls me 'Hugabillity Reid', I've recently done a revue and who is married to Jan Waters) got into absolute knots, like I did about the whole thing. We got into a space capsule and hoped to disappear before we were discovered laughing again, because we'd only be ticked off, and that programme was really like being back at school.

This book almost had no ending. Or, at least, no happy ending, and I'm all for those. Some time ago a clairvoyant called Kim Tracey asked if she could come to my house. She brought stones called Runes. I had never heard of them, but it's a very old way of fortune telling. You yourself arrange them in a circle, and they look like beautifully carved dominoes. She told me a lot of very revealing things about myself and I was enchanted by her. She was with her daughter and her manager, and she loved my surroundings.

The time came when Lulu, one of my dottier cats, was missing. I said to Kim, 'I'm terribly worried.' I rang her up, because she lives in Chatham. I said, 'I can't find Lulu.' She said, 'Oh, she's all right: she's not very happy, but she will be back, but maybe not for two or three days.' She did come back, not very happy, but she was all right.

It was coming up to the last day's work on my story, when my cat Dimly gave me a terrible turn. I hadn't seen him for three days, and normally he comes as soon as I call him. They mostly all do, though Muriel and Sir Harry, his brother and sister, are apt to wander a bit; but not Dimly. I got so desperate that I rang Kim up and told her he was missing and how worried I was. He's a friendly little cat, and he would go off with anybody who had a funny twig in their hand or who stroked him. I really couldn't understand what had happened, and I got up at 5 o'clock on Sunday morning looking for him and calling and calling.

It was about midday when I rang her. She said, 'It seems a silly thing to say, Beryl, but it's something connected with water, and he's shut in. Is there a boatyard near you?' I said, 'Oh, yes, but there's nobody there just now. I don't think he'd be shut in there.' He didn't come home that night, and I telephoned her on the Monday morning. She said, 'Get dressed and go round to the boatyard now, because I'm quite certain that that's where he is.'

I did exactly as she told me. I walked round to the boatyard with Muriel and Sir Harry. I was rather nervous, because we were on what's called the Big Road, Old Ferry Drive. They cried and cried, and I said, 'Oh, do be quiet, because I won't know if I hear Dimly.' I looked in all the boats, then I got to a locked-up shed – and there was Dimly, not quite as large as life, a little bit thinner. I couldn't see how I could get him out, because it had a padlock on it and it was glass with metal bars going down. Behind the glass was chicken wire, so I couldn't break the glass and offer to repay them or anything.

I found an iron bar and with all my strength I pulled at the bottom of the door until there was just room for Dimly's head to come out. It was such an extraordinary relief. He was not quite three then: he was going to be three on my birthday, 17 June. It was such a joy to have him back and I'm so grateful to Kim for helping me. I rang her up immediately, and she said, 'Oh, it's so lovely to be *right* sometimes.' She takes all her obviously great gifts with a pinch of salt, but she's a very strong and lovable person, and really caring.

And now my heart's beating properly again, because I've had a dry mouth and my heart bumping, when I thought I would never see the little fellow again. And here he is, as large as life, and perhaps nervous – but quite cheeky.

What's the key to my life? Well, you can't really sum it up in a phrase, but really what I most treasure is the gift not only to be happy, but to *know* when I'm happy at the time. Right back in childhood I had this gift, and it's never deserted me. One day I said to my mother, 'It's such a lovely day! Oh Mummy, it's a really lovely day.' And she said, 'Well, Beryl, you're getting your share of it!'

Appendix One:

Theatre

North Regional Follies, summer season. Professional debut, as Soubrette-Impressionist. Presented by Fred Rayne. With Horace and Edna Mashford. Floral Hall, Bridlington; May to second week September 1936

Aladdin, as Genie of the Ring, Fairy, Second Boy, Principal Girl. Presented by Jack Gillam. With Reginald Vincent, Vera McLean. Tour, from Hippodrome, Salford; 24 December 1936; Metropole, Openshaw; King's Palace, Preston

Arnold Crowther Show, summer season, as School Girl Impressionist, and presenting 'My Radio', acts written by Arnold Crowther. Presented by Jack Gillam. With Crowther, 'Horace', Six Zio Angels. Arcadia, Scarborough; May 1937

Variety for Hyman Zahl, Al Burnett. Dates included County, Bedford, with Nellie Wallace; Argyll, Birkenhead, with Billy Reid and His Accordion Band, Dorothy Squires. Also on bills with Max Miller, Harry Champion, Billy Russell, G. H. Elliott, Randolph Sutton, Robb Wilton, Billy Bennett, George Formby Jnr. Sunday concerts for Butlin's, Skegness; 1937–1940

Cine-Variety, following talent contest at Paramount Cinema, Manchester. 5-a-Day; Paramount, Tottenham Court Road; Astoria, Brixton: Astoria, Old Kent Road etc; 1938

Blue Skies, touring revue, presented by Ernest Binns. With Olivia Jevons, Brian Seymour. Home Counties; Lancashire, including St Helen's; 1938

Mother Goose, as Gretchen, pantomime tour, presented by Ernest Binns. With Harry Orchard. Lancashire; December 1938

Summer Season, as Soubrette-Impressionist. With Pat Cross, Hal Swain. Church Hall, Saltburn; May 1939

Variety with Flotsam and Jetsam, presented by them. Repertory Theatre, Scarborough; October 1939

Little Bo Peep, as Bo Peep, presented by Repertory Theatre, Swindon; December 1939

ENSA Tour, as Soubrette-Impressionist, presented by Basil Dean. With Koringa, playing Armed Forces Camps, US Air Bases etc; 3 years from 1940

Will Fyffe Show, touring variety road-show, presented by Harry Bright. With the Dagenham Girl Pipers, Bert Brownbill. Home Counties; Scotland, including Empire, Glasgow; 1942

Dave Morris Show, summer season, as Soubrette-Impressionist, presented by Lawrence Wright. With the Norman Thomas Trio. North Pier, Blackpool; May 1941

Cinderella, as Ugly Sister, presented by Tom Arnold. With Jack Buchanan as Buttons, Jean Gillie, Fred Emney, Adèle Dixon (later Kitty Reidy), Nat Jackley, Elsie Percival (later Marianne Lincoln). Sheffield opening; December 1941, postponed due to bombing; returned there after opening Manchester. Subsequently Empire, Liverpool; December 1942; Theatre Royal, Birmingham; December 1943

Variety for Moss Empires throughout the British Isles, from mid-forties

The Sleeping Beauty, as Trixie, presented by Tom Arnold. With Douglas Byng, Betty Frankiss. Theatre Royal, Nottingham; December 1944

Mother Goose, as Gretchen, presented by Tom Arnold. With Douglas Byng, Wilfred Pickles, Tessa Deane, Georgette Bishop. Empire, Liverpool; December 1945

Betty, musical comedy, Moss Empires Tour, as Estelle, presented by Harry Benet. With Jean Inglis, Elsie Prince, Jack Lester, Hilda Campbell-Russell, Betty Leslie-Smith; spring 1946

The Half-Past Eight Show, second lead in summer season, presented by A. Stewart Cruikshank for Howard &

Wyndham, directed Charles Ross. With Dave Willis, Jack Tripp (joined half-way through season), Hope Jackman, Jimmy Plant, Helen Carrera. Theatre Royal; Edinburgh; May 1946. Subsequently with Harry Gordon as lead. King's, Glasgow; May 1947

The Gaiety Whirl, second lead in autumn–winter season, presented by Eric Popplewell, directed Jack Barton. With Robert Wilson (later Dave Willis), Jack Tripp, Joan Mann. Gaiety, Ayr; Autumn 1947

Mother Goose, as Gretchen. Story by J. Hickory Wood, presented by Prince Littler, directed Ellis Holland. With George Gee, Jill Manners, Archie Glenn, Sylvia Lane. Hippodrome, Bristol; 24 December 1949. Subsequently Hippodrome, Brighton; 23 December 1950

Clifford Stanton Show, summer season. With Mary Brooks, Bill Footer. New, Newquay; May 1949

Roy Barbour Show, principal comedienne in summer season. Presented by Catlin's. With The Burt Twins. Wellington Pier Pavilion, Great Yarmouth; May 1950

Mother Goose, as Gretchen, presented by A. Stewart Cruikshank for Howard and Wyndham, directed Freddie Carpenter. With George Lacy, Victoria Elliott. Royal Court, Liverpool; 24 December 1951

After the Show, revue, by Peter Myers and Alec Grahame. Presented by New Watergate Theatre Club. With Robert Dorning, Maeve Leslie, Allan Gabriel. Watergate, WC2; March 1951. Transferred by John Regan Managements, by arrangement with Dare Clingberg & John K. Gibson, directed by John Regan, assisted Christopher Hewett, to St Martin's; April 1951

Sunday Concert, as 'Interlude'. With Isobel Baillie, Phyllis Sellick and Cyril Smith. Royal Albert Hall; Festival of Britain 1951 (May–June)

These Radio Times, leading lady in one-year tour, presented by Moss Empires. With Max Wall, the Hedley Ward Trio, including Chiswick Empire; September 1952

First Edition, revue, devised and directed by Ronnie Hill, staged Ian (Marc) Stuart. With Nicholas Parsons, Petra

Davies, Robert Bishop, James Gilbert, Barbara Leigh. New Watergate Theatre Club; 11 March 1952

Second Edition, ditto, staged by Lionel Blair; summer 1952

Autumn Revue, devised and directed by Ronnie Hill, presented by Ian Tucker for New Watergate Theatre Club, staged James Browne. With Barry Sinclair, Bill Pertwee, Pamela Charles; 27 October 1952

Educating Archie, as Monica, later Marlene, in touring road shows for Moss Empires. With Peter Brough, Archie Andrews, other members of team; from 1952 to 1954

Music for the Millions, variety tour presented by Harold Fielding. Acts included the Hedley Ward Trio, Kay Cavendish. Floral Hall, Scarborough; 15 June 1953, on through Bournemouth, Llandudno, Harrogate, Cheltenham; summer dates 1954, 1955

Goody Two-Shoes, as Marlene. Presented by Bob & Maurice Kennedy. Hippodrome, Dudley; 24 December 1955

The World's the Limit, leading lady in revue with storyline by James Gilbert and Julian More. Devised, directed Ronnie Hill, presented John Counsell. With Peter Graves, Patrick Cargill, James Sharkey, Roderick Cook, Isabel George. Theatre Royal, Windsor; 7 June 1955

Rockin' the Town, revue, presented by Val Parnell, directed by Robert Nesbitt. With Harry Secombe, Winifred Atwell, Alma Cogan. London Palladium; May 1956

Aladdin, as Marlene, presented by S. H. Newsome, devised, directed, choreographed Pauline Grant. With Eve Boswell, Joe Church, Sonny Jenks, Dennis Noble. Coventry Theatre; 24 December 1956

The Dream House, as the Fortune Teller, by Philip King & Faulkland Carey, presented by Melville Gillam. With Bill Owen, Elizabeth Spriggs, Sheila Shand-Gibbs, Pamela Charles. Connaught, Worthing; 24 June 1957

Tonight at 8.30, three playlets by Noel Coward: 'Brief Encounter', 'Red Peppers', 'Still Life', directed by Hugh Goldie, presented John Counsell. With Graham Payn. Theatre Royal, Windsor; 19 August 1957

Jack and the Beanstalk, as Marlene. Presented by Tom Arnold, devised, directed E. Kelland-Espinosa. With Reg Dixon, Audrey Jeans. Hippodrome, Birmingham; 24 December 1957

Nude with Violin, as Cherry-May Waterton. By Noel Coward, presented by John Counsell for Windsor Repertory Company, directed by Joan Riley. With Peter Graves, Noel Dyson. Theatre Royal, Windsor; 19 May 1958

Witch Errant, as Gertrude Blunt. By R. A. Dick, presented by Melville Gillam, directed Guy Vaesen. With Gerald Flood, Angela Browne. Connaught, Worthing; 23 June 1958

Music for the Millions, variety tour, presented by Harold Fielding. Acts incl. Kenneth Earle and Malcolm Vaughan, Bernard Miles. Winter Gardens, Bournemouth; from July 1958

Jack and the Beanstalk, as Marlene. Presented by Tom Arnold, devised and directed E. Kelland-Espinosa. With Audrey Jeans, Joe Black, Billy Whittaker. Theatre Royal, Nottingham; 24 December 1958

One to Another, revue. By John Mortimer, N. F. Simpson, Harold Pinter, John Cranko, Dorothy Parker et al., presented by J. Baxter Somerville, directed Eleanor Fazan. With Patrick Wymark, Barbara Evans, Sheila Hancock, Patricia Bredin, Joe Melia. Theatre Royal, Margate; 30 June 1959: Lyric Opera House, Hammersmith; 15 July 1959; Apollo; 19 August 1959

Fun and Games, revue. Presented by Stewart Cruikshank, for Howard & Wyndham, directed Dick Hurran. With Bill Maynard, Ivor Emmanuel, Jean Bayliss. Royal Court, Liverpool; 22 December 1959

Green Room Rag, Pinter's 'Black And White' sketch from 'One To Another', with Sheila Hancock. Adelphi; 2 May 1960

It's the Tops, summer show. Presented by Tom Arnold, devised, directed E. Kelland-Espinosa. With Derek Roy, Gary Miller. The Lido, Cliftonville, Margate; 24 June 1960

Night of 100 Stars, midnight revue, in aid of Actors' Orphanage. Staged by Charles Russell. Incl. Beatrice Lillie, Sybil Thorndike, Richard Attenborough, Donald Sinden. London Palladium; 21 July 1960

The Pied Piper of Hamelin, as Grand Duchess Marlene, Electress of Dresden. Presented by S. H. Newsome, devised, directed and choreographed Pauline Grant. With Ken Dodd, Janie Marden. Coventry Theatre; 26 December 1960

On the Avenue, revue. By Arthur Macrae, Paul Dehn. Presented by H. M. Tennent, directed William Chappell. With Joan Heal, George Rose. Alexandra, Birmingham; 17 April 1961; Globe; 21 June 1961

Summer Startime, brief variety tour with Reg Dixon. Palace, Manchester; 7 August 1961

Something New, revue, presented by Leonard Schach. With John Boulter, Francois Swart. Hofmeyr, Cape Town, South Africa; 6 December 1961

The '62 Spring Show, revue. Presented by S. H. Newsome, directed Joan Davis. With Jimmy Edwards, Joan Regan, the Dallas Boys, Clark Brothers. Coventry Theatre; 3 April 1962

Let's Make a Night of It, summer show. Presented by Richard Stone, directed Bill Roberton. With Craig Douglas, Billy Burden. White Rock Pavilion, Hastings; 18 June 1962; Knightstone, Weston-super-Mare; 6 July 1962

S. H. Newsome's Autumn Spectacular, revue. Presented by Leslie A. MacDonnell for S. H. Newsome, directed Joan Davis. With Jimmy Edwards, Adèle Leigh, the Dallas Boys. Palace, Manchester; 22 October 1962

Royal Variety in the presence of HM Queen Elizabeth II. With Jimmy Edwards, Peter Brough, Michael Bentine; 14 December 1962

Mother Goose, as Marlene, maid to Jack Tripp's Mother Goose. Presented and directed by Derek Salberg. With Frank Ifield, Ted Rogers, the Dallas Boys, Allen Christie. Alexandra, Birmingham; 22 December 1962

All Square, revue. By Alan Melville. Presented by Linnit and Dunfee Ltd, directed Charles Hickman. With Naunton Wayne, Joyce Blair, Robin Hunter, John Warner, Julian Holloway, Nicky Henson. New, Oxford; 8 April 1963; Vaudeville; 25 April 1963

Night of 100 Stars, midnight revue for Actors' Charitable Trust.

Staged by Charles Russell. Incl. Richard Burton, Elizabeth Taylor, Jessie Matthews, Anna Neagle, Coral Browne, Leslie Caron. London Palladium; 18 July 1963

Autumn Spectacular, revue. Presented by Leslie A. MacDonnell for S. H. Newsome, directed Joan Davis. With Jimmy Edwards, Reg Varney, the Raindrops. Hippodrome, Bristol; 18 July 1963; Empire, Liverpool; 14 October 1963

Mother Goose, as Marlene. Presented by Derek Salberg, directed by Allen Christie. With Ted Rogers, Jack Tripp, the Dallas Boys. Grand, Wolverhampton; 24 December 1963

Night of 100 Stars, midnight revue for Actors' Charitable Trust. Staged by Charles Russell. Incl. Judy Garland, the Beatles, Frankie Vaughan. London Palladium; 24 July 1964

Victorian Music Hall, presented by John Counsell. With Ronnie Corbett, Jamie Phillips. Theatre Royal, Windsor; 31 August 1964

Dick Whittington, as Marlene. Book by Phil Park, David Croft. Music, lyrics Cyril Ornadel; Beryl Reid's material George Evans, Derek Collyer. Presented by Tom Arnold, directed Louis Barber from the production by E. Kelland-Espinosa. With Tommy Cooper, Gary Miller, Billy Whittaker. Golders Green Hippodrome; 24 December 1964

The Killing of Sister George, as June Buckridge. By Frank Marcus. Presented by the Old Vic Theatre Trust for Michael Codron, directed Val May. With Eileen Atkins, Lally Bowers. Theatre Royal, Bristol; 20 April 1965: Duke of York's; 17 June 1965: St Martin's; 18 April 1966; presented by Helen Bonfils and Morton Gottlieb; Belasco, New York; 5 October 1966

Blithe Spirit, as Madame Arcati. By Noel Coward. Presented by H. M. Tennent Ltd, by arrangement with Arthur Cantor and the Yvonne Arnaud Theatre, directed Nigel Patrick. With Phyllis Calvert (later Ursula Howells, Rosemary Martin), Peter Gray (later Patrick Cargill), Amanda Reiss. Yvonne Arnaud, Guildford; 2 June 1970; Globe; 23 July 1970; O'Keefe Center, Toronto; January 1971

Fall In the Stars, Charity for the Army Benevolent Fund before Princess Anne. Organized by Harry Secombe, presented Louis Benjamin. Incl. Vera Lynn, John Mills, Coral Browne, Bill Fraser, the Beverley Sisters. London Palladium; 19 April 1971.

Repeated 1 April 1973 before Princess Margaret, incl. Harry
Secombe, Ronnie Corbett, Joan Greenwood, Geraint Evans.

Spring Awakening, as Frau Bergmann. By Frank Wedekind,
translated by Edward Bond. Presented by the National
Theatre, directed Bill Bryden. With Cyril Cusack, Peter Firth,
Veronica Quilligan, Jenny Agutter. Old Vic; 28 May 1974.
Tour: Oxford Playhouse; 1 July 1974

Those Good Old Days, Sunday music hall, Sundays only.
Presented by Robert Luff Holdings, in association with MAM
Productions Ltd. With Arthur Askey, Walter Landauer.
Pavilion, Bournemouth; 30 June 1974

Romeo and Juliet, as the Nurse. By William Shakespeare.
Presented by the National Theatre, directed Bill Bryden. With
Peter Firth, Veronica Quilligan, Michael Kitchen. Key,
Peterborough; 31 July 1974; Old Vic; 28 August 1974

Entertaining Mr Sloane, as Kath. By Joe Orton. Presented by
Eddie Kulukundis, Michael White, directed Roger Croucher
(later Lindsay Anderson). With Malcolm McDowell (later
Kenneth Cranham), Ronald Fraser (later Harry H. Corbett),
James Ottaway. Royal Court; 17 April 1975; Duke of York's;
2 June 1975

Il Campiello, as Donna Katherina. By Carlo Goldoni,
translated Bill Bryden, Susannah Graham-Jones, directed by
Bryden. Presented by the National Theatre Company. With
Michael Gough, Peggy Mount, Stephen Rea. Olivier Theatre
at the National; gala opening in the presence of HM Queen
Elizabeth II, 25 October 1976

Counting the Ways, vaudeville. By Edward Albee. World
première, presented by the National Theatre Company,
directed Bill Bryden. With Michael Gough. Olivier
Theatre at the National; 6 December 1976; Lyttleton,
21 January 1977

The Way of the World, as Lady Wishfort. By William Congreve.
Presented by the Royal Shakespeare Company, directed John
Barton. With Judi Dench, Michael Pennington, Roger Rees.
Aldwych; 27 January 1978

The Rivals, rehearsals as Mrs Malaprop interrupted by an
accident at home. The Prospect Theatre Production of

Richard Brinsley Sheridan's comedy, directed by and costarring Anthony Quayle, opened with Margaret Courtenay deputizing. The Old Vic; 10 September 1978

Born in the Gardens, as Maud. Written, directed by Peter Nichols (later Clifford Williams). Presented by Bristol Old Vic Trust for Eddie Kulukundis and John Wallbank (Knightsbridge Theatrical Productions Ltd) and Archie Stirling and Howard Panter (Archie Stirling Ltd). With Barry Foster, Peter Bowles, Jennie Linden (later Jan Waters). Theatre Royal, Bristol; 29 August 1979; Globe; 23 January 1980

The School for Scandal, as Mrs Candour. By Richard Brinsley Sheridan, presented by Duncan C. Weldon with Paul Gregg and Lionel Becker for Triumph Apollo Productions, directed by John Barton with Peter Stevenson. With Donald Sinden, Michael Denison, Dulcie Gray, Judy Buxton, Sebastian Shaw, Bill Fraser, Michael Siberry. Grand, Leeds; 30 November 1982; Theatre Royal, Haymarket; 7 January 1983

A Little Bit on the Side, revue. Sketches by Alan Melville, Harold Pinter, Eric Merriman, Victoria Wood, Ronald Wolfe et al.; lyrics by Norman Newell, music Cyril Ornadel, Roger Webb. Presented by Duncan C. Weldon with Paul Gregg and Lionel Becker for Triumph Apollo Productions Ltd, by arrangement with the Yvonne Arnaud Theatre, directed William Chappell. With Jan Waters, Janet Mahoney. Yvonne Arnaud, Guildford; 31 August 1983; tour

The School for Scandal, as Mrs Candour. By Richard Brinsley Sheridan, presented by Duncan C. Weldon with Paul Gregg and Lionel Becker for Triumph Apollo Productions, directed by John Barton with Peter Stevenson. With Donald Sinden, Michael Denison (later John McCallum), Dulcie Gray, Nicola Pagett, Clive Francis, Harold Innocent, Bill Fraser, Michael Siberry. Duke of York's; 15 December 1983

Gigi, as Mamita. Book and lyrics by Alan Jay Lerner, from the novel by Colette. Music by Frederick Loewe. Presented by Peter Baldwin, Helen Montague, Louis Benjamin, Jerome Minskoff, directed John Dexter. With Jean-Pierre Aumont, Amanda Waring, Sian Phillips. Lyric; 11th September, 1985

Appendix Two:

Film

Abbreviation: B & W – black and white. Main players listed. Dates quoted refer to first British showing following year of production, where different. Subjects listed in the order filmed.

1 *Spare a Copper*. Associated Talking Pictures Production. Directed by John Paddy Carstairs, associate producer Basil Dearden also screenplay, with Roger MacDougall, Austin Melford, Basil Dearden. B & W. As George Formby's musical 'opposition', soprano in pince-nez, in comedy number. 79 mins. Dorothy Hyson, George Merritt, Ellen Pollock, John Warwick, Bernard Lee. December 1940.

2 *The Belles of St Trinian's*. Launder and Gilliat Production/ British Lion. Directed and produced by Frank Launder and Sidney Gilliat, also screenplay, with Val Guest. B & W. 91 mins. Inspired by Ronald Searle's drawings of monstrous schoolgirl tribe. As Miss Wilson, science and maths mistress. Alastair Sim as Headmistress Miss Fritton. George Cole, Hermione Baddeley, Irene Handl, Renee Houston, Joyce Grenfell, Betty Ann Davies. September 1954.

3 *The Extra Day*. William F. Fairchild Production/British Lion. Directed, produced and screenplay by Fairchild. Eastman Colour. 83 mins. As Beryl, Fan Club Member, with Shani Wallis, of singer Dennis Lotis' Appreciation Society. About the reshooting of a lost film, starring himself and France's Simone Simon: Richard Basehart as the American assistant director, Laurence Naismith the European director. (US title: *Desperate Hours*) 1955. March 1956.

4 *Two Way Stretch*. Shepperton Production/British Lion. Directed by Robert Day, producer M. Smedley Aston. Screenplay by John Warren, Len Heath. B & W. 87 mins.

271

As Miss Pringle, prison visitor to the jail where conman Peter Sellers is incarcerated, hatching a plot for a million-pound diamond heist with old lag Wilfrid Hyde-White. Bernard Cribbins, Maurice Denham, David Lodge, Liz Fraser, Irene Handl. Working title: 'Nothing Barred'. 1959. January 1960.

5 *The Dock Brief.* MGM – British production. Directed by James Hill, producer Dimitri de Grunwald. Screenplay by Pierre Rouve from play by John Mortimer. B & W. 90 mins. As Doris Fowle, raucous wife of peace-loving seed merchant Richard Attenborough, who murders her for excessive joviality with lodger David Lodge. Peter Sellers the incompetent lawyer of the title. US: *Trial and Error.* August 1962.

6 *Star!* Robert Wise Production/20th-Century Fox. Directed by Robert Wise, producer Saul Chaplin. Screenplay by William Fairchild. De Luxe Colour. Todd-AO. 174 mins. As Rose, tippling music hall girlfriend of Bruce Forsyth, playing Gertrude Lawrence's father. Julie Andrews as eponymous heroine. Michael Craig, Richard Crenna, Daniel Massey as Noel Coward. Reissued in USA as *Those Were the Happy Times,* 1967. July 1968. 1983: CB5 Fox-Video.

7 *Inspector Clouseau.* United Artists production. Directed by Bud Yorkin, producer Lewis J. Rachmil. Screenplay by Tom and Frank Waldman from Blake Edwards and Maurice Richlin's original character, herein played by Alan Arkin, on the trail of a plot to steal all the money in Switzerland. As Mrs Weaver, a Scot married to Police Inspector Frank Finlay, yet amorously pursuing Clouseau. Colour. Patrick Cargill, Barry Foster, Clive Francis. November 1968.

8 *The Assassination Bureau.* Michael Relph and Basil Dearden Production. Directed by Basil Dearden, produced by Relph, also written, with Wolf Mankowitz. Technicolor. Elaborate black comedy set in Paris at the turn of the century with Oliver Reed as prospective victim and Diana Rigg as feminist investigative journalist. As Madame Otero, bordello keeper. Telly Savalas, Curt Jurgens, Philippe Noiret, Warren Mitchell, Jess Conrad. 1968. March 1969.

9 *The Killing of Sister George.* George Palomar International And Associates and Aldrich Co. Inc. Production. Directed and produced by Robert Aldrich. Screenplay by Lukas Heller from play by Frank Marcus. Metrocolor. 135 mins. Top billed as

soap opera heroine of the title, transposed for screen version
from radio to TV actress about to be written out of her series,
with consequent repercussions in her private life with lover
Alice 'Childie' McNaught, played by Susannah York. Coral
Browne, Patricia Medina, Ronald Fraser, Hugh Paddick.
1968. March 1969.

10 *Entertaining Mr Sloane*. Canterbury Films Production/
Anglo-Amalgamated. Directed by Douglas Hickox, producer
Douglas Kentish. Screenplay by Clive Exton from play by Joe
Orton. Technicolor. 94 mins. Top billed as Kath, ageing
nymphomaniac vying with Harry Andrews as brother Ed for
the affections of Peter McEnery, playing the sleazily dishy
young lodger of the title, who murders their senile Dadda,
Alan Webb. 1969. London première 1 April 1970 in the
presence of Princess Margaret, Countess of Snowdon.
Released June 1970.

11 *The Beast in the Cellar*. Tigon British Production, in
association with Leander. Directed and screenplay by James
Kelly. Producer Graham Harris. Colour. 89 mins. Top billed
as Ellie, the timid one of two spinster sisters with a living
family skeleton below stairs, with Flora Robson as the
dominant Joyče Ballantyne. Tessa Wyatt, John Hamill, T. P.
McKenna. Filmed 1969 as 'Young Man, I Think You're
Dying', title changed to 'Are You Dying, Young Man?'
Released May 1971 as half of double horror bill with 'Blood
On Satan's Claw'.

12 *Psychomania*. Benmar – Scotia-Barber Production. Directed
and screenplay by Don Sharp. Producer Andrew Donally.
Colour. 90 mins. As Mrs Latham, dabbler in the occult, who
pledges the soul of her infant son, played when grown-up by
Nicky Henson, to the Devil, in return for the secret of Eternal
Life. Costarring George Sanders as butler Shadwell, emissary
from Hades, in his last film. Shot 1971 under titles 'The Frogs'
and 'The Living Dead'. Released March 1973 as half of double
horror film with 'The Baby'.

13 *Dr Phibes Rises Again*. American International Pictures
Production/MGM–EMI. Directed by Robert Fuest,
screenplay by him with Robert Blees. Producers Samuel Z.
Arkoff, James H. Donaldson. De Luxe Colour. 88 mins. Guest
role as Mrs Ambrose, scheming travel agent in comedy-horror

thriller starring Vincent Price as the diabolical Doctor.
October 1972.

14 *Father, Dear Father*. Rank Organization Production.
Directed by William G. Stewart, producer Peter J. Thompson.
Screenplay by Johnnie Mortimer, Brian Cooke, based on the
TV series. Colour. Multivista. 99 mins. Guest role as Mrs
Stoppard, charlady to Patrick Cargill, who persuades herself
that he is about to propose to her. Donald Sinden also
guesting. Natasha Pyne, Ann Holloway, Noel Dyson, Ursula
Howells, Richard O'Sullivan. 1972. May 1973.

15 *No Sex Please – We're British*. Columbia–Warner Production.
Directed by Cliff Owen, producer John Woolf. Screenplay by
Brian Cooke, Johnnie Mortimer and Anthony Marriott, from
his play with Alistair Foot. Colour. 91 mins. As Bertha,
costarring with Ronnie Corbett's eccentric Runnicles in film
version of longest-running stage farce: a flood of unsolicited
pornographic material has to be hidden from her when staying
with son Ian Ogilvy and daughter-in-law Susan Penhaligon.
Arthur Lowe as the glamorous but strait-laced lady's suitor.
July 1973.

16 *Joseph Andrews*. Woodfall Production for United Artists.
Directed by Tony Richardson from his screenplay with Allan
Scott, Chris Bryant from Henry Fielding's 18th-century novel.
Producer, Neil Hartlay. Colour. 99 mins. As Mrs Slipslop,
sluttish personal maid to the licentious lady lusting over the
young footman of the title. Costarring with Ann-Margret and
Peter Firth in these roles, also Michael Hordern and Jim Dale,
with an all-star cast. 1976. April 1977.

17 *Rosie Dixon – Night Nurse*. Belling-Parsons Production/
Columbia–Warner. Directed by Justin Cartwright from his
screenplay with Christopher Wood. Producers Davina Belling,
Clive Parsons. Colour. 88 mins. Top billed as Matron in
hospital farce, introducing Debbie Ash in the title role. Arthur
Askey, John Junkin, John LeMesurier, Liz Fraser. 1977.
February 1978.

18 *Carry On, Emmanuelle*. Hemdale Production. Directed by
Gerald Thomas, screenplay by producer Peter Rogers.
Technicolor. 88 mins. Guest role as Mrs Valentine, dominant
mother of spineless Larry Dann. Usual 'Carry On' team,
including Kenneth Griffiths, impotent diplomat husband of

Suzanne Danielle in title role, Joan Sims, Kenneth Connor, Peter Butterworth. 1978. January 1979.

19 (Short) *A Late Flowering Love*. Charles Wallace Co. Picture Production. Directed, produced and screenplay by Charles Wallace, based on poems by John Betjeman and narrated by him: 'Agricultural Caress', 'Myfanwy', 'A Subaltern's Love Story', 'Invasion Exercise on the Poultry Farm'. In latter, as horsey country lady in jokey reprise of her Sister George relationship with Susannah York, who prefers John Alderton. Eric Morecambe, Jenny Agutter, John LeMesurier. Colour. 21 mins. 1980. Released August 1981 as supporting feature to *Raiders of the Lost Ark*.

20 *Yellowbeard*. Orion Pictures Production. Directed by Mel Dariski, producer Carter de Haven. Screenplay by Graham Chapman, Bernard McKenna, Peter Cook. De Luxe Colour. 96 mins. As Lady Lambourn, wife to Cook's noble Lord, she is abducted and raped in the bushes by Chapman as the fearsome pirate of the title. Other guest stars include Susannah York, James Mason, Madeline Kahn, Peter Boyle, Cheech and Chong, Eric Idle, John Cleese, Spike Milligan and Marty Feldman in his last film. September 1983.

21 *The Doctor and the Devils*. Brooksfilms Production. Directed by Freddie Francis, screenplay by Ronald Harwood, based on the story of Burke and Hare. Producer Jonathan Sanger, associate Geoffrey Helman. Colour. Guest role as Mrs Flynn, victim of the Doctors. Timothy Dalton, Jonathan Pryce, Twiggy, Julian Sands, Stephen Rea, Phyllis Logan, Sian Phillips. Filmed at Shepperton Studios from January 1985 for nine weeks.

Appendix Three:

Awards and Nominations

1966: Tony Award (New York), Best Performance by a Female Lead in a Straight Play for *The Killing of Sister George*, as June Buckridge

1969: Golden Globe Nomination, Best Actress for film *The Killing of Sister George*, as June Buckridge

1974: Plays and Players Nomination, Best Supporting Actress for *Spring Awakening*, as Frau Bergmann, and *Romeo and Juliet*, as the Nurse

1977: Plays and Players Nomination, Best Supporting Actress for *The Way of the World*, as Lady Wishfort

1979: BAFTA Nomination, Best TV Actress for *Tinker, Tailor, Soldier, Spy*, as Connie Sachs

1980: SWET Award (London), Best Comedy Performance by an Actress for *Born in the Gardens*, as Maud

1982: BAFTA Award, Best TV Actress for *Smiley's People*, as Connie Sachs

1984: Plays and Players Nomination, Best Actress for *The School for Scandal*, as Mrs Candour

Appendix Four:

Discs and Cassettes

Unless otherwise specified, the date given refers to the recording.

HMV BD 1337 Produced by Wally Ridley May 1955; Rel. July 1955	'Tin Pan Alley Ball' Single 45 RPM Featuring Beryl Reid as Marlene. Side B: Monologue by Ronnie Wolfe, over music by Ken Mackintosh & his Orchestra.
MUSIC FOR PLEASURE MFP 1627/8 Norman Newell Record Production October 1965	'Alice In Wonderland' All-star LP 33⅓ RPM Adapted by Pauline Grant from book by Lewis Carroll. Narration by Dirk Bogarde. Beryl as the Duchess sings, Side One (e) 'Speak Roughly to your Little Boy', with Dorothy Squires as the Cook. Side Two (d) 'Love Makes the World Go Round'. Lyrics Norman Newell, Music Philip Green Orchestra, MD Brian Fahey.
MUSIC FOR PLEASURE MFP 1066 Norman Newell Record Production October 1965	'Hello, Dolly!' LP 33⅓ RPM Beryl stars as Dolly Levi with Arthur Haynes to sing, Side One (1) 'I Put My Hand In' (with Orch. & Chorus); (3) 'Put on Your Sunday Clothes' (with Tony Adams, Richard Fox and Co.); (5) 'Motherhood March' (with Patricia Routledge, Sylvia King); (6) 'Dancing' (with Patricia Routledge, Tony Adams, Richard Fox). Side Two (1) 'Before the Parade Passes By' (with the Co.); (3) 'Hello Dolly!' (with the Co.); (5) 'So Long,

Dearie'; (6) 'Finale' (with Arthur Haynes and Co.). Music, Lyrics Jerry Herman. Orchestra, MD Alyn Ainsworth.

HMV Pop 1489 Norman Newell Record Production November 1965	'Love Makes the World Go Round' Single 45 RPM (Newell–Green) 'When the Circus Comes to Town' With Brian Fahey and Orch. (West–Wittstatt) With Geoff Love and Orch.
EMI STATESIDE SSL 10233 Produced by Michael Kidd for 20th-Century Fox Records 1967 Original Soundtrack Album Rel. July 1968	'Star!' LP 33⅓ RPM Robert Wise's Film Biopic of Gertrude Lawrence Beryl as Rose, girlfriend of her father Side One (3) 'Piccadilly' (with Julie Andrews, Bruce Forsyth) (Williams–Sievier–Morande)
COLUMBIA SX 6299 Produced by Norman Newell Late summer 1968	'One Man's Music' The Songs of Noel Gay LP 33⅓ RPM A Tribute to Noel Gay by Des O'Connor, Beryl Reid, Norman Wisdom. Beryl sings Side One (4) 'I Took My Harp to a Party (Cater–Gay); (3) 'Only a Glass of Champagne' (Wimperis–Gay) With the Mike Sammes Singers, Brian Fahey and his Orchestra.
COLUMBIA SCX 6299	As above. Single 45 RPM
MAJOR– MINOR Budget LP SMC P5005 Produced by Norman Newell January 1969	'Mame' LP 33⅓ RPM Beryl stars as Mame Denis, sings, Side One (2) 'It's Today'; (3) 'Open a New Window'; (5) 'My Best Girl' (with Keith Knight); (6) 'We Need a Little Christmas' (with Charlie Young, Pat Whitmore, Keith Knight). Side Two (2) 'Bosom Buddies' (with Joan Turner); (4) 'That's How Young I Feel'; (5) 'If He Walked into My Life'; (6) 'Finale'

(with the John McCarthy Singers). Music,
Lyrics Jerry Herman.

CONTOUR
Musical
Rendezvous Ltd
2870140
Produced by
Norman Newell
August 1971

'Bedknobs And Broomsticks' LP 33⅓ RPM
Walt Disney Production.
Beryl Reid, Hugh Paddick, Rita
Williams Singers.
Side 1 (3) 'The Age of Not Believing'; (5)
'Don't Let Me Down' (with Hugh
Paddick); (6) 'Portobello Road' (with Hugh
Paddick, Rita Williams Singers).
Side 2 (1) 'The Beautiful Briny' (with Hugh
Paddick, Rita Williams Singers); (2) 'A
Step in the Right Direction' (with Rita
Williams Singers); (4) 'Substitutiary
Locomotion' (with Hugh Paddick); (5)
'Finale' (with Hugh Paddick, Rita Williams
Singers). Words and Music R. M. and R. B.
Sherman. Orchestra, MD Brian Fahey.

PINNACLE
STORY-
TELLER
SERIES
P 9002
Produced by
Andrew
Gardner
September 1971
Rel. November
1971

'Traditional Fairy Stories' Cassette.
By Helen Cresswell.
Storyteller Beryl Reid.

PINNACLE
STORY-
TELLER
DS/90/6016
Rel. Autumn
1972

'Dick Whittington and other Fairy Stories'
Cassette.
By Helen Cresswell.
Storyteller Beryl Reid.

PINNACLE
STORY-
TELLER
P 90002
1972

'Famous Fairy Tales' Cassette.
By Alan Hankinson
Introduced by Andrew Gardner.
Storyteller Beryl Reid.

EMI

'Cinderella' LP 33⅓ RPM

STARLINE SRS 5148 Produced by Norman Newell for David Paradine Productions Rel. December 1972	Presented by Storyteller David Frost. Book by Jan Butlin. Beryl as Ugly Sister sings, Side Two (4) 'Sister, Sister, Sister' (arr. Brian Fahey) with Barbara Windsor. Lyrics Norman Newell, Music Cyril Ornadel. Orchestra, MD Chris Walker.
PYE NSPL 18423 Produced by Paul Ciani for BBC TV October 1973 Soundtrack Album Rel. January 1974	'Smike!' LP 33⅓ RPM Beryl as Mrs Steele/Mrs Squeers in Pop Musical adapted for TV by John Morley and Paul Ciani, freely based on *Nicholas Nickleby* by Charles Dickens. Side One (5) 'Dotheboys Hall' (with Andrew Keir & Chorus); (6) 'We've got the Youngsters' Interests at Heart'. Side Two (2) 'Brimstone and Treacle' (with Chorus); (6) 'Dotheboys Rock' (with Andrew Keir, Leonard Whiting, Christine McKenna: Ian Sharrock & Chorus. Music and lyrics by Roger Holman and Simon May.
MUSIC FOR PLEASURE MFP 50174 Produced by Norman Newell August 1974 A Supertunes Production Assistant Producer on last two records Gil King	'Beryl Reid Music Hall Singalong' LP 33⅓ RPM Side One (1) 'Fall in and Follow Me' (Mills–Scott); (2) 'The Honeysuckle and the Bee' (Fitz–Penn); (3) 'Burlington Bertie from Bow' (Hargreaves); (4) 'If You Were the Only Girl in the World' (Grey–Ayer); (5) 'Oh! Oh! Antonio!' (Murphy–Lipton); (6) 'Moonstruck!' (Monckton). Side Two (1) 'Who Were You with Last Night?' (Sheridan–Godfrey); (2) 'Hold Your Hand Out, Naughty Boy!' (Murphy–David); (3) 'I Live in Trafalgar Square' (Murphy); (4) 'I'll Be Your Sweetheart' (Dacre – arr. Bolton); (5) 'Only a Glass of Champagne' (Wimperis–Gay); (6) 'Don't Dilly Dally on the Way' (Collins–Leigh).
LISTENING FOR	'Little Grey Rabbit' Cassette. By Alison Uttley.

PLEASURE
TCLFP 7031
Produced by
Graham
Goodwin
June 1978
Rel. August
1978

Storyteller Beryl Reid.

Appendix Five:

Selected Radio and TV Appearances 1936–1985

Children's Hour, Guest, doing impressions, in three series. With Wilfred Pickles, Violet Carson at the piano. BBC Manchester; from 1936

A Quarter of an Hour with Beryl Reid, Own series. BBC Manchester; from 1937

Workers' Playtime, Many times guest. Lunchtime shows for war and post-war factory workers. Introduced, produced by Bill Worsley, later John Foreman. Piano, James Moody. Home; early 1940s to approx. 1952

Variety Bandbox, Many appearances. Resident comics over years, Frankie Howerd, Derek Roy, Reg Dixon, Vic Wise, Arthur English, Harry Locke, Billy Ternent and Cyril Stapleton bands. Producer, John Foreman, and others. General Forces Network, then Light; 1940s to 1952

Music Hall, with Jewel and Warriss, Lizbeth Webb, Radio Revellers. Producer, Bill Worsley. Home; 31st March, 1951

Starlight Hour, Guest on twenty programmes. Alfred Marks, Peter Yorke, et al. Script, Sid Colin, additional material from Lionel Harris, Ronnie Wolfe. Presented by Brian Reece, later Fayne and Evans. Producer, Roy Speer. Light; from 7th May, 1951

Vic's Grill, Guest in six programmes with host Vic Wise, Norman Wisdom. Occasionally John Hanson. Producer, Bill Lyon-Shaw. Music, Eric Robinson. BBC TV; 18th April to 27th June, 1951

Diversion, Miniature revue with Turner Layton, Lorrae Desmond, Peter Glover. Producer, Bill Lyon-Shaw. BBC TV; 20th July, 1951

Educating Archie, in character of Monica, later Marlene, created for her by Ronnie Wolfe. Original scripts, Sid Colin and Eric Sykes. Starring Peter Brough, Archie Andrews. Guests over years include Harry Secombe, Max Bygraves, Norman Wisdom, Benny Hill, Alfred Marks, Ronald Chesney, Hattie Jacques and Julie Andrews. Producers, Roy Speer, Joy Leslie-Smith. Started 18th September 1952; on 11th November, 1954, programme called *Archie's the Boy*, with first-time credits of 'Monica' and 'Marlene'. Light; September, 1952 to 1956

The Star Show, Introduced by Joe Linnane. With Jack Watson, Googie Withers, John McCallum, Derek Roy. Producers, Tom Ronald and Michael North. Home; 27th September, 1952

The Centre Show, Guest in Christmas Variety for HM Forces, from Nuffield Centre. Jack Warner. Producers, Kenneth Carter and Mary Cook. Music, Steve Race, Malcolm Lockyer. BBC TV; 23rd December 1952

Henry Hall's Guest Nights, Guest in many shows with other personalities and band. Producer, Alastair Scott-Johnson. Home; new run from 25th September, 1953, but started in early 1950s

Variety Playhouse, Guest, music-hall type programme. Producer, Tom Ronald. Appeared through 1953 and 1954. Home. As 'Marlene from the Midlands' on 18th December, 1953

Christmas Service Show, TV theatre for HM Forces. Introduced by Benny Hill. Many guests, Shirley Abicair, Diana Day. Producer, Kenneth Carter. BBC TV; 21st December, 1953

Garrison Theatre, Guest in show from HMS *Greenock*, with Hedley Ward Trio, Alma Cogan, introduced by Bob Monkhouse. Producer, Barrie Edgar. BBC TV; 12th February, 1954

Showcase, with Benny Hill. Guest with Jeremy Hawk and others. Also artistes new to TV. Producer, Kenneth Carter. BBC TV; 26th April, 1954

Welcome Home to Her Majesty the Queen and Prince Philip from Commonwealth Tour. Introduced by Jack Buchanan and Margaret Lockwood. Peggy Ashcroft, Michael Redgrave, Max Bygraves etc. Producer, Tom Ronald. Home and Light; 15th May, 1954

Benny Hill Show, with Alma Cogan, Jeremy Hawk. Producer, Kenneth Carter. Three shows. BBC TV; 15th January to 12th March, 1955

Wilfred and Mabel Pickles' Silver Wedding, 25th Wedding celebrations shared by BBC Radio and TV. Guest, with Vera Lynn, Jack Train, Dorothy Ward, Eric Portman. Produced by Brian Tesler. 20th September, 1955

Musical Cheers, Guests hosted and produced by Noele Gordon. ITV; Saturday afternoons, mid-1950s

Tea with Noele Gordon, with regular guests. Producers, Noele Gordon, Stephen Wade. ITV. Long running programme; from 11th July, 1956

Billy Cotton Band Show, Guest with Bill Cotton, Alan Breeze. Produced by Bill Cotton, Jnr. BBC TV; 11th June 1957

Mr Bowling Buys a Newspaper, as Alice the maid, in strange, violent tale. Hugh Sinclair, as Mr Bowling. Written by Donald Henderson. Producer, Stephen Harrison. George Howe, Eric Chitty. BBC TV; 15th June 1957

Lunch Box, Guests hosted by Noele Gordon. Producers, Jack Barton, Reg Watson. Jerry Allen trio. ITV; July, 1957 and others

Sunday Night at the London Palladium, Guest with Harry Secombe and others. *Beat the Clock*, compered by Tommy Trinder. Presenter, Val Parnell. Producer and director, Stephen Wade. ITV; 16th September, 1957; many times subsequently

The Most Likely Girl, playing Arethusa Wilderspin, most likely to succeed in Society, marry a Lord, etc. Written by Robert Bishop, with Noele Gordon and Barbara Couper, and occasional guest 'victim'. Comedy in six parts. Produced, directed by Cecil Petty. ITV; from 23rd September, 1957

'Good Evening, Each', Weekly series by Ronald Wolfe, David Climie, Frank Roscoe, produced by Roy Speer. With Ken Platt. Light; 29th April, 1958

Ted Ray Show, Guest, sketches incl. Helga the Wren, produced by Barry Lupino. With Joan Turner, Kenneth Connor. BBC TV; 10th May, 1958

M & B, as Marlene, Beer Commercial Series by Dorland Advertising, Transferred from Midlands. ITV; 1958

Henry Hall Show, Guest, sketches incl. the Sponging Relative. With Wim Sonneveld, Elisabeth Welch. Produced by Ned Sherrin. BBC TV; 9th June, 1958

Beryl Reid's Monday Night Requests, Record Programme Series. Radio Luxembourg; October, 1958

Educating Archie, Return as Monica, in Christmas Special with Peter Brough. Light; December, 1958

Saturday Spectacular, Guest on Frankie Vaughan Show, as Forecaster Lady Pamela, presented by Bernard Delfont. With the King Brothers, Henny Youngman. ITV; 6th December, 1958

A–Z, Presented by Alan Melville, through alphabet of world of entertainment. This week, letter 'R'. Recorded interview with Ginger Rogers. James Robertson Justice, Ronnie Ronalde. Produced, Bryan Sears. BBC TV; 10th June, 1959

Sunday Night at the Prince of Wales, Guest 'Spanish Maid' from 'One To Another', presented by Bernard Delfont, produced by Ken Carter. With Bernard Bresslaw. ITV; 2nd August, 1959

Wednesday Magazine, Mainly for Women series. Reading a story. Also David Jacobs, Janette Scott, H.E. Bates, Robert Kee. Produced by Lorna Pegram. BBC TV; 28th August, 1959

Be My Guest, The Joan Regan Show, with Dickie Valentine, Elizabeth Larner. BBC TV; 11th May, 1960

Laughline, On panel of new cartoon contest. With Digby Wolfe, Bill Owen, Barry Took, Kenneth Williams. Produced by Ned Sherrin, Brian Marker. BBC TV; 25th May, 22nd June, 21st September, 1960

Parade, First edition of new showbiz magazine programme. Guest, with Jacqueline Delman, Joyce and Lionel Blair, Anna Quayle. Introduced by Alan Melville. Produced by Bryan Sears. BBC TV; 5th October, 1960

London Lights, Guest in weekly series, The Life of, compered by Jack Watson, produced by Trafford Whitelock. Light; October to December, 1960

Fifth Anniversary Gala Programme from the Midlands, Guest, ITV; 17th February, 1961

Flying High! From the Royal Air Force Station, Brampton, Huntingdon, presented by Richard Maddock. With Anne Shelton, Martin Lukins. Light; 21st August, 1961

Twelfth Night, as Maria. By William Shakespeare, produced by Val Gielgud, Cedric Messina. With Jimmy Edwards as Sir Toby Belch, Rachel Gurney, June Tobin, Alan Wheatley. Home; 6th January, 1962. Repeat 1964

The Merry Wives of Windsor, as Mistress Quickly. By William Shakespeare produced by Cedric Messina. With Jimmy Edwards as Sir John Falstaff, Moira Lister, June Tobin. Home; 23rd April, 1962

Midland Profile. Interviewed by Noele Gordon, Ivor Jay. ITV; 11th May, 1962

Let's Make A Night Of It. Extracts from Summer Show, with Craig Douglas, Billy Burden, Elsye Monk Trio. BBC TV (Bristol); 11th July, 1962

The Dickie Henderson Show: The Visit, as Miss McDonald. Executive writer: Jimmy Grafton, directed by Bill Hitchcock. ITV; 28th November, 1962

Desert Island Discs, Interviewed by Roy Plomley. Home; 24th June, 1963

Big Night Out, Guest, introduced by Mike and Bernie Winters. With Terry Scott, Jill Day, the King Brothers, Lionel Blair. ITV; 31st August, 1963

Man O' Brass, as Bessie Briggs. Situation Comedy series by Ron Watson, produced by Douglas Moodie. With Wallas Eaton. BBC TV; 28th November, 1963

The Hen House, as Mrs. Teresa Fanwyn. Comedy Playhouse, by George Evans, Derek Collyer, produced by Michael Mills. With Barbara Windsor, Dermot Kelly. BBC TV; 10th January, 1964

The Good Old Days, from City Varieties, Leeds. 'Burlington Bertie', produced by Barney Colehan. With Jack Tripp, Val Doonican, Jo, Jac and Joni. BBC TV; 14th February, 1964 Chairman Leonard Sachs; subsequently 1965, 1973

Bold As Brass, as Bessie Briggs in further episodes of the life of 'The Briggs' by Ron Watson in a new general comedy series by David Climie, produced by Philip Barker. With Jimmy Edwards, Stephane Grappelli. BBC1; 4th April, 1964

Don't Say A Word, Panel Game, devised by Mike Stokey, directed by Daphne Shadwell. Special Guest with John Alderton. Host Ronan O'Casey. ITV; 6th September, 1964

Who Is Mary Morison?, as Maggie. Written and produced by Douglas Moodie inspired by the life of Robbie Burns. With Jess Conrad, Angela Douglas, Maggie Fitzgibbon, Anita Harris, Susan Maughan. BBC2; 15th January, 1965

Not So Much A Programme, More A Way Of Life, Satirical Revue, sketches incl. Woman's Hour Interviewer, Dr. Finlay's 'Janet'. Chairman David Frost. With Eartha Kitt, John Bird, Cleo Laine. Produced by Ned Sherrin. BBC1; 26th February, 1965

'BBC-3', Satirical Revue, Sketches incl. 'Naked as Nature Expected'. Chairman Robert Robinson. With Lynda Baron, Patrick Campbell, Denis Norden, Produced by Ned Sherrin. BBC1; 2nd October 1965

Petticoat Line, Guest, intermittently during the run of panel programme from the feminine viewpoint. In the Chair, Anona Winn. With Renée Houston. Home; October, 1965, yearly until 1972

Call My Bluff, Contest of Words and Wit, on Kenneth Horne's team with Alan Melville vs Frank Muir with Joyce Grenfell, Bernard Braden. Referee Robin Ray. Devised by Mark Goodson, Bill Todman, produced by Bryan Sears. BBC2; 3rd February, 1966. On Robert Morley's Team 16th June 1966

P. G. Wodehouse's 'The World Of Wooster': Jeeves And The Indian Summer Of An Uncle, as Mrs. Wilberforce. Adapted from the short story by Michael Pertwee, produced by Michael Mills, in association with Peter Cotes. With Ian Carmichael, Dennis Price, Fabia Drake. BBC1; 15th February, 1966

The Frankie Howerd Show, as Gilda La Peche, the perennial Film Starlet, by Ray Galton and Alan Simpson, produced by Duncan Wood. With Warren Mitchell, Arthur Mullard, Rita Webb. BBC1; 1st March, 1966

Fault On The Line, as Madge. By Jennifer Phillips, produced by Leslie Magahey. With Patricia Hayes. Home. 22nd April, 1966

The Val Doonican Show, Guest, Special Material by Ronnie Taylor and Val Doonican, produced by John Ammonds. With Kenny Ball and his Jazzmen, Harry Bailey. BBC1; 29th May, 1966, subsequently 1968, 1972

Duggie, as Kate Reilly. Love Story, by Robin Smyth, directed by Alastair Reid, produced Pieter Rogers. With Judy Parfitt, Ray Lonnen, Angela Richards, Ida Barr. ITV; 12th July, 1966

Tony Awards Show. Best performance by an Actress in a Straight Play, as June Buckridge in 'The Killing Of Sister George', presented by Kirk Douglas, Shubert Theatre, New York. ABC TV; 26th March, 1967

Dee Time, Guest on Chat Show hosted by Simon Dee. Directed by Sydney Lotterby. With Donald Peers. BBC1; 11th May, 1967

Juke Box Jury. Record Selection Programme, Guest with Vince Hill. Chairman David Jacobs. Devised, produced by Peter Potter. BBC1; 19th August 1967

Show of the Week, Beryl Reid anthology of outstanding sketches, produced in Colour by Robin Nash, staged by William Chappell, Charles Hickman. With Gary Miller, William Mervyn, Raymond Francis, Avril Elgar. BBC2; 16th September, 1967: *Late Night Line-Up*, Discussion of above show and career

Before the Fringe, Guest in retrospective revue, produced by Robin Nash, introduced by Alan Melville. With Hermione Baddeley, Dora Bryan, Douglas Byng. BBC2; 18th September, 1967; BBC1; 26th August, 1968

The Bird's Nest, as Teresa Fanwyn. By George Evans, Derek Collyer, produced by John Browell. With Heather Chasen, Arthur Howard. Radio 4; 20th September, 1967

Bruce Forsyth Show, Guest, Script Sid Green, Dick Hills, produced by Keith Beckett. With Engelbert Humperdinck. ITV; 24th September, 1967

The Very Merry Widow: Square Meals at Round Tables, Guest Star. By Alan Melville, produced by Robin Nash. With Moira Lister, Donald Hewlett, Molly Urquhart, Rosamund Greenwood. BBC1; 4th December, 1967

The Good Old Days, from City Varieties, Leeds. 'We Live in Trafalgar Square', Tramp, with John Hewer, produced by Barney Colehan. Chairman, Leonard Sachs. BBC1; 29th December, 1967; subsequently 1973

Mrs. Capper's Birthday, as Hilda Capper. By Noel Coward, adapted by William Marchant. Directed by Guy Verney, produced by Leonard White. With Arthur Lowe, Sylvia Coleridge, Jill Dixon, George Baker, Maudie Edwards. ITV; 31st January, 1968

Beryl Reid Says 'Good Evening!', Revue Series with Hugh Paddick, sketches by Arthur Macrae, Alan Melville, Harold Pinter et al. Staged by William Chappell, produced by Robin Nash. BBC1; 4th March, 1968; subsequently weekly till 8th April, 1968

View By Appointment, as Rene Jelliot. Comedy Playhouse. By Jennifer Phillips, produced by Robin Nash. With Hugh Paddick, Derek Fowlds, Pauline Collins. BBC1; 3rd May, 1968

The Eamonn Andrews Show, Guest. Produced by Gordon Reece. With Michael Bentine, Ian Carmichael: ITV; 26th May, 1968; 28th November, 1968

Movie-Go-Round, Guest Interview, script, produced by Lyn Fairhurst. 'Star!' Radio 2; 14th July, 1968. 'Sister George' Interview, 28th July, 1968, subsequently 1969

Johnnie Carson Show; Dick Cavett Show (CBC), Guest on these and other TV chat programmes in New York; 1–3 February, 1969

Edward The Confessor, as Mrs. Blaxhill. Armchair Theatre, by Leigh Vance produced by Henry Caplan. With Alfred Burke, Ian Holm. ITV; 24th February, 1969

Max, Guest, Script by Spike Mullins, Barry Cryer, Dick Vosbrugh, Joe Steeples, produced by William G. Stewart. With Max Bygraves, Aimi Macdonald. ITV; 9th April, 1969

Wink To Me Only, as Rene Jelliot. Situation Comedy Series, with Hugh Paddick as Sid Jelliot. Episode 1 'The Lost Chord' with Peter Butterworth. By Jennifer Phillips, produced by

Douglas Argent. BBC1; 11th June, 1969: subsequently weekly till 9th August, 1969

It's Sunday Night, Guest, David Jacobs Chat Show, produced by David Bell. With Alfred Marks, Frankie Vaughan, Mary Tyler Moore. BBC1; 15th June, 1969

Join Jim Dale, Guest, Script by Barry Cryer, Jim Dale. Producer-director Dennis Vance. ITV 3rd July, 1969

Sound Screen '69. Script, produced by Lyn Fairhurst. Extracts presented by Tony Bilbow from films starring Reid, Crawford, Davis, Stanwyck. Radio 2; 5th September, 1969

The Trouble With You, Lillian. As Madge, Situation Comedy Series by Jennifer Phillips, produced by Keith Williams. With Patricia Hayes. Radio 4; 1. 'The Quick Recovery' 6th October, 1969

Cinderella, as Ugly Sister Marlene. Produced by Freddie Carpenter, directed by Peter Whitmore. With Jimmy Tarbuck, Anita Harris, Jack Tripp, Allen Christie BBC1; Christmas Day, 1969

While We're On The Subject (Show Business). Reminiscences, with Wilfred Pickles, Charles Chilton. BBC2; 27th January, 1970

Woman's Hour. Guest, Introduced by Marjorie Anderson. With Dorothy Dickson, Richard Chamberlain. Radio 4; 13th May, 1970

The Rivals, as Mrs Malaprop. Play of the Month. By Richard Brinsley Sheridan, produced by Cedric Messina, directed by Basil Coleman. With Andrew Cruickshank, Jeremy Brett, Jenny Linden, John Alderton, T.P. McKenna. BBC1; 17th May, 1971.

For Love Of A Lady, Title role, Comedy Parade, by Philip Learoyd, produced by John Cassels. With Brian Rix, Elspet Gray, Campbell Singer. Radio 4; 31st January, 1971

The Misfit . . . On Paperback Revolutionaries, as Mrs. Low Road Jones. By Roy Clarke, directed by James Gatward, produced by Dennis Vance, with Ronald Fraser, Patrick Newell, Freddie Jones. ITV; 8th March, 1971

Storyteller, reading 'The Landlady', by Roald Dahl. Produced by Bill Wyatt. BBC2; 20th March, 1971

The Commuters' Tales, telling 'The Tale of the Midwife' by Richard Gordon to Brian Hewlett and Patrick Tull. Produced by David Hatch. Radio 4; 21st June, 1971

Father, Dear Father: Housey-Housey, as Beryl Pretty. By Johnnie Mortimer and Brian Cooke, directed and produced by William G. Stewart. With Patrick Cargill, Natasha Pyne, Noel Dyson, Ann Holloway, Hugh Paddick. ITV; 29th June, 1971

The Edward Woodward Hour, Guest, Script by Eric Merriman, directed and produced by Reginald Collin. With Nina. ITV; 4th August, 1971

Choice Of Paperbacks, Reviewing *KissKiss* and reading from the work of St. Teresa of Avila. With Norman St. John Stevas, presented by Jacky Gillott, produced by Rosemary Hart. Radio 4; 1st September, 1971

Will Amelia Quint Continue Writing 'A Gnome Called Shorthouse'?, as Best Selling Writer Quint. By Roy Clarke, produced by Jacqueline Davis, directed by James Gatward. With Norman Rossington, Richard Vernon, Geoffrey Chater, David Warbeck, Sheila Steafel. ITV; 28th September, 1971

Harry Secombe Show, Guest, incl. Anne of Cleves to Secombe's Henry VIII. Programme associate Jimmy Grafton, produced by Terry Hughes. BBC1; 2nd October, 1971, subsequently 1972

The Marty Feldman Comedy Machine, Guest, directed by John Robins, produced by Larry Gelbart. With Randy Newman, Spike Milligan, Hugh Paddick. ITV; 18th December, 1971

Stars On Christmas Sunday, reading the Nativity Story, Directed by Len Lurcock, executive producer Jess Yates. With Petula Clark, the Beverley Sisters. ITV; 26th December, 1971, subsequently 1972

The Goodies, Guest, incl. Mrs. Desirée Carthorse, anti-filth campaigner. With Tim Brooke-Taylor, Graeme Garden, Bill Oddie. BBC2, 31st December 1971

Patrick, Dear Patrick, An Evening with Patrick Cargill and his Guests, incl. Queen Victoria, Monica. Script Editor Peter Dulay, directed and produced by William G. Stewart. With Bernard Cribbins, Nina, Joyce Carey, Patrick Macnee. ITV; 26th January, 1972

Show Of The Week, Guest, duetting with Harry Secombe. Julian Orchard, Nana Mouskouri. BBC2; 20th April, 1972

Pete Murray's Open House, Guest Interview. Radio 2; 26th May, 1972

Alcock And Gander, as Marigold Alcock. Situation Comedy Series by Johnnie Mortimer and Brian Cooke, directed and produced by Alan Tarrant. With Richard O'Sullivan, John Cater, ITV; 5th June 1972: subsequently weekly till 10th July, 1972

Out Of The Box, Guest, Quiz programme for the BBC's 50th Anniversary, directed by Peggy Walker. With Denis Norden, Alan Melville, Bill Cotton. BBC2 25th September, 1972

Trapped: Chez Madame Thompson, in the title role, by Jack Gerson. Directed and produced by Liam Hood. With Laurence Naismith, Leigh Lawson. ITV; 25th October, 1972

The Reg Varney Revue, Guest, incl. Monica, Detective Shirley Holmes. Script Dick Vosburgh, Wally Malston, Garry Chambers, David Cumming. Directed and produced by Bryan Izzard. With Adèle Leigh, Pat Coombs, David Lodge. ITV; 25th November, 1972

The Generation Game, Guest, Script by Tony Hawes, produced by Alan Tarrant, James Moir, With Bruce Forsyth, Anthea Redfern. BBC1; 2nd December, 1972

Rainbow: 'Party Food', telling the story of 'Birthday Soup'. ITV; 8th December, 1972, subsequently 1983

A Royal Television Gala Performance of 'The Harry Secombe Show', Guest, before H.M. Queen Elizabeth II and H.R.H. the Duke of Edinburgh. Presented by Bill Cotton Jnr. With Jim Bailey, Anna Moffo. BBC1; 25th July, 1973

Russell Harty Plus, Guest, Editor Tanya Bruce-Lockhart, directed by Mike Mansfield, produced by Derek Bailey. With Malcolm McDowell, Robert Robinson, Alan Price. ITV; 12th August, 1973: *Harry Secombe Show*, produced by Colin Charman, BBC2, 12 August 1973; also BBC 1, 22 December 1973

Looks Familiar, Guest, devised and compiled by Denis Gifford. Directed by Anthony Parker, produced by David Clarke. Chairman Denis Norden. With Harry Fowler, Cardew

Robinson. ITV; 13th August, 1973, subsequently 1977, 1980, 1983

The Best Of 'Good Afternoon' Guest, on female comedians. Interviewed by Ken Ashton. With Arthur Askey. ITV; 21st August, 1973

Michael Parkinson Show, Guest Interview. With Buddy Rich. BBC1; 27th October, 1973

Riceyman Steps, as Violet, dramatisation by James Duckett of novel by Arnold Bennett Radio 4; directed by Anthony Cornish 14th November, 1973

Smike!, as Mrs. Squeers and Headmaster's wife Mrs. Steele; Pop musical based on Charles Dickens' 'Nicholas Nickleby' by John Morley and producer Paul Ciani, Music and lyrics by Roger Holman, Simon May. With Andrew Keir, Leonard Whiting, Perry Clayton, Joel Cooper. BBC2; 26 December 1973

Any Questions?, Guest on Current Affairs Discussion, produced by Michael Bowen from Halewood, Lancashire. Chairman David Jacobs. With Lord Greenwood, Steve Race, Alan Haselhurst, MP. Radio 4; 18th January, 1974, and subsequently

Sounds Familiar, Guest, programme devised and compiled by Denis Gifford, produced by John Cassells. Chairman Barry Took, with Barry Cryer, Hubert Gregg, Jesse Lasky. Radio 2; 14th February, 1974

Des O'Connor Entertains, Guest, as Marlene. With Peters and Lee. Directed and produced by Colin Clews. ITV; 12th March, 1974

Does The Team Think? Guest on Panel. From an idea by Jimmy Edwards, produced by Edward Taylor. With Edwards, Ted Ray, Arthur Askey. Radio 4; June 4th, 1974

Wogan's World, Guest on Chat Show, BBC1; 7th July, 1974

The Comediennes. Guest from past recordings, with Gracie Fields, Marie Lloyd, Beatrice Lillie, Hermiones Baddeley and Gingold et al. Introduced by Nan Winton, produced by John Cassels. Radio 4; 1st January 1975

This Is Your Life, Guest on Geoff Love programme. Introduced by Eamonn Andrews, directed by Robert Reed. ITV; 8th January, 1975

The Apple Cart, as Amanda, Postmistress General. Play of the Month. By George Bernard Shaw, adapted and produced by Cedric Messina. With Nigel Davenport, Helen Mirren, Peter Barkworth, Bill Fraser. BBC1; 18th January, 1975

Good Afternoon, Interview by Mavis Nicholson. BBC1; 17th July, 1975

When We Are Married, as Maria, by J.B. Priestley, directed by David Giles. With Thora Hird, Eric Porter, Richard Pearson, Patricia Routledge, Ronnie Barker. BBC1; 29th December, 1975

This Is Your Life. Subject, introduced by Eamonn Andrews, directed by Mike Dormer, produced by Philip Casson. With Pat Kirkwood, Jack Tripp, Andrew Gardner. ITV; 17th March, 1976

Hughie's Full House, as Heckler in cod Music Hall history. Directed and produced by Ronald Fouracre from Richmond Theatre. With Hughie Green, Bernard Bresslaw, Renée Houston, Pat Coombs, Yvonne Marsh. ITV; 28th April, 1976

The Andy Stewart Show, Guest. With Andy Stewart, Hughie Green. ITV; 16th July, 1976

London–New York, as Guest on the London side of Dick Cavett Show, produced by Steve Minchin. With Peter Cook, Warren Mitchell, Johnny Speight, Carroll O'Connor, Edward Lear, Debbie Reynolds, Eamonn Andrews. ITV; 8th September, 1976

Fall In, The Stars, London Palladium. Sketch with Harry Secombe, produced by William Chappell in the presence of H.M. Queen Elizabeth the Queen Mother. With Vera Lynn, Johnnie Ray, John Gielgud, John Mills et al. ITV; 15th May, 1977

Night Of 100 Stars, Guest, 'Burlington Bertie', in Jubilee Concert at Olivier. With Jessie Matthews, John Gielgud, Elaine Stritch, Dora Bryan et al. BBC1; 5th June, 1977

Pause For Thought, Religious broadcast, Radio 4; 25th July, 1977

Tell Me Another, True Tales from the World of Show Business, Guest of Dick Hills. Directed by John Coxall. With Marti Caine, Roy Hudd, Thora Hird, Millicent Martin. ITV; August 25th 1977 and subsequently

The 78 Show, Panellist on Disc Quiz, compiled, and produced by John Dias. Chairman Shaw Taylor, with Vivian Ellis, Clifford Mollison. Radio 2; 5th October, 1977

Beryl Reid. Script by John Mortimer, N. F. Simpson, Joe Orton, Arthur Macrae, produced by Robin Nash, artistic direction by William Chappell. With Malcolm McDowell, John Standing, Derek Fowlds, Susan Engel, Avril Elgar. BBC2; 12th December, 1977. Repeated 5th April 1978

Flint as Victoria. Play of the Month. By David Mercer, directed by Peter Wood, produced by David Jones. With John LeMesurier, Julie Covington, Dandy Nichols, Peter Bowles. BBC1; 15th January, 1978

Two's Company: The Pet, as Mrs. Shelton, by Bill Macilwraith. Directed by John Reardon, produced by Humphrey Barclay. With Elaine Stritch, Donald Sinden. ITV; 5th February, 1978

Saturday Night At The Mill, Guest, Directed by Roy Norton, produced by Roy Ronnie. With David Essex, Patrick Moore, Kenny Ball and his Jazzmen. BBC1; 1st April, 1978

Those Wonderful TV Times, Guest in TV Nostalgia Quiz, Written by Norman Shaw, directed and produced by Anthony J. Bacon. With Janet Brown, Charlie Drake, Norman Vaughan, Cardew Robinson. ITV; 3rd September, 1978

She Must Be Joking! Omnibus Special on Female Jokers, produced by Jeff Parks. With Hylda Baker, Marti Caine, Christine Pilgrim. BBC1; 28th December, 1978

Beryl Reid's Christmas Collection, Sketches, poems, monologues, from the Redgrave Theatre, Farnham, produced by Brian Patten, artistic direction by William Chappell. Radio 4; Christmas Eve & Christmas Day, 1978

Out With The Old, In With The New, Part 1: Some Wonderful Scottish Girls, directed by Jim McCann, executive producer Bryan Izzard. With Janet Brown, Rikkie Fulton, Lulu, Aimi Macdonald, Molly Weir. ITV from Glasgow; New Year's Eve, 1978

Be My Guest, Record programme from Wraysbury. Radio 2; 10 January, 1979

Blankety Blank, Guest in first of Quiz Series, produced by

Marcus Plantin, hosted by Terry Wogan. With Jack Douglas, Michael Parkinson, Ian Wallace, Diane Keen, Lorraine Chase. 1st February, and subsequently 29th March, 10th May, 6th September, 4th October, 25th December, 1979

Beryl Reid, Script by Noel Coward, N.F. Simpson et al.; scene from Congreve's 'Way Of The World'. Produced by Robin Nash, artistic direction by William Chappell. With Patricia Hayes, Norman Rossington, Sheila Steafel. BBC2; 5th February, 1979. Repeated 18th December 1979; 10th May 1980

The Ronnie Corbett Special, Singing 'Style' with Corbett. Script by Eddie Braben, produced by Michael Hurll. With Jim Davidson, Lou Rawls, the Wurzels. BBC1; 4th May, 1979

Celebrity Squares, Guest in Quiz Game devised by Ian Messiter, Howard Imber. Directed and produced by Glyn Edwards. Chairman Bob Monkhouse, with Lorraine Chase, Spike Milligan, William Rushton, Magnus Pyke. ITV; 26th May and subsequently 9th, 16th, 23rd June, 1979

Dick Emery's Comedy Hour, Guest, as Ada in sketch with Emery, by Eric Merriman. Directed, produced Keith Beckett. ITV; 6th June, 1979

Funny You Should Ask, Guest, with scriptwriter Jimmy Perry, producer James Casey. Produced by Bob Oliver Rogers. Radio 2; 6th August, 1979

Tinker, Tailor, Soldier, Spy, as Connie Sachs, dramatized by Arthur Hopcraft from the novel by John le Carré, directed by John Irvin. Part 3 With Alec Guinness. BBC2; 24th September, 1979

An Honourable Retirement, as The Landlady. Film scripted by Donald Churchill, directed by Tom Clegg, produced by Robert Lowe. With John LeMesurier, Philip Locke, Hilary Mason. ITV; 4th November, 1979

Give Us A Clue, Guest as Mother Christmas in Charades Programme, directed by Ian Bolt, produced by Juliet Grimm. Host Michael Aspel. With Lionel Blair, Una Stubbs, Dickie Davies. ITV; Christmas Eve, 1979

Looks Familiar, Guest, directed and produced by Roy Clark. With Denis Norden, Roy Hudd. ITV; 21st February, 1980

Comedy Tonight: Frank Muir Recalls 50 Years of Revue, Re-creating Cicely Courtneidge sketch 'Laughing Gas'. Directed and produced by Michael Mills. With Sheila Hancock, Frankie Howerd, Harry H. Corbett. ITV; 1st April, 1980

Nationwide. Interviewed by Frank Bough. BBC1; 19th June, 1980

Woman's Hour, Guest, introduced by Maureen Staffer. Radio 4; 3rd July, 1980

Betjeman's Britain. Dramatizing the poems of the Poet Laureate, directed and produced by Charles Wallace. With Eric Morecambe, Susannah York, John Alderton, Jenny Agutter. ITV; 25th August, 1980. Repeated as 'A Late Flowering Love'. Channel 4; 3rd March, 1985

Peter Cook And Co, Guest, Script by Peter Cook, directed and produced by Paul Smith. With John Cleese, Terry Jones, Rowan Atkinson. ITV; 14th September, 1980

Blankety Blank, Guest in Comedy Quiz Game hosted by Terry Wogan. Directed by Stanley Appel, produced by Alan Boyd. With Ray Alan, Pat Coombs, Liza Goddard. BBC1; 18th September, 9th October, 9th November, Boxing Day, 1980

Nanny Knows Best, as Nanny Price. Situation comedy by Anne Valery, directed by Bob Hird, produced by Susi Hush. With Wanda Ventham, Peter Bowles. ITV; 14th October, 1980

Rhubarb, Rhubarb! Guest in film for ITV, written and directed by and starring Eric Sykes, produced by David Clark. With Jimmy Edwards, Charlie Drake, Hattie Jacques, Bill Fraser, Roy Kinnear, Norman Rossington. 15th December 1980

Agony: Arrivals And Departures, as Cherry Lightfoot. By Stan Hey, Andrew Nickolds, directed and produced by John Reardon. With Maureen Lipman, Simon Williams, Maria Charles. ITV; 25th January, 1981

Miss Lambert's Last Dance, by Jennifer Phillips, directed by Anthony Cornish. In the title role. With Anne Stallybrass, Martin Friend. Capital Radio; 8th February, 1981

Get Up And Go!, as Beryl, Landlady to Stephen Boxer and Mooncat, in Series for the Under Fives. By Rick Vanes,

Shirley Isherwood, directed and produced by Lesley Rogers, subsequently by Len Lurcock. ITV; 9th April, 1981; subsequently 1982 and 1983

Queenie's Channel, as Queenie. Afternoon Theatre by David Wheeler, directed by Margaret Etall. With Alan Dudley, Sheelah Wilcocks. Radio 4; 15th July, 1981

Blankety Blank, Guest in Comedy Quiz Game hosted by Terry Wogan. Directed by Geoffrey Posner, produced by Marcus Plantin. With Lenny Henry, David Jacobs, Roy Kinnear, Madeline Smith, Tracey Ullman. BBC1; 3rd September, 1981

Worzel Gummidge: Muvvers' Day, as Sarah Pigswill. By Keith Porterhouse and Willis Hall, directed and produced by James Hill. With Jon Pertwee, Una Stubbs, Geoffrey Bayldon, Lorraine Chase. STV; 31st October, 1981

Does the Team Think?, Panellist on TV version of radio series, chaired by Tim Brooke-Taylor, produced by Robert Reed, associate Eric Merriman. With Jimmy Edwards, Frankie Howerd, William Rushton. 14th January, 1982

Dr Who, 'Earthshock', as Captain Briggs, by Eric Saward. With Peter Davison, James Warwick and Clare Clifford. BBC1; 4 episodes from 8th March, 1982

Gloria Hunniford, Guest. Radio 4; 10th August, 1982

Smiley's People, as Connie Sachs, by John le Carré and John Hopkins, directed by Simon Langton, produced by Jonathan Powell. With Alec Guinness, Eileen Atkins, Bernard Hepton, Norma West. BBC2; 4th September, 1982

Play It Again, interviewed by Tony Bilbow on her favourite films, directed by Terry Steel. ITV; 10th November, 1982

The Studio, as a woman in love with an artist, visiting his studio when he's not there. 10-minute soliloquy by James Windsor, directed by Glyn Dearman. Radio 3; 15th November, 1982

The Irish RM, as Mrs. Knox, series adapted by Rosemary Anne Sisson from the stories by Somerville and Ross. A James Mitchell Production, directed by Robert Chetwyn. With Peter Bowles, Faith Brook, Bryan Murray, Anna Manahan. Channel 4; 13th January, 5th February, 1983

Desert Island Discs, Interviewed by Roy Plomley, produced by Derek Drescher. Radio 4; 5th February, 1983

The Practical Book Review, Pet Care, Reviewing books on cats, directed by Juliet Miller, produced by Barbara Derkow. With Pat Fairon. Channel 4; 14th February, 1983

Comediennes, introduced by Richard Anthony Baker, produced by Alan Owen. With Tessie O'Shea, recordings Cicely Courtneidge, Suzette Tarri. Radio 2; 11th March, 1983

British Academy Awards, hosted by Frank Bough and Selina Scott in the presence of H.R.H. Princess Anne at Grosvenor House. BBC1; 20th March, 1983. *BAFTA Award* for Best Television Actress of the Year for 'Smiley's People'.

Cuffy, as Matron in 'Cuffy and a Holiday', by Francis Essex, directed/produced by Paul Harrison. With Bernard Cribbins, Jack Douglas. ITV; 20th March, 1983

Private Lives, Interviewed by Maria Aitken, directed by David G. Croft, produced by Lavinia Warner. With Kingsley Amis, Peter Skellern. BBC2; 29th May, 1983

Carling Black Label, as the Fortune Teller, presented by Wight Collins. With Britt Ekland. ITV; July, 1983

Looks Familiar, Guest, devised and compiled by Denis Gifford, directed and produced by Robert Reed. Chairman Denis Norden. With Roy Hudd, Billy Dainty. 29th July, 1983

Blankety Blank, Guest in Comedy Quiz Series, hosted by Terry Wogan, directed by David Taylor, produced by Marcus Plantin. With Roy Kinnear, Ruth Madoc, Patrick Moore, Freddie Starr. BBC1; Christmas Day, 1983

Wind in the Willows, as the voice of the Magistrate, adapted by Rosemary Anne Sisson, from the book by Kenneth Grahame. Directed by Mark Hall, also producer with Brian Cosgrove. With Ian Carmichael, Michael Hordern, David Jason, Richard Pearson, Una Stubbs. BBC2; 27th December, 1983

The Time of Your Life, Subject of flashback to September, 1952, directed by Henry Murray, hosted by Noel Edmonds. With Peter Brough, Ronald Wolfe (also material by), Ronald Chesney, Nat Temple & his Orchestra, Dennis Lotis, Lita Roza. BBC1; 20th April, 1984

Post Office, as herself in promotional film. April, 1984

On the Market, Guest cook on Susan Brookes and Trevor Hyett's marketing programme, directed by Nick Peake, produced by Marian Nelson. ITV; 28th April, 1984

Whose Baby? On panel of guessing quiz, hosted by Bernie Winters, Schnorbitz, with Su Pollard, Maureen Lipman. ITV; 10th May, 14th May, 1984

Des O'Connor Show, Guest, directed by Brian Penders. With Arthur English. ITV; 21st May, 1984

Minder, as authoress Ruby Todd in 'Second Time Around', directed by Francis Megahey. With George Cole, Dennis Waterman, Bill Maynard. ITV; 26th September, 1984

Start the Week with Richard Baker, Guest, with Jon Pertwee. Produced by Ian Strachan. Radio 4; 22nd October, 1984

Ken Bruce Show, Guest. Radio Scotland; 22nd October, 1984

Brian Hayes Show, Interview. LBC; 23rd October, 1984

Guest, British Forces Broadcasting Service; 23rd October, 1984

Guest, Capital Radio; Radio London; 26th October, 1984

John Dunn Show, Guest. Producers David Vercoe, Phil Hughes. Radio 2; 2nd November 1984

Wogan, Guest, produced by Geoffrey Posner, directed by Kevin Bishop. With Gore Vidal, Rabbi Lionel Blue. BBC1; 3rd November, 1984

Breakfast Time, Star Guest of the day. With Frank Bough, Nick Ross. BBC1; 9th November, 1984

Round Midnight, Brian Matthews' Guest. Radio 2; 14th November, 1984

Children in Need, Charity Appeal. BBC1; 23rd November, 1984

Blankety Blank, Guest in Comedy Quiz Game hosted by Les Dawson. Produced by John Bishop, directed by David Taylor. With Bonnie Langford, Bertice Reading, Stan Boardman, Henry Kelly, Cyril Smith. BBC1; 7th December, 1984

The Woodland Gospels, as Batty Bat. By Jeremy Lloyd, dramatized for radio by Brian Sibley, directed by John

Forrest, produced by Graham Gauld. With David Langton,
Jeremy Lloyd, Clive Swift, Nigel Davenport, Leslie Phillips.
Radio 4; 23rd December, 1984

Educating Archie, Repeat of the 1954 broadcast, produced by Roy
Speer. Script by Ronald Wolfe, Eric Sykes, additional material
by Walter Ridley, starring Peter Brough, Archie Andrews. With
Bernard Miles, Harry Secombe, Hattie Jacques, Ronald
Chesney, BBC Revue Orchestra, conducted by Harry
Rabinowitz. Radio 4; 13th January, weekly to 10th February,
1985

Questions, Guest on panel compered by David Jacobs. With
Gerald Kaufman and Clare Francis TVS; 21st January, 1985

Aspel & Company, Guest, produced by Helen Fraser, directed by
Nicholas Vaughan-Barrett. With Victoria Wood, Sebastian
Coe. ITV; 23rd February, 1985

Favourite Things, Interviewed by Roy Plomley, photographed at
Honeypot Cottage. Produced and directed by Michael Kerr.
Start of series: BBC2; 24th February, 1985

This is Your Life, Guest on Harry Andrews programme,
introduced by Eamonn Andrews, produced by Malcolm Morris.
With John Gielgud, Gina Lollobrigida, Joyce Redman,
Anthony Quayle, Joan Collins. ITV; 6th March 1985.

Late Starter, as Helen Magee, by Brian Clarke, produced by
Ruth Boswell, directed by Barry Davies. With Peter
Barkworth, Julia Foster, Rowena Cooper, Jimmy Jewel.
BBC1; 29th March to 12th April, 1985

Forthcoming Appearances

Bernard Miles on the Halls, Guest. ITV

The Secret Diary of Adrian Mole Aged 13¾, as Grandmother Mole.
Film scripted by Sue Townsend from her book, directed and
produced by Peter Sasdy. With Gian Sammarco in the title
role, Julie Walters, Bill Fraser. ITV; autumn 1985

Bergerac: Low Profile, as Miss Broome; series created by Robert
Banks Stewart, story by Roger Davenport. Produced by
Jonathan Alwyn, directed by David Reynolds. With John
Nettles, Terence Alexander, Louise Jameson. BBC1; autumn
1985

Index

Letter A before a number denotes relevant Appendix credits, chronologically listed, applying *only* to names included in the text. Roman numerals ix indicate Illustrations between pages 112 and 113; x stands for those between pages 176 and 177

Grateful thanks to David Cutlack for invaluable help in collating and typing material for the Index. E.B.

BESTSELLING NON-FICTION FROM ARROW

All these books are available from your bookshop or newsagent or you can order them direct. Just tick the titles you want and complete the form below.

☐	THE GREAT ESCAPE	Paul Brickhill	£1.75
☐	A RUMOR OF WAR	Philip Caputo	£2.50
☐	A LITTLE ZIT ON THE SIDE	Jasper Carrott	£1.50
☐	THE ART OF COARSE ACTING	Michael Green	£1.50
☐	THE UNLUCKIEST MAN IN THE WORLD	Mike Harding	£1.75
☐	DIARY OF A SOMEBODY	Christopher Matthew	£1.25
☐	TALES FROM A LONG ROOM	Peter Tinniswood	£1.75
☐	LOVE WITHOUT FEAR	Eustace Chesser	£1.95
☐	NO CHANGE	Wendy Cooper	£1.95
☐	MEN IN LOVE	Nancy Friday	£2.75

Postage _____

Total _____

ARROW BOOKS, BOOKSERVICE BY POST, PO BOX 29, DOUGLAS, ISLE OF MAN, BRITISH ISLES

Please enclose a cheque or postal order made out to Arrow Books Ltd for the amount due including 15p per book for postage and packing both for orders within the UK and for overseas orders.

Please print clearly

NAME ....

ADDRESS ....

....

Whilst every effort is made to keep prices down and to keep popular books in print, Arrow Books cannot guarantee that prices will be the same as those advertised here or that the books will be available.